Bread for Believers

Bread for Believers

The Foundations For Growth—What Every Christian Needs To Know

Curtis Hutson

SWORD of the LORD PUBLISHERS

P.O.BOX 1099, MURFREESBORO, TN 37133

Copyright, 1982, by
SWORD OF THE LORD PUBLISHERS

ISBN 0-87398-082-4

Enlarged Edition: April, 1988

This Printing 1997

Printed and Bound in the United States of America

Introduction

I often tell my students that Dr. Curtis Hutson is the best preacher in America. That is a staggering statement, to call anyone the best of anything. But that is my conviction based on being a member of the Forrest Hills Baptist Church and listening to the sermons of Dr. Hutson for over two years.

I go further to tell my students to read his sermons, listen to his tapes and open their hearts to his message. Dr. Curtis Hutson is a great example of expository preaching with a powerful, yet warm, appeal.

A few years ago I wrote a book that I never published. My working title was *The Ten Greatest Baptist Pulpiteers and How They Prepare*. In that book, I included a chapter on Dr. Curtis Hutson. The criteria I used in judging great pulpiteers apply to Curtis Hutson.

First, I believe great pulpiteers get results from their preaching. Therefore, for a man to be a great preacher, he has to have built a great church: meaning people walk the aisles, get baptized, and the church membership grows.

Everyone knows that Curtis Hutson took the Forrest Hills Baptist Church when they were running approximately 30 people and when he left they were averaging over 3,000 weekly in the morning attendance. I have seen the church in action and know that they had a great bus program and Sunday school outreach. I have often said that what built Forrest Hills Baptist Church was Dr. Hutson's sermons; they attracted people to come and hear about the Saviour Jesus Christ. There are many other reasons why I feel that Curtis Hutson is a great pulpiteer, yet the church he built alone is enough to qualify him as being a great pulpiteer in America.

Before I leave this subject, let me say a word about the phrase that is often heard: "He is a great preacher, but he can't build a church." I am not sure that that is a true statement. If a pastor is a great preacher, his sermons will attract people to Jesus Christ; and the church will grow.

Second, Dr. Hutson is a great preacher because he expounds the Word of God. As I listened to him week by week, I was amazed at the doctrine that he knew and preached. Obviously, Dr. Hutson did not make his sermons a theology class. Anyone who knows theology recognizes the doctrines of the Word of God are like the foundation of a building—necessary to hold the superstructure but always out of sight. What makes Dr. Hutson a great preacher is his knowledge of doctrine and his ability to communicate it practically.

The third criterion of a great preacher is balance: Balance between knowledge and application; between scholarship and everyday language; between motivation and explanation; between the Old Testament and the New; between biographical and devotional preaching; and, lastly, between the head and the heart. Dr. Hutson is a great preacher because of the balance in his preaching.

Fourth, great pulpiteers preach beautiful sermons. I am amazed at the beauty of Dr. Hutson's sermons. He can stop and give a small incident from everyday life. Once he told the story of a barefoot boy crossing a plowed field in South Carolina. I could almost feel the dust coming between my toes as he told the story. Later, when in the same sermon he began to describe the beauties of Heaven, I appreciated the adjectives and similes, evidence of great preaching.

Fifth, a great pulpiteer gives evidence of spiritual power in the pulpit. To be one of the greatest preachers in the world, a man has to be a channel for the convicting work of the Holy Spirit as he brings men to the altar to get saved. Spiritual power means Jesus Christ must be magnified. When a man preaches on the cross of Jesus Christ, people must come for its cleansing. Spiritual power motivates people to godly living and Christian service. After having sat under the preaching of Curtis Hutson on a weekly basis, I discovered that, when he came to bat, he always got a hit. I don't remember that he ever struck out in this aspect.

Great preaching is communication. Therefore, a great pulpiteer must know the English language, illustrations, gestures, and freedom in the pulpit. Dr. Hutson has all of these; and those who have heard him preach, want to hear him again.

I learned another thing from the preaching of Dr. Hutson—the principles of the Word of God. He does not just preach devotional messages and make you feel good or feel bad according to your experience. Dr. Hutson usually brings a man to a biblical principle of the Christian life. I found in listening to him that I was motivated to base my life on the principles of the Word of God. Hence, listening to Dr. Hutson I grew in my Christian life.

Great preaching makes you love the Bible. For a couple of years before joining Forrest Hills Baptist Church, I had become lax in my dedication to read the Bible through every year. Dr. Hutson preached on Acts 17:11 and asked that we make a commitment to read the Bible through every year. That was five years ago, and I have read the Bible through at least once and sometimes twice each year since. This was because of his preaching.

Finally, there seem to be many more things that make a great pulpiteer. I could talk of all these; yet, when looking at all the criteria of a great preacher, Curtis Hutson has not failed in any.

To conclude, Curtis Hutson is a great preacher because hundreds of young men and women have walked forward to dedicate their lives to full-time Christian service through his preaching. We read in Genesis 1:11 that each produces "after his kind." Therefore, I know that Curtis Hutson is called of God; because when he is preaching, other young people are called of God. Curtis Hutson is producing after his kind.

I trust that many will read this book and preach greater sermons. If that happens, the impact of this book will be greater than any of us realize.

January, 1982   Elmer L. Towns
            Dean of Liberty Baptist Seminary
            Lynchburg, Virginia

Table of Contents

What Is a Believer?

CHAPTER ONE

"He that believeth on the Son hath everlasting life: and he that believeth not the Son shall not see life; but the wrath of God abideth on him."—John 3:36.

What is the determining factor in salvation? Exactly what does a person have to do to be saved? The Bible doesn't leave us in the dark. The answer is in the Word of God.

In Acts 16:30, 31 the Philippian jailor asked Paul and Silas, "Sirs, what must I do to be saved? And they said, Believe on the Lord Jesus Christ, and thou shalt be saved. . . ."

The jailor was asking, "What one thing is absolutely necessary for my salvation?" And the Bible answer was, "Believe on the Lord Jesus Christ. . . ."

In John 3:36 Jesus divides the world into two groups: "He that believeth on the Son hath everlasting life: and he that believeth not the Son shall not see life; but the wrath of God abideth on him." Here are those who believe on the Son and those who believe not on the Son. Those who believe have everlasting life according to the promise of God; and those who believe not shall not see life, but the wrath of God abides on them.

In John 3:18, Jesus again divides the world into two groups:

"He that believeth on him is not condemned [not under sentence]: but he that believeth not is condemned already, because he hath not believed in the name of the only begotten Son of God." Here again, Jesus says there are two groups—those who believe and those who believe not. Those who believe have the sentence lifted, and they are not condemned. Those who believe not are under the sentence of sin, which is the second death, because they have not believed on the name of the only begotten Son of God.

In Galatians 3:26 the Bible says, "For ye are all the children of God by faith in Christ Jesus." This passage says that every child of God is a child of God by faith. Romans 5:1 says, "Therefore being justified by faith, we have peace with God through our Lord Jesus Christ."

Time and space do not permit me to share with you all the verses that say believing, or faith, is the determining factor in salvation. There are at least 153 verses in the Bible that make *believing the determining factor in salvation.* Mark 16:16 says, ". . . he that believeth not shall be damned." So if the Bible is true, faith in the Lord Jesus Christ is the determining factor in salvation.

I've heard or read a number of sermons on "saving faith," but the Bible never puts "saving" before faith. Jesus, not faith, is the Saviour. Faith is an attitude of the soul through which Jesus saves.

The Bible never tells us to believe and be saved. It is always careful to say, "Believe *on the Lord Jesus Christ,* and thou shalt be saved" or "Whosoever believeth *in him* should not perish, but have everlasting life" or "He that believeth on *the Son* hath everlasting life." It's the object of faith that makes faith important. Faith in the wrong thing could result in a person's damnation.

Now, since faith is the determining factor in salvation, it is important to know what faith is.

As far as I know, there is only one definition of faith recorded in the Bible—Hebrews 11:1. But there are many illustrations of faith in the Bible. The best one is in Hebrews 12:2, where we find the expression, "Looking unto Jesus. . . ."

I. FAITH IS NOT LOOKING **AT** JESUS BUT LOOKING **UNTO** JESUS

Almost everyone will admit that Jesus Christ existed, that He was a real person. Every time we date a check, we admit the existence of Christ. Faith is not looking at Jesus as a historical personage.

James 2:19 says "the devils also believe and tremble." Even the demons admit the existence of Christ. In Acts 19:15 the evil spirit in the man said, "Jesus I know, and Paul I know; but who are ye?" No, faith is not looking *at* Jesus; it is looking *unto* Jesus, which is another way of saying depending on Jesus.

Suppose someone cosigned for you to borrow money. If you fail to pay, the authorities could put you in jail. And suppose the money came due and you had nothing with which to pay. You call your cosigner. "Bob, I've got problems. You know that note you signed for me? Well, the money is due, and I can't pay it."

Your friend replies, "Don't worry about it. Just look to me!" He means, "Just depend on me. I'll pay it."

Jesus Christ says that we owe a sin debt. Romans 6:23 says, "For the wages of sin is death." And Jesus says if we pay what we owe, we must die and go into Hell and stay there forever. But He adds, "Don't worry about it. You just look to Me."

Isaiah 53:6 says, ". . . the Lord hath laid on him the iniquity of us all." Two thousand years ago God took every sin you have or ever will commit, and God Almighty laid those sins on Jesus Christ. While Jesus was bearing your sins in His own body, God punished Him in your place to pay the debt that you owe as a sinner.

Jesus uttered seven things while He hung on the cross. The sixth utterance was, "It is finished." Nothing can be added to it; nothing can be taken from it. It's complete!

His death made full payment for your sins. And now He says to each of us, "Look to Me! Believe that I did die on the cross for you. Believe that I did pay your sin debt. Look to Me, and all is well."

Faith is not looking *at* Jesus; it is looking *unto* Jesus, depending on Jesus, relying on Jesus, putting the matter of your salvation in His hands and trusting Him to get you to Heaven.

II. FAITH IS LOOKING AWAY FROM EVERYTHING ELSE AND LOOKING **ONLY** TO JESUS

Martin Luther translated Hebrews 12:2, "Off-looking unto Jesus . . . ," which means looking away from everything else and looking only to Jesus. It means looking away from your works.

How long do you think one would have to work to earn Heaven? Read the description of Heaven in Revelation 21 and 22. Why, the Bible says Heaven's streets are pure gold, so pure it's like transparent glass. Earth has no way of refining gold that pure. If you worked ten million lifetimes, you couldn't begin to earn Heaven. And the Bible says in Ephesians 2:8, 9, "For by grace are ye saved through faith; and that not of yourselves: it is the gift of God: Not of works, lest any man should boast."

And consider this: If a man worked to stay out of Hell, the very motive would render the work ineffective. He would be working from a motive of fear. According to I Corinthians 13, all work must be motivated by love. Paul said in verse 3, "And though I bestow all my goods to feed the poor, and though I give my body to be burned, and have not charity [or love], it profiteth me nothing." So if a person worked to stay out of Hell, the motive would render the work ineffective.

A boy once asked an old preacher, "Sir, what can I do to be saved?"

The preacher replied, "Son, you're too late."

"What!" exclaimed the boy, "too late to be saved?"

"No," said the preacher, "too late to do anything. You see,

son, Jesus did it all two thousand years ago."

Now I believe in good works, but not as an instrument of salvation. We don't work to be saved; we work because we are saved.

> I would not work my soul to save,
> For that my Lord hath done,
> But I would work like any slave,
> For love of God's dear Son!

"Off-looking unto Jesus" means I look away from my righteousness and only to Jesus. I'm for living right. We ought to live as clean, as moral and as pure as we possibly can. But it is "not by works of righteousness which we have done, but according to his mercy he saved us, by the washing of regeneration, and renewing of the Holy Ghost" (Titus 3:5). Isaiah 64:6 says that "all our righteousnesses are as filthy rags." Now the Bible doesn't say the worst we do is like filthy rags but the best we do. There is no way that anyone could ever be righteous enough to earn Heaven. We would have to be perfect, and there are no perfect people.

The Methodist evangelist Sam Jones once asked a congregation, "Does anyone here know a perfect person?"

A lady raised her hand.

"Yes. Do you know a perfect person?"

"Well," answered the lady, "I've never met her, but my husband talks about her all the time. She was his first wife."

The truth is, no one is perfect. Jesus said, "They that are whole have no need of the physician, but they that are sick: I came not to call the righteous, but sinners to repentance" (Mark 2:17). Faith is looking away from our righteousness and looking only to Jesus. We don't get better to get saved. We get saved to get better, and we can't get better until we do get saved.

A stanza from my favorite hymn says:

> My hope is built on nothing less
> Than Jesus' blood and righteousness;
> I dare not trust the sweetest frame,
> But wholly lean on Jesus' name.

"Off-looking unto Jesus" means looking away from our church membership and looking only to Jesus. Everyone who accepts Jesus Christ as Saviour should join a church. But you don't join the church to become a Christian. Being in the church won't make a Christian out of you anymore than getting into the garage will make an automobile out of you. I'm a church member, and every saved person ought to join a Bible-believing church. Acts 2:41 says, "Then they that gladly received his word were baptized: and the same day there were added unto them about three thousand souls."

On the other hand, if one depends on the fact that he belongs to the church to get him to Heaven, he will go to Hell through the church. In Matthew 7:22,23 Jesus said:

"Many will say to me in that day, Lord, Lord, have we not prophesied in thy name? and in thy name have cast out devils? and in thy name done many wonderful works? And then will I profess unto them, I never knew you: depart from me, ye that work iniquity."

According to the Bible many will miss Heaven even though they were church members and worked hard, and some even preached or prophesied in Jesus' name—they will miss Heaven because instead of totally, fully, completely trusting Jesus Christ, they trusted their works.

"Off-looking unto Jesus" means you look away from your baptism and look only to Jesus. Now every person who accepts Jesus Christ as Saviour ought to be baptized, but baptism is not an instrument of salvation. It is an outward expression of an inward experience. It's like putting the wedding band on the finger after we are married. It doesn't marry us, but it shows everybody that we are married. Being baptized doesn't save you; but it is an outward symbol telling others that you believe in the death, burial and resurrection of Christ.

The man who is depending on his baptism to get him to Heaven will go to Hell through the baptistry. Now why do I say that? Because John 3:36b says, ". . . and he that believeth not the Son shall not see life; but the wrath of God abideth on him."

Friend, Jesus Christ says if you're not depending on, believing, trusting, relying on the Son, you shall not see life: but the wrath of God abides on you. The man who is trusting his church membership or his baptism or his reformation or anything else other than Jesus Christ will miss Heaven. John 3:18 says, ". . . he that believeth not is condemned already, because he hath not believed in the name of the only begotten Son of God." There is no promise to those who partly believe on Christ and partly on something else.

Someone asked, "But doesn't the Bible say in Mark 16:16, 'He that believeth and is baptized shall be saved'?"

Yes, but the next expression says, ". . . he that believeth not shall be damned."

You see, *believing is the determining factor,* not being baptized. That is like saying, "He that getteth on the jet plane, and sitteth down, shall fly to Jacksonville, Florida; but, he that getteth not on the plane, shall not fly to Jacksonville." It is the getting on that gets us there, not the sitting down. But anyone with sense knows if you get on, you ought to sit down.

If you've trusted Jesus Christ as Saviour, you ought to be baptized. But you should not be thinking that baptism saves you. If you do, you are not trusting Jesus Christ but baptism. Faith is looking away from everything else and looking only to Jesus.

III. FAITH IS NOT EXPERIENCING A FEELING BUT RELYING ON A FACT

I've dealt with people who doubted their salvation because they did not think they had the proper feelings at the time of conversion. There is not a verse in the Bible that tells a man exactly how he has to feel in order to be saved. As a matter of fact, the Bible never says you have to feel any way to be saved. Acts 16:31 says, "Believe on the Lord Jesus Christ, and thou shalt be saved."

When we were first married, we drove back to my wife's home.

Some friends were in the yard. When we got out of the car, someone asked, "How does it feel to be married?"

I said, "I feel exactly like I did a few minutes ago, before we got married." But I was just as married as the fellow who had some great feeling.

Not everyone reacts the same to the same experience. Driving home from a revival meeting one night, a car overturned in front of us. Several people were badly injured. Some who saw it cried; others ran to help, while some buried their faces in their hands. One lady fainted. Now they all saw the same thing and had the same experience but reacted differently.

I've seen people cry when they trusted Christ. I've been with others who smiled, while others laughed, and some even shouted; but they all had the same experience. They all trusted Jesus Christ as Saviour. Faith is not having some particular feeling; it is depending on a fact.

Now here's the fact: Two thousand years ago Jesus Christ died for us. He bore our sins in His own body. God punished Him in our place to pay the debt that we owe. Whether we ever do anything about it or not, it is still a fact.

What we must do is believe that fact and depend on, rely on, trust in Him and what He did for our salvation.

If I were not a Christian and wanted to be, I would simply pray this prayer:

> Dear Lord Jesus, I know that I am a sinner. I do believe that You died for me. And here and now, I trust You as my Saviour. From this minute on, I'm depending on You to get me to Heaven. Help me to live for You and to be a good Christian.

After praying, I would accept what God says in the Bible— that I do have everlasting life because I'm trusting Jesus Christ for my salvation. "He that believeth on the Son *hath* everlasting life..." (John 3:36). I would accept what God says, whether or not I ever had any feelings.

Once you make that decision and trust Christ, perhaps some feeling will come. But whether the feeling comes or not, the Word of God is still true. God cannot lie!

When you trust Him, you will have everlasting life. *The determining factor in salvation is believing, trusting, depending on, relying on the Lord Jesus Christ.*

F. G. Penetecost said, "Two and two is four—that's mathematics. Hydrogen and oxygen form water—that's chemistry. 'Believe on the Lord Jesus Christ, and thou shalt be saved'— that's revelation."

Said Pentecost: "You ask how do I know?"

"Well," he said, "the burden of proof lies with you. Put two and two together and see if you don't have four. Put hydrogen and oxygen together and see if you don't have water. And believe on the Lord Jesus Christ and see if you won't be saved."

The Believer's Security

CHAPTER TWO

Nearly everywhere I go I find people troubled because they do not know that they are secure. They think that because of their sins, their negligence, their failing to endure to the end, or some other reason, they may lose their salvation.

Those who think they are saved now but could lose their salvation later have one of two problems: First, they are trusting to some degree in their works to save them; or, second, they do not understand that by trusting Jesus Christ as Saviour their destiny is in the hands of God.

Perhaps they have taken the word of someone whom they trust, or they have not studied the Bible carefully and do not realize that God has determined that all who believe on Him have everlasting life and will go to Heaven when they die.

The first group—those who believe that leading a poor Christian life will result in the loss of their salvation—actually need to have the plan of salvation made clear to them. Somehow they have not completely understood that Jesus Christ fully paid for all our sins when He died on the cross and that our conduct or good works have nothing to do with salvation.

Of course, we ought to live good; and God has ways of dealing with disobedient children. But we are saved by trusting Jesus Christ as Saviour. John 3:36 says, "He that believeth on the Son hath everlasting life . . . ." It is a clear-cut problem of "grace or works." Ephesians 2:8, 9 makes it plain: "For by grace are ye saved through faith; and that not of yourselves: it is the gift of God: Not of works, lest any man should boast."

The second group needs to study carefully what the Bible says about the security of the believer.

With that in mind, let me share with you several thoughts.

I. GOD PROMISED AND PRODUCED ETERNAL LIFE

John 3:14-16 says:

"And as Moses lifted up the serpent in the wilderness, even so must the Son of man be lifted up: That whosoever believeth in him should not perish, but have eternal life. For God so loved the world, that he gave his only begotten Son, that whosoever believeth in him should not perish, but have everlasting life."

Again, in Titus 1, verse 2, we read: "In hope of eternal life, which God, that cannot lie, *promised* before the world began." First John 2:25 says, "And this is the *promise* that he hath *promised* us, even eternal life."

Now when God promises something, He is bound by His honor to produce. If He did not produce what He promised, He would sacrifice His honor and integrity. But what God promised He produced.

The Bible says in I John 5:10, 11:

"He that believeth on the Son of God hath the witness in himself: he that believeth not God hath made him a liar; because he believeth not the record that God gave of his Son. And this is the record, that God hath given to us eternal life, and this life is in his Son."

John 10:27-29 says:

"My sheep hear my voice, and I know them, and they follow

me: And I give unto them eternal life; and they shall never perish, neither shall any man pluck them out of my hand. My Father, which gave them me, is greater than all; and no man is able to pluck them out of my Father's hand."

And we read in Romans 6:23: "For the wages of sin is death; but the gift of God is eternal life through Jesus Christ our Lord." God promised and God produced eternal life for the believer.

II. THE BELIEVER HAS EXACTLY WHAT GOD PROMISED AND PRODUCED

Many Scriptures make it unmistakably plain that the man who is trusting Jesus Christ as Saviour has eternal life. John 5:24 says, "Verily, verily, I say unto you, He that heareth my word, and believeth on him that sent me, *hath* everlasting life...." Notice the Bible does not say, "He that believes on the Son will have..." but "hath"—present tense. That means the man who is trusting Jesus Christ completely for salvation has everlasting life now. It is not something that God promised him provided he meets certain additional conditions but something he has the moment he believes on Christ.

But notice that Jesus goes a little further than saying we have everlasting life and makes it doubly sure in John 5:24, "Verily, verily, I say unto you, He that heareth my word, and believeth on him that sent me, hath everlasting life, and shall not come into condemnation; but *is* passed from death unto life."

In addition to saying that the believer has everlasting life the moment he believes, Jesus adds the promise that he shall not come into condemnation; that is, the sentence of sin will never be put on the believer again.

The condemned criminal is the man who has been arrested, tried and had sentence passed upon him. He is under the sentence. He is condemned. The sentence for sin is death. "The wages of sin is death..." (Rom. 6:23). That death is described as the second death, the lake of fire. "Death and hell were cast into the lake of fire. This is the second death" (Rev. 20:14).

But now Jesus says the man who believes on Christ not only has had the sentence lifted, he is not condemned. But He further promises that "he shall not come into condemnation...." The sentence of sin will never again be placed on the believer.

He goes even further in John 5:24 and says, "...but is passed from death unto life." Not that he is going to pass from death to life, but the one who believes on the Lord Jesus Christ has already passed from death unto life. John 3:36 says, "He that believeth on the Son *hath* everlasting life." Here again we have the word "hath"—present tense. The one who believes on the Son has everlasting life now. Everlasting life is not something God promises in the future, but it is the present possession of every believer.

Now "everlasting" and "eternal" do not mean a short duration—life for a day, a week, a month, a year, nor even a hundred years—but life for all time and all eternity.

The word "everlasting" in John 5:24 and John 3:36 which describes the life of the believer is the same word "everlasting" in Romans 16:26 that describes the duration of God, "...according to the commandment of the everlasting God." If God Himself is everlasting, then the life of the believer is everlasting.

More than forty-five times the terms "eternal life" and "everlasting life" are used in the Bible. If the believer has anything, he has everlasting life; for that is precisely what God promised and God produced.

III. GOD NOT ONLY GIVES ETERNAL LIFE, BUT PROMISES THAT THE BELIEVER WILL NEVER PERISH

John 10:28 says, "And I give unto them eternal life; and they shall never perish, neither shall any man pluck them out of my hand."

When you look up in the *Strong's Concordance* the word "never" in John 10:28, you find that it comes from four different

Greek words which, spelled in English letters, are OUME, EIS, HO and AION. Looking up each of these words in turn in the same *Strong's Concordance* you find that OUME (#3364) means, "not at all, by no means, in no case, never." EIS (#1519) means, "place, time, purpose." HO (#3588) means "male, female, or (even) neuter." AION (#165) means, "perpetually, eternally."

Put the meanings of all these root words together; and you find that when Christ said "never" here in this verse, it carries with it very powerful assurance—more than the word "never" ordinarily carries with it in our minds.

Looking at John 10:28 with this additional light we could write it this way and give it the emphasis Christ did when He spoke it: "And I give unto them eternal life; and they shall NOT AT ALL, BY ANY MEANS, IN ANY CASE, IN ANY PLACE, AT ANY TIME, FOR ANY PURPOSE, WHETHER THEY ARE MALE OR FEMALE, PERPETUALLY AND ETERNALLY, ever perish...."

IV. BELIEVERS ARE KEPT BY GOD, THEY DO NOT KEEP THEMSELVES

The Bible makes it plain again and again that the believer is kept by God. If we had to keep ourselves, we could be lost again and probably would be. In one of Spurgeon's sermons he said, "If it should ever come to pass that sheep of God could fall away, alas my fickle, feeble soul would fall ten thousand times a day."

No, we cannot keep ourselves. Thank God, we are kept by God Himself! In II Timothy 1:12 Paul said, "For I know whom I have believed, and am persuaded that he is able to keep that which I have committed unto him against that day." Here the apostle says, "I am persuaded [thoroughly convinced] that he is able to keep that which I have committed unto him."

It is my business to trust Jesus Christ as Saviour; it is His business to keep me. First Peter 1:3-5 says:

"Blessed be the God and Father of our Lord Jesus Christ, which according to his abundant mercy hath begotten us again unto

a lively hope by the resurrection of Jesus Christ from the dead, To an inheritance incorruptible, and undefiled, and that fadeth not away, reserved in heaven for you, Who are kept by the power of God through faith unto salvation ready to be revealed in the last time."

These verses tell us that the inheritance is reserved for us and we are reserved or kept for the inheritance. When the Bible says, "To an inheritance incorruptible...," it means that it will not corrupt, will not decay, but will last. It will be there when we get there. Peter continues, "To an inheritance incorruptible and undefiled, that fadeth not away...."

There have been occasions on earth when men have received a great inheritance; but when the lawyers, the courts, and the State were finished, the majority of the inheritance had faded away. But the Bible says our inheritance "fadeth not away." Then he continues: "...reserved in heaven for you." It is reserved. No one can take it. It is yours if you have trusted Jesus Christ as Saviour.

Not only is the inheritance reserved in Heaven for you, but the Bible says you "are kept by the power of God through faith unto salvation...." The word "salvation" here denotes our final redemption, when we are saved from the very presence of sin, that is, when Jesus Christ comes for us and we see Him and are made exactly like Him.

No, the believer does not and could not keep himself. God keeps him. John 10:28 says, "And I give unto them eternal life; and they shall never perish, neither shall any man pluck them out of my hand." The believer is in the hand of God, and no man can pluck him out.

Several years ago I was discussing eternal security with another preacher. In the course of the conversation I read John 10:28, "...neither shall any man pluck them out of my hand."

The preacher interrupted and said, "Yes. But the Bible does not say that we cannot ourselves get out of His hand."

I responded, "You do not build doctrine on what the Bible

doesn't say; you build it on what the Bible *does* say. And the Bible says, 'neither shall any man pluck them out of my hand.' You are a man, aren't you?"

"Why, yes," he answered.

"Then you could not pluck yourself out of His hand either because the Bible says 'any man.'"

John 6:39 says, "And this is the Father's will which hath sent me, that of all which he hath given me I should lose nothing, but should raise it up again at the last day." It is God's will that no saved person will ever be lost. He says He will "lose nothing." And since we are at least something, this means that we can never be lost again.

Colossians 3:3 says, "For ye are dead, and your life is hid with Christ in God." According to this verse, the believer is under double lock and key.

I heard an old preacher illustrate this verse by saying:

> Suppose you had three barrels—a big barrel, a medium-sized barrel and a little barrel. You take the little barrel and put it into the medium-sized barrel, then put the medium-sized barrel into the big barrel. Then in order to get to the little barrel you would have to tear open the big barrel and the medium-sized barrel.
>
> God is the big barrel. Jesus is the medium-sized barrel, and I'm the little barrel. My life is hid with Christ in God. And before the Devil could get to me, he would have to tear away the big barrel and the medium-sized barrel. And before he could ever do that, I would have already slipped away to Glory!

V. JESUS IS THE SAVIOUR

He is referred to as "Saviour" at least twenty-four times in the New Testament. One time is Titus 2:13, "Looking for that blessed hope, and the glorious appearing of the great God and our Saviour Jesus Christ."

Now what is a saviour?

Suppose you are drowning. You are in the middle of the ocean. Suppose someone threw you a book entitled *Three Easy Lessons on How to Swim.* Would he be a saviour? No. Perhaps you could call him an educator, but you could not call him a saviour.

Suppose another man came by, got out of his boat, jumped in alongside you and demonstrated various swimming strokes, showing you exactly how to swim. Would he be a saviour? Of course not. He might be a good example and give a good demonstration, but he is not a saviour.

What if he lifted you into his boat, dried you off, gave you dry clothing, fed you, took you within ten miles of the shore, and then threw you out again into the ocean? Would he be a saviour? Absolutely not!

A saviour is one who takes you safely all the way to the shore.

When God says He gives you eternal life and He will never cast you out or lose you, He means what He says, because He is a true Saviour.

If you do not trust Christ as Saviour, if you do not put your case in His hands and solely depend on Him to get you to Heaven, then you will miss Heaven. John 3:36 says, "He that believeth not the Son shall not see life; but the wrath of God abideth on him." On the other hand, if you do trust Christ as your Saviour, Him only and nothing else, then you will go to Heaven, because He is a Saviour.

He is not one who teaches you how to save yourself; He is the One who saves you. "For the Son of man is come to seek and to *save* that which was lost" (Luke 19:10).

No verse in the Bible teaches that God places the believer in a position to be saved PROVIDED he does other things. The Bible says He saves the believer. "For whosoever shall call upon the name of the Lord shall be saved," says Romans 10:13.

Eternal security is not a totally separate doctrine from salvation. If you are not saved forever, then you are not saved at all.

VI. JESUS DIED FOR ALL OUR SINS

Many of those who believe that one can lose his salvation think that one loses it for some sin committed after he was saved.

Several years ago I had an unforgettable experience. It was Thursday night, and I was out soul winning. I had been asked to make a visit at a certain address. When I knocked, I was greeted by a friendly gentleman in a business suit. Inside, I saw four other men.

I had been there only a few minutes when one of the men remarked, "Oh, you Baptists! You believe once saved, always saved. You are wrong about that." I knew then that the men were preachers, and that I had been invited to the home simply to argue eternal security.

I said, "Now, men, I do not use the expression 'once saved, always saved.' But I do believe in the eternal security of the born-again believer, i.e., the man who has trusted Jesus Christ as Saviour is secure. He can never lose his salvation."

"Oh," they argued, "yes, he could." I quoted a number of verses, and they quoted other verses back to me.

After some time I asked, "Well, if a man could be lost after he is saved, what would he have to do to be lost?"

Immediately one of them responded, "Get out into sin." The others agreed.

I said, "All right. You are saying that if a man goes back into sin after he is saved, then he is lost."

"Yes," was their quick reply.

"All right. Answer several questions for me. First, you did invite me here tonight to argue about eternal security, didn't you?"

"That's right."

"You knew that Thursday night is the night I always go soul winning, didn't you?"

"Yes, we did."

"Don't you think it would be a good thing if you had let me go soul winning tonight instead of inviting me here for the sake of arguing about eternal security?"

They agreed it would.

I continued, "You men are preachers. Don't you think it would have been good to have gone soul winning instead of setting up this meeting with me?"

They agreed.

I opened my Bible to James 4:17 and read, "Therefore to him that knoweth to do good, and doeth it not, to him it is _____." And I asked them to read the last word. They stuttered a moment and quoted other verses. I said, "No. No. I want you to tell me what James 4:17 says, 'To him that knoweth to do good, and doeth it not, to him it is _____.' What?" Finally one of them said, "Sin."

"Then according to this verse, you are sinning right now. Because you know it would have been good had you gone soul winning and allowed me to go ahead with my soul-winning visits tonight, according to this verse you are all sinning; and according to your teaching, you are all lost."

"Oh, no," they were quick to reply.

"But you have admitted that you are sinning."

"Oh, we know it. But, we have not sinned enough yet," said one of them.

I smiled and said, "Take this Bible and show me where it teaches how much sin you have to commit to be lost."

Of course they could not find such a verse.

The truth is, Jesus Christ died for all our sins. First Peter 2:24 says, "Who his own self bare our sins in his own body on the tree. . . ." Isaiah 53:6 says, "The Lord hath laid on him the iniquity of us all." And II Corinthians 5:21 says, "For he hath made him to be sin for us, who knew no sin; that we might be made the righteousness of God in him."

Every sin that I have ever committed or ever will commit was laid on Jesus two thousand years ago, and He died on the cross to pay my sin debt and to suffer for my sins.

Once I told a lady that; and she said, "I can understand how He died for my past sins; but I cannot understand how He died for my future sins that I have not even committed yet."

I smiled and said, "Lady, when Jesus Christ died, all your sins were future. You were not even born."

God Almighty dealt with me as a sinner two thousand years ago when He poured out His wrath on Jesus Christ, as Jesus bore my sins in His own body on the tree.

After you trust Jesus Christ as Saviour, God will never again deal with you as a sinner. From that point on all His dealings will be as with a son.

VII. GOD CHASTISES THE BELIEVER WHO SINS

Look at Hebrews 12:6-8:

"For whom the Lord loveth he chasteneth, and scourgeth every son whom he receiveth. If ye endure chastening, God dealeth with you as with sons; for what son is he whom the father chasteneth not? But if ye be without chastisement, whereof all are partakers, then are ye bastards, and not sons."

Notice in these verses the words "son" and "sons," and the expression, "God dealeth with you as with sons."

From the moment you trust Jesus Christ as Saviour, God will never again deal with you as a sinner but as a son. And the Bible plainly says, "He chasteneth every son whom he receiveth." If the believer sins after he is saved, then God will chastise him.

Sometimes this chastening takes the form of sickness or even death, as in the case of I Corinthians 11:30: "For this cause many are weak and sickly among you, and many sleep."

Not all sickness is chastening. But in many cases it is. God's chastening takes various forms which I will not have space to discuss in this article. But I want to make this point: Chastisement is never payment for sin. It is child-training. God may chastise you, but Jesus Christ paid for your sins at Calvary two thousand years ago.

Let me illustrate.

Suppose I say to my son, Tony, "Now, Son, don't play ball in the front yard. You may break the big window in the front of the house."

While I am away in a revival meeting, my son disobeys me, plays ball in the front yard, and breaks a window. When I get home I ask, "Son, did you break that window?"

"Yes, Dad, I did."

"Did I tell you I would spank you if you broke it?"

"Yes, Sir, you did."

"Then I will have to do what I told you. Now you come with me."

I take my son into the back room and give him a good spanking. Does the spanking pay for the window? I don't care how much I spank the boy, it will never pay for the window. When I finish chastising him, I will have to reach into my pocket, take out the money, and pay the man to replace the window. I chastised my boy, but I paid for the window.

If the believer sins after he is saved, God will chastise him. But the chastisement is not payment for sin. Jesus Christ paid for our sins two thousand years ago when He died on the cross.

There is no end to hypothetical questions. I've been asked over and over again, "But what if. . .?" "What if. . .?" A man asked me one day, "What if a man gets out into open, known sin, and then on the way home runs his car into a telephone pole and is killed before he has time to confess his sin and get right with God? Do you mean to tell me that man is saved?"

I answered, "Yes, if he had trusted Jesus Christ as his Saviour, he is saved. He may have gone to Heaven with a red face, but he was saved. I must say what the Bible says, 'He that believeth on the Son hath everlasting life.'"

The man continued, "But he didn't have time to get right with God, and God didn't have time to chastise him."

I said, "What do you mean, 'God didn't have time to chastise him'? He killed him!"

First Corinthians 5:5 says, "To deliver such an one unto Satan for the destruction of the flesh, that the spirit may be saved in the day of the Lord Jesus." The premature death of a believer is the ultimate in Christian chastisement.

Trust Jesus Christ as Saviour Today

If you have never trusted Christ as your own personal Saviour, let me plead with you to trust Him today. Realize that you are a sinner and accept the clear teaching of the Bible that Jesus Christ died on the cross to pay our sin debt, then trust Him completely for your salvation.

The Bible says in John 3:36, "He that believeth on the Son hath everlasting life. . . ." And again, look at John 3:18, "He that believeth on him is not condemned. . . ." The word "believe" means to trust, to depend on, to rely on.

Will you completely trust Jesus Christ as your Saviour? If so, pray this simple prayer: "Dear Lord Jesus, I know that I am a sinner. I do believe that You died for me, and the best I know how, I do trust You as my Saviour. From this minute on, I'm depending on You to get me to Heaven. Now help me live for You and be a good Christian. Amen."

If you prayed that simple prayer, then I can promise you, on the authority of God's Word, that you have everlasting life. "He that believeth on the Son hath everlasting life. . . ."

The Believer and Doubt
CHAPTER THREE

"**W**hosoever believeth that Jesus is the Christ is born of God: and every one that loveth him that begat loveth him also that is begotten of him. By this we know that we love the children of God, when we love God, and keep his commandments. For this is the love of God, that we keep his commandments: and his commandments are not grievous. For whatsoever is born of God overcometh the world: and this is the victory that overcometh the world, even our faith. Who is he that overcometh the world, but he that believeth that Jesus is the Son of God? This is he that came by water and blood, even Jesus Christ; not by water only, but by water and blood. And it is the Spirit that beareth witness, because the Spirit is truth. For there are three that bear record in heaven, the Father, the Word, and the Holy Ghost: and these three are one. And there are three that bear witness in earth, the Spirit, and the water, and the blood: and these three agree in one. If we receive the witness of men, the witness of God is greater: for this is the witness of God which he hath testified of his Son. He that believeth on the Son of God hath the witness in himself: he that believeth not God hath made him a liar; because he believeth not the record that God gave of his Son. And this is the *record, that God hath given to us eternal life, and this life is in his Son. He that hath the Son hath life; and he that hath not the Son of God hath not life. These things have I written unto you that believe on the name of the Son of God; that ye may know that ye have eternal life, and that ye may believe on the name of the Son of God."* —I John 5:1-13.

I call your attention to verse 13, the verse often used when leading someone to the assurance of salvation:

"These things have I written unto you that believe on the name of the Son of God; that ye may know that ye have eternal life, and that ye may believe on the name of the Son of God."

I am alarmed at the number of people who are afraid to express assurance of salvation. There is either one of two reasons for that: first, they actually have doubts about it; or, second, they think it is presumptuous to say, "I know I am saved." I don't know of any other reason a person would fear to express the assurance of salvation.

I was saved when I was eleven years old, but I did not have assurance until in my early twenties. I could have had assurance the very day I was saved, but I didn't have it. No one showed me from the Bible how to be sure. For the first years after I was saved, when I felt good, I would think, *Well, I am saved now. Boy, I feel great.* Then I would have days of depression and would wonder, *Am I really saved? Maybe I just thought I was saved.* And I would doubt again. I was up and down...up and down...up and down...never really sure.

I went through life as an animated question mark. Then one day I learned the truth about assurance of salvation and got straightened out into an exclamation point. Now I know beyond a shadow of a doubt that I am saved, and I even know why I know I am saved.

It is possible for a person to doubt salvation. In II Peter, chapter 1, we read where Peter said, "Add to your faith virtue; and to virtue knowledge; And to knowledge temperance; and to temperance patience; and to patience godliness; And to godliness brotherly kindness; and to brotherly kindness charity" (vss. 5-7). He goes on to say, "But he that lacketh these things . . . cannot see afar off, and hath forgotten that he was purged from his old sins" (vs. 9). That is, if you do not add these things, you will get to the place where you will doubt that you are saved.

John the Baptist is an example of doubt in the Bible. He was imprisoned; and his disciples came to him and said, "Listen, Jesus is here doing mighty works." John said, "Go and ask Him, Are you the Christ, or should we look for another? I am not sure." John said, "I have my doubts." When you doubt, it doesn't mean you are lost; it just means you lack assurance. On the banks of the Caddo Lake near the Louisiana border not far from Marshall, Texas, is a little village named Uncertain. Imagine how confusing it is when a resident of this place visits in other lands. He is asked, "Where do you live?"

The fellow says, "Uncertain."

"You mean you are not certain where you live?"

"Yes, I am certain that I live in Uncertain."

A lot of Christians are certain they live in uncertain.

I. THE CONSEQUENCES OF DOUBT

First, when a man doubts his salvation, there is no fullness of joy. First John, chapter 5, verse 13, says:

"These things have I written unto you that believe on the name of the Son of God; that ye may know that ye have eternal life, and that ye may believe on the name of the Son of God."

That same epistle, in chapter 1, verse 4, says:

"These things write we unto you, that your joy may be full."

Why was First John written? Was it written that your joy may be full? Or was it written that ye may know that ye have eternal life? Both. Assurance of salvation and fullness of joy are

Siamese twins. You cannot separate them. It is absolutely impossible to have fullness of joy without having assurance of salvation. Doubt not only produces a lack of joy in the Christian life; but it hinders service. D. L. Moody said, "I have never known a Christian who was any good in the work of Christ who did not have assurance of salvation."

I've read that during the first part of the construction of the world's largest bridge in San Francisco, no safety devices were used; and twenty-three men fell to their deaths. During the construction of the last part of that bridge, a safety net was constructed at the cost of $100,000. At least ten men fell into the net and were saved. But the interesting thing is that the workers got twenty-five percent more done once they were assured they were safe.

It is the same way in Christian work. A man cannot put his all into the service of God and really go after souls until he is sure he is saved.

I will never forget when I got it settled. I am S-A-V-E-D! Today, tomorrow, day after tomorrow and twenty years from now, I am saved! And I don't have to worry about falling.

When we doubt, it destroys our joy. When we doubt, it destroys our usefulness. When we doubt, we cannot win souls. Over and over the Bible tells of those who, after meeting the Saviour, went immediately to find their loved ones and bring them to Christ.

Philip, for instance, in John, chapter 1, found Nathanael, his brother. And then Andrew found his brother Simon. And the woman at the well, after drinking the living water, ran to town and said, "Come, see a man, which told me all things that ever I did." These were people who first knew they had met the Master. They knew they were saved. There is an old story about a little fellow standing by the side of the road when a man came by who was lost. The stranger asked, "Say, fellow, how do you get to town?"

The little boy said, "I don't know."

"Where is Route 20?"

"I don't know."

"Where does this road go?"

"I don't know."

"What is the name of this street?"

"I don't know."

"Boy, you don't know anything, do you?"

The little fellow said, "I know I ain't lost."

And until you know you "ain't" lost, you are not going to win others to Christ.

When one doubts salvation, it not only kills his joy and his usefulness and keeps him from winning souls; but he never really gets active in fighting against sin. It is hard to resist the Devil until you know you are his opponent.

Martin Luther's battle with the Devil was a real battle. The Devil was a real person to him. It is said that there is a stained place on the wall of Martin Luther's study where once he took an inkwell and threw it where he thought the Devil was standing. The people who are doing something in this country are those who have settled the matter of salvation. They know that they know they are saved!

II. THE CAUSE OF DOUBT

Why do people doubt salvation? Some doubt because they don't remember *when* they were saved. I am not sure I like the song we used to sing some time ago:

"It was on a Monday Somebody touched me—" and everybody saved on Monday would stand.

Then we would sing, "It was on a Tuesday Somebody touched me—" and everybody saved on Tuesday would stand.

"It was on a Wednesday . . .," etc.

We sang until we mentioned every day of the week. And you stood on the day of the week that you were saved.

I don't remember whether it was Monday, Tuesday, Wednesday, Thursday, Friday, Saturday or Sunday when I was saved. I didn't like the song because I couldn't stand without lying.

Then some thought I wasn't saved because I couldn't remember the day I was saved. That actually caused me to doubt my salvation.

I have heard people testify in church, "Oh, bless God! I was saved October 5, 1921, in the south end of the cornfield. I was plowing old Alex, and I stopped at ten minutes after eleven and got down on my knees, prayed two hours and three minutes and eight seconds. Jesus Christ came into my heart, and I have been saved ever since."

I thought, *Boy, that is wonderful! I wish I had a testimony like that!* In fact, I made up a testimony one time but didn't have the nerve to give it.

In the country church in the day meetings they would give a certain day and certain time when they were saved, and the Devil would get on my shoulder and say, "You are not saved because you don't remember when it happened."

Do you know, I would go for months thinking, *Well, I am not saved because I can't remember the day.* And there are a lot of folks like that.

I have heard people say, "If you can't remember the day you were saved, then you are not saved." Well, let me turn it around. If you can't remember the day you were born, you are not born.

"But," you say, "I know I was born. I have a birth certificate." So have I. A spiritual one, too. I will tell you about it in a few minutes. Some people doubt because they don't remember the day.

Suppose I go to the bank to cash a check. "Listen, I need twenty dollars for something. I want to write a check."

"Well, Mr. Hutson, do you remember the day and hour you made your deposit?"

"No, I don't remember the exact day."

"I'm sorry. You don't have any money in this bank."

"What do you mean?"

"Well, you can't remember when you made your deposit, so you don't have money here." Listen, I have money there whether I can remember when I made the deposit or not.

I don't remember the exact day I trusted Jesus as Saviour either. I was eleven years old, or about eleven. I remember that. I remember it was at night, and I was on an old iron bedstead in the front bedroom of a five-room, frame house. I remember that. But that is about all I can remember. Are you telling me I am not saved? I have news for you. My ability to remember is not the basis of my assurance.

What about the poor Christians who become so forgetful in their latter years they can hardly remember their names? Are you telling me they are not saved?

What about the fellow who goes to the hospital, is put under an anesthetic, and doesn't know what he is saying? He forgets everything. You mean, while he has forgotten everything and is sick and doesn't know anything, he is not saved? No, he is just as saved as he ever was.

His ability to remember has nothing to do with whether or not he is saved.

A lot of people are very forgetful. They are like the fellow who went in to see the doctor. "Doctor, there is something wrong with me. I can't remember anything."

The doctor said, "Sit down here and tell me all about it."

The man replied, "Tell you about what?"

Some doubt because they can't remember when they were saved. Others doubt because they didn't have the same experience someone else had. Sometimes in the country church when folks got saved, they shouted. I have seen folks, after praying and trusting Christ, hug people and shout, "Glory to God! Hallelujah!" I would sit in the back of the church as a little boy and think, *I must not be saved. I didn't do anything like that. That woman ran up and down the church aisle shouting. I didn't do that when I got saved. I must not be saved.*

I didn't have their experience. I found that all people in the Bible didn't have the same experiences either. When Matthew was saved, he was sitting at the receipt of customs collecting taxes for the Roman government. Jesus came by and said, "Follow me." He got up and followed Him—saved. No big experience, no shouting, no hugging of necks, no handshaking, no right hand of fellowship, and no voting into the church.

Paul is riding a donkey. A light shines out of Heaven, and a voice speaks out of Heaven, "Saul, Saul, why persecutest thou me?" Then God knocks Paul off the donkey to the ground, and he goes blind. A man has to lead him around to the street called Straight. Then a man comes in and prays with him. The scales fall off his eyes and he can see.

So Paul says, "If you weren't riding a donkey when you got saved and if a light didn't shine from Heaven, if you didn't hear a great voice saying, 'Saul, Saul, why persecutest thou me?' if you didn't get knocked to the ground and blinded for three days, you are not saved." Do you know some preachers do that? They want everybody to have their same experience. If you didn't have their experience, you are not saved. That kind of teaching is not in the Bible. The Bible says in John 3:36, "He that believeth on the Son hath everlasting life." It does not say, 'He that believeth on the Son and has a certain experience has eternal life.' It does not say, 'He that believeth on the Son and has a certain feeling has eternal life.' Nor does it say, 'He that believeth on the Son and remembers the day and hour he did so has everlasting life.' What it does say very simply and plainly is, "He that believeth on the Son hath everlasting life." Feeling or no feeling, experience or no experience, memory or no memory, one has everlasting life the moment he trusts Jesus Christ as Saviour.

We don't all have to have the same experience. But if you put your faith in Jesus Christ, you are just as saved as the fellow who jumped up and down and shouted and ran up and down the church aisle. I heard a fellow say, "I know I am saved. I felt something cold go up my back, and my hair stood on end."

I said, "Well, some fellows couldn't get saved because they don't have any hair." (In fact, I could only get half saved!)

Some doubt because they don't remember when they were saved. Some doubt because they didn't have the same experience somebody else had. And others doubt because of their feelings. When I got saved, I must say, I did feel good. I had a heavy burden; and when the Lord saved me and I knew my sins were forgiven, it was as if a mountain had been rolled off my chest. Now, I don't tell that often because some young person, or maybe some older person, will think, *I didn't feel as if a mountain were rolled off my chest, so I must not be saved.* There was a feeling, and I thank God for the feeling. As a matter of fact, I feel pretty religious right now. But there were days when I didn't feel too good, and the Devil would say, "You don't feel like you did the night you got saved, do you?"

"No, Devil, I don't."

"Are you sure you are saved?"

"Well, I don't know. I thought I was. Now I don't know."

"Where is all the joy you had?"

"I don't know."

"Are you sure you are saved?"

"I don't know."

I've learned since then that we don't base the assurance of salvation on our changing feelings.

We base the assurance of salvation on the unchanging Word of God.

> **For feelings come and feelings go,**
> **And feelings are deceiving.**
> **My warrant is the Word of God—**
> **Naught else is worth believing.**

> **Though all my soul should feel condemned,**
> **For want of some sweet token,**
> **There is One greater than my heart,**
> **Whose Word cannot be broken.**

> **I'll stand on His unchanging Word,**
> **Till soul and body sever,**
> **For though all things should pass away**
> **His Word shall stand forever.**

I do not know I'm saved because I feel good. I know I am saved because God said so in His Word. And I feel good because I know I am saved.

I remember when I married. We went to the preacher's house. He had forgotten we were coming, so he had a housecoat on when we arrived. He said, "Can I help you?"

I said, "I hope so. We came to get married."

"Oh, that is right. You were coming to get married."

My wife's cousin stood with her, and she was the only one there besides us and the preacher. He said, "Do you take this woman, whom you hold by the right hand, to be your lawful wedded wife?" (I think he said that! I don't remember what he said.) When he looked at me quizzically I said, "I do."

Then he asked Gerri, "Do you take this man, whom you hold by the right hand, to be your lawful wedded husband?"

I could feel her hand shaking as it tightened up on mine, then loosen up. I didn't know whether she was about to turn loose and run or not! But she said, "I do."

He said, "I now pronounce you husband and wife in the presence of God and these assembled witnesses." (I didn't see any witness except her cousin.)

We walked out of the house, and I said to myself, "I am married!"

We got in the car and stopped by to see some friends. Do you know what they said? "Well, how does it *feel* to be married?"

I said, "I don't know. No particular feeling." Now do you suppose I wasn't married because I didn't have a feeling? Certainly not!

I was just as married when I said, "I do," as I am today after thirty-four years of married life.

"Well, I hope I am saved. I don't know whether I had the right feeling or not."

Listen, your feelings fluctuate. They are up and down. Forget your feelings and take what God said, and stand on it. Some doubt because of feelings. Be my feelings what they will, Jesus is my Saviour still.

III. THE CURE FOR DOUBT

The cure for doubt is God's Word. First John 5:13 says, "These things have I written unto you that believe on the name of the Son of God; that ye may KNOW that ye have eternal life...."

Suppose I ask a fellow, "Are you married?"

He says, "I sure hope so. I have been living with this woman twenty-one years, and we have six kids. Man, I hope I am married! But I am not sure. I have my doubts."

What would you think of a fellow like that? You would think him a candidate for the insane asylum, wouldn't you?

Everybody who is married knows it. I never met a fellow who said, "I hope I am married," or "I think I am married." Everybody I ask says, "Yes," or "No."

I know I am married because I have a piece of paper. They call it a marriage certificate. It says that on a certain day Curtis Wiley Hutson of Decatur, Georgia, was united in marriage to Barbara Geraldine Crawford.

How do you know you are saved? Let's see what the Bible says.

"These things have I written unto you that believe on the name of the Son of God; that ye may know that ye have eternal life...."—I John 5:13.

Now what did He say? "These *feelings* have I given you that you may know..."? "*This vision* have I given you that you may know..."? No.

"These things have I written unto you...that ye may know." We have something better than feelings. We have the written Word of God.

When you buy something, you want it in black and white. You want it in writing.

You go to buy a house—"I will pay you so much for that house."

"Okay. Put it down in black and white. Put it in writing."

You go to buy a car. "Give me a sales contract. Put it in black and white."

Did you know that your salvation is down in writing? That is better than feelings because Isaiah 40:8 says, "The grass withereth, the flower fadeth: but the word of our God shall stand for ever." Mark 13:31 says, "Heaven and earth shall pass away: but my words shall not pass away."

The written Word is better than feelings because feelings pass away, but the Word of God never passes away. Feelings change, but the Word of God never changes.

Jesus, how can I *know* I am saved? "These things have I written unto you...that ye may know...." What did He write?

John 3:36: "He that believeth on the Son hath everlasting life."

All right, Jesus, I believe on the Son. I believe He died for me. I believe that on the cross He suffered my Hell and paid my debt. I trust Jesus as my Saviour. Now, in writing, God Almighty says I have everlasting life. I know I have it because He wrote it in the Bible.

Romans 10:13: "Whosoever shall call upon the name of the Lord shall be saved."

All right, I called upon Him. He said if I call, I am saved. I know I am saved because He said so and put it in the Bible in writing.

John 3:16: "...that whosoever believeth in him should not perish, but have everlasting life." He wrote it. If you believe on Him, you have everlasting life and shall never perish. I know I am saved because of what He wrote.

"These things have I *written* unto you that believe on the name of the Son of God; that ye may know that ye have eternal life...."

If you have doubts about your salvation at this moment, there are only two things you can possibly doubt: either you doubt that you have trusted Him, or you doubt that He meant what He said.

I led a lady to Christ who was near seventy. I will never forget it. She was one of the most difficult to lead to the assurance of salvation. After she had prayed and said, "I will trust Jesus Christ as Saviour," then I said to her, "Now then, Mrs. So-and-So, if you died today, would you go to Heaven?"

"I hope so."

"Hope?"

"Yes, I hope I will."

"That means you have some doubts?"

"That is right."

I said, "There are only two things you can doubt. You either doubt that you trusted Him completely for salvation or you doubt that God meant what He said. Now which one do you doubt?"

She said, "Well, I don't doubt that God meant what He said."

I said, "There is only one thing left that you could doubt and that is that you trusted Him. You prayed and told Him you would trust Him, you would depend on Him to get you to Heaven. Now did you mean it?"

She began to smile. "I see it! I don't doubt that I trusted Him, and I don't doubt that He meant what He said when He said I would have everlasting life. I have to have everlasting life! He said it in the Bible, so it has to be true." Then she began to smile more and said, "I have everlasting life! I would go to Heaven if I were to die. And there is no doubt about it. I know I am saved."

"Why do you know you are saved?" I asked.

"Because God Almighty said so in the Bible."

I said, "When the Bible ceases to be true, you will be lost. But as long as the Bible is true, you are saved."

I had rather have what the Bible says for the assurance of my salvation than to have every angel in Heaven come down to earth and tell me I am saved.

Suppose Gabriel came down from Heaven and said, "Dr. Hutson, I want to tell you that you are saved, you have everlasting life, and when you die, you are going to Heaven."

I would say, "Gabriel, I am glad you came. That is a long trip for you to make, and I appreciate your coming. But you didn't need to come. I have something better than your word. I have the very Word of God."

I had rather have the Bible than a tape recording of God's voice. I would play it on the tape recorder and hear, "Curtis, you are saved"; but I would always think some nut put that on tape.

I had rather have the written Word than have God call me on the telephone. If He called me on the phone and said, "Curtis, this is God. I want to tell you that you are saved," I wouldn't believe it. You wouldn't either. You would think some nut had called you. You would never believe it was God.

> **How firm a foundation, ye saints of the Lord,**
> **Is laid for your faith in His excellent Word!**
> **What more can He say than to you He hath said,**
> **To you who for refuge to Jesus have fled?**

I had rather have the Bible for the assurance of salvation because it is what God gave me. "These things have I *written* unto you that believe on the name of the Son of God; that ye may know that ye have eternal life. . . . "

If you have trusted Christ and say, "I hope I am saved," you are saying, "I hope God told the truth." You are implying that God may have lied about it.

I am more sure that I am saved than I am that I am alive. I am more sure that I am saved than I am that I am married. Why? Because I have better assurance for it. I have God Almighty's written Word that has never changed and never will change.

A preacher once asked me, "You mean the Bible is all you have for your assurance?" I said, "Yes, do you have anything better?" He thought a minute and replied, "Well, I don't guess so."

Latch onto this and hang onto it.

If some friend says you are not saved, do not believe him; believe the Bible. If your feelings seem to say you are not saved, do not believe your feelings; believe the Bible. Even if you get to thinking that you are not saved, do not believe your thinking; believe the Bible.

Friends have deceived you, feelings have deceived you, even your thinking has deceived you. But the Word of God has never deceived anyone and never will. The Bible is true: "He that believeth on the Son hath everlasting life."

> **Blessed assurance, Jesus is mine!**
>   **Oh, what a foretaste of glory divine!**
> **Heir of salvation, purchase of God,**
>   **Born of His Spirit, washed in His blood.**
> **This is my story, this is my song,**
>   **Praising my Saviour all the day long;**
> **This is my story, this is my song,**
>   **Praising my Saviour all the day long.**

In conclusion, if you will answer three questions honestly, I can tell you whether or not you are saved.

1. Do you know that you are a sinner, that you have sinned, that you are not perfect?

2. Do you believe that Jesus Christ died on the cross for your sins, just like the Bible says in John 3:16?

3. Are you trusting Jesus Christ to take you to Heaven? By that I mean, are you depending on Him, relying on Him, as your only hope of salvation? If you can answer "yes" to all three questions, then I guarantee you, on the basis of the Word of God, that you have everlasting life, you will never perish, you will go to Heaven when you die.

Here it is again: "He that believeth on the Son hath everlasting life: and he that believeth not the Son shall not see life; but the wrath of God abideth on him" (John 3:36).

You are either believing or not believing. If you are believing, you have everlasting life. If you are not believing, you shall not see life, but the wrath of God abides on you.

That is as simple and as plain as it can possibly be. If you are not sure you have trusted Him, then trust Him now. Tell Him in your own words: "Dear Lord Jesus, I know that I am a sinner, and I do trust You for my salvation."

The Believer and Sin

C H A P T E R   F O U R

Everyone who trusts Christ as Saviour is saved, but everyone who is saved is not the same. Some Christians live victoriously, while others live in defeat. Some are happy and excited, while others are discouraged and depressed. Some go on regardless of failure, while others allow failure to get them down. What is the difference?

The difference is not that one is more accepted than the other. The ground for acceptance is the same for all. We must remember that it is impossible for anyone to make himself acceptable to God. God does not accept us because of our good works or good living. He does not accept us because of what we do, don't do, or promise to do. The Bible says in Ephesians 1:6, "He hath made us accepted in the beloved." The only thing that satisfied God for our sins was the death of Jesus Christ on the cross, and the only person God accepts is the one who trusts in Jesus and His finished work at Calvary.

This is illustrated in an Old Testament story recorded in Exodus 12. The angel of the Lord was to pass through Egypt, and the first-born in every house was to die. But God instructed the Israelites to kill an innocent lamb and sprinkle blood on the doorposts of their houses. God said in Exodus 12:13, "When I see the blood, I will pass over you." Suppose some family hung their baptismal certificates on the door. Would they have been safe? Absolutely not! God did not say, "When I see your baptismal certificates, I will pass over you." He said, "When I see the blood, I will pass over you."

Suppose others had hung their Sunday school pins on the door, signifying their faithful attendance at the local church. Would they have been safe? No. God did not say, "When I see your faithful church attendance, I will pass over you."

They could have hung a list of their achievements on the door or maybe a list of their good works, but the only people who were safe were those who were trusting in the shed blood of the sacrifice. And the only people whom God accepts are those who are trusting Jesus as Saviour.

When we put our faith in Christ, Him alone and nothing else, we are "made...accepted in the beloved." And since everyone is accepted on the same basis, then no one is more accepted than the other. All who have trusted Christ have the same standing with the Father. When we trust Jesus as Saviour, God accepts us just like He accepts Christ because He accepts us in Christ, in the Beloved.

We are so accustomed to accepting people because of what they are and rejecting them for what they are not that somehow we believe God must operate that way, too. But if God accepted us because of what we were or were not, or because of what we did or did not do, then no one would be accepted. Isaiah 64:6 says, "But we are all as an unclean thing, and all our righteousnesses are as filthy rags; and we all do fade as a leaf; and our iniquities, like the wind, have taken us away." Since all have been accepted alike, on the same basis and forever, then why are Christians different? Why are some victorious while others are defeated? One is no more saved than the other nor is he more a child of God than the other. All those who trust Christ have been justified; they have everlasting life, and are all the sons of God. So what is the difference?

The difference is in what we do about our sins after we are saved. Discouragement may be the Devil's most effective tool against the believer, and the one thing he uses most to discourage us is our failure to be everything God wants us to be.

Now let's face the facts. Every Christian sins. The Bible says in I John 1:10, "If we say that we have not sinned, we make him a liar." The best Christians in the Bible sinned. David sinned. Noah sinned. Lot sinned. Peter sinned. And the list goes on.

The difference in Christians is not that one sins and the other doesn't. No, we all fail. But the difference is in what we do with our sins.

Several years ago I led a policeman to Christ. The next Sunday he came to church and joined for baptism. For several weeks he didn't miss a single service. As a matter of fact, he was one of the first ones to arrive at the church. In no time at all, he was attending soul-winning visitation; and I remember so well several visits he and I made together. He got so excited about soul winning that he kept a supply of gospel tracts in his pocket. When he stopped people for speeding, he would give them a ticket and a gospel tract. Some of these people later came to the church, and this young Christian led several to Christ.

A few months later, I missed him in the church services. When I went to visit, he was sitting on the front porch. I inquired as to why he had been absent from church, and very sadly he said, "I can't live it." He explained that he had done some things that Christians shouldn't do, things that were unbecoming to a Christian life.

I shared with him I John 1:9 and explained that the believer should confess his sins. "Yes, I know," he said, "but God is tired of my asking forgiveness for the same thing over and over again! And I have decided to drop out of church until I know I can live it."

His story is one that has happened thousands of times. The Devil had discouraged him because of his failure in the Christian life. The greatest blunder Christians make is not their failure in trying to live for Christ, but their failure to understand God's provision for sin.

Let's look at several important Bible facts.

I. CHRIST DIED ON THE CROSS FOR ALL OUR SINS

I cannot overemphasize that fact. It needs to be shouted from every housetop in the community; it needs to be told over and over again. There is not a sin, no matter how small or how great, that Jesus did not die for. The Bible says in Isaiah 53:6, ". . . and the Lord hath laid on him the iniquity of us all." The Scripture says in I Peter 2:24, "Who his own self bare our sins in his own body on the tree . . . ." And II Corinthians 5:21 says, "For he hath made him to be sin for us, who knew no sin; that we might be made the righteousness of God in him." When I was a young Christian, I got the idea that Jesus died for my past sins—that is, the sins I committed before I was saved. But somehow I could not see that He died for my future sins. I thought that I must suffer, be discouraged, defeated, sorrowful, and depressed for any sin I committed after trusting Christ as Saviour. After years of defeat, I finally realized that Jesus died for all my sins—past, present, and future; and I could sing:

> My sin—oh, the bliss of this glorious tho't—
> My sin—not in part, but the whole—
> Is nailed to the cross and I bear it no more,
> Praise the Lord, praise the Lord, O my soul!

The songwriter certainly knew what he was talking about when he wrote:

> Why did they nail Him to Calvary's tree?
> Why? tell me, why was He there?
> Jesus the Helper, the Healer, the Friend—
> Why? tell me, why was He there?
>
> All my iniquities on Him were laid—
> He nailed them all to the tree.
> Jesus the debt of my sin fully paid—
> He paid the ransom for me.

The greatest truth that ever coursed through my brain is the truth of the substitutionary death of Jesus on the cross. There is not a sin great or small, past, present or future for which Jesus did not die. There is no sin that you will ever commit which has not already been paid for by Christ's substitutionary death at Calvary.

God does not find it difficult to forgive us. As a matter of fact, He does not forgive sin; He forgives the sinner. "Forgive" means to bear the burden, and the burden of our sin was laid on Jesus two thousand years ago. At Calvary He bore the burden of our guilt and satisfied the just demands of a holy God. The price of forgiveness has already been paid. All God wants us to do is accept it freely.

It is an insult to God not to accept the payment He provided in Jesus Christ.

II. GOD DOES NOT MAKE US PAY FOR OUR SINS

To be sure, He chastens us; but chastisement is not payment for sin. We will talk about that later. The death of Jesus on the cross was full payment for the sins of the whole world. The Bible says in I John 2:2, "And he [Christ] is the propitiation for our sins: and not for our's only, but also for the sins of the whole world." That simply means that the death of Jesus on the cross satisfied God for all sins which have ever been committed or ever will be committed.

Isaiah 53:5 says, "He was wounded for our transgressions, he was bruised for our iniquities: the chastisement of our peace was upon him; and with his stripes we are healed." The word "transgress" means to cross the line. Jesus was wounded for every time we crossed the line. Every person who ever lived has at times deliberately and willfully disobeyed the commands of God. We have crossed the line, but Jesus was wounded for every time we crossed the line. He was bruised for our iniquities.

We sometimes sing the invitational hymn:

> **Jesus paid it all,**
> **All to Him I owe;**

> **Sin had left a crimson stain,**
> **He washed it white as snow.**

It is not easy for us to accept the fact that the death of Jesus Christ is complete payment for our sins. We somehow feel that we must at least suffer for some of them. While Jesus was hanging on the cross, He uttered seven things. The sixth utterance was, "It is finished" (John 19:30). I have read that the expression is one Greek word, *tetelestai,* a word used for business transactions. When this word was written across a bill, it meant "paid in full."

I have also read that it is the word of an artist. After working for months on a painting, when the final touch has been made to the canvas, the artist stands, stares with complete satisfaction, and says, *"tetelestai,"* meaning it is completed. Nothing can be added to it, and nothing can be taken from it.

In his song, "Hallelujah, What a Saviour!" Philip P. Bliss wrote:

> **Lifted up was He to die,**
> **"It is finished," was His cry;**
> **Now in Heav'n exalted high;**
> **Hallelujah! what a Saviour!**

"It is finished," are the most important words in the Bible to understand; but they are also the most misunderstood words. The world is filled with religions that have never understood the meaning of Jesus' cry, "It is finished." They do not believe that Jesus completely paid for our sins, so they add something to His finished work as a requirement for salvation. They either add sacraments, rituals, ceremonies or good works. But when Jesus died on the cross, everything necessary for our salvation was done: " 'Tis done: the great transaction's done; I am my Lord's, and He is mine."

The Bible says in Isaiah 53:10, "Yet it pleased the Lord to bruise him; he hath put him to grief: when thou shalt make his soul an offering for sin...." Jesus paid for all our sins, not simply the sins we committed before we were saved, but the sins

we will commit tomorrow and the next day and for as long as
we shall live.

I have heard preachers say, "If you sin, you will pay for it,"
but that is not taught in the Bible. If we paid for any sin we
would have to die, go into Hell, and stay there forever. You see,
God has only one payment for sin. Romans 6:23 says, "The wages
of sin is death." That death is described in the Bible in Revelation 20:14 as the second death. Here the Scripture says, "Death
and hell were cast into the lake of fire. This is the second death."

I mentioned earlier that God does chasten His children, but
chastisement is not payment for sin; it is child correction.
Hebrews 12:6 states, "For whom the Lord loveth he chasteneth,
and scourgeth every son whom he receiveth." Once we trust
Christ as Saviour, God never deals with us again as a sinner.
From that moment on, He deals with us as sons. Let me see if
I can illustrate this truth.

Suppose I caution my son about his careless driving and warn
him that if he wrecks the car I will deal with him. Some time
later he wrecks the automobile. And let's suppose I give him
an old-fashioned spanking (or, as my father would say, whipping). Did the spanking pay for the automobile? Absolutely not.
After I spank my son, I still have to pay the body shop to repair
the automobile. I paid for the repair, but I spanked my son so
he would be more careful about his driving.

God chastens believers. However, the chastening never pays
for our sins. Jesus paid for all our sins when He died on the cross,
so God does not make us pay for them.

III. HOW DO WE OBTAIN FORGIVENESS?

The first epistle of John, containing 5 chapters and 105 verses,
was written to believers. First John 5:13 says, "These things
have I written unto you that *believe* on the name of the Son of
God. . . ." One of the most blessed verses in the Bible for Christians is I John 1:9, "If we confess our sins, he is faithful and
just to forgive us our sins, and to cleanse us from all unright-

eousness." All we need do to obtain forgiveness and cleansing is confess our sins. To confess does not mean to beg, plead or live in misery until we convince God that we mean business; it simply means that we agree with God about our sin and freely accept His forgiveness.

The moment we trust Christ as Saviour, we are permanently accepted in the Beloved. But if we sin after we are saved, we need forgiveness and cleansing in order to maintain fellowship with God. Sonship is one thing; fellowship is quite another. First John 1:7 says, "If we walk in the light, as he is in the light, we have fellowship one with another, and the blood of Jesus Christ his Son cleanseth us from all sin."

Unconfessed sin in the believer's life causes loss of joy. David prayed, in Psalm 51:12, "Restore unto me the joy of thy salvation." He also prayed in verse 7, "Purge me with hyssop, and I shall be clean: wash me, and I shall be whiter than snow." He continued in verse 8, "Make me to hear joy and gladness; that the bones which thou hast broken may rejoice."

David was out of fellowship with God. He was not a happy, victorious Christian because he had not confessed his sins and obtained forgiveness and cleansing.

Martin Luther used to say, "Keep short accounts with God." It was his way of saying, "Don't let sin pile up in your life." One reason Christians should pray every day is to obtain forgiveness and cleansing for the sins of that day. It is best to confess the sin immediately. The moment you are aware of sin is the time to confess it.

You need not kneel to pray. You can pray while driving or sweeping the floor or washing dishes. All you need do is simply say, "Dear Lord, I realize I have sinned," and then tell Him what you did that was sinful and say, "Dear Lord, I confess this as a sin because I want to be forgiven and cleansed." Then simply accept His forgiveness.

I often say, "Lord, I know I'm forgiven and cleansed because You said so in the Bible, and You cannot lie about it." When

you confess sin, you can be sure you are forgiven. That is
exactly what the Bible says, and God cannot lie.

But confession brings more than forgiveness.

IV. CONFESSION ALSO BRINGS CLEANSING

First John 1:9 not only promises forgiveness, but also cleansing for those who confess their sins. "If we confess our sins, he
is faithful and just to forgive us our sins, and to *cleanse* us from
all unrighteousness." It is one thing to be forgiven and quite
another to be *cleansed*.

I have illustrated this truth by telling the story of the little
girl who got dressed for Sunday school; and while her mother
and father were dressing, she went outside. Walking too near
the mud, she slipped and fell into it. Running back into the
house, she asked her mother's forgiveness. Quickly the mother
said, "You are forgiven," but she went beyond forgiveness. She
took the muddy clothes off the little girl, gave her another bath,
washed and blow-dried her hair, and put a clean dress, clean
socks and shoes on her. In other words, she fixed her back like
she was before she fell into the mud. She forgave her and
cleansed her. And when the little girl arrived at Sunday school,
no one ever knew she had fallen into the mud.

When we confess our sins, God not only forgives, but *cleanses*
us. Isaiah 43:25 says, "I, even I, am he that blotteth out thy
transgressions for mine own sake, and will not remember thy
sins." Isaiah 44:22 says, "I have blotted out, as a thick cloud,
thy transgressions, and, as a cloud, thy sins." And Psalm 103:12
reminds us, "As far as the east is from the west, so far hath he
removed our transgressions from us." That is an immeasurable
distance! You can travel east or west forever because there are
no east or west poles. But you cannot travel north or south
forever.

When we confess our sins, they are blotted out; they no longer
exist.

For several years, my wife has been asking me to buy her a

microwave oven. Not being too excited about the idea, I tried to discourage it. But every time she visited a friend who had one, she came home talking about a microwave oven. Finally last year I gave in and bought her one for Christmas.

Several weeks went by before I had an occasion to use it. One day my coffee was cold, and I started to pour it out and get a fresh cup when my wife reminded me that I could heat it in a few seconds in the microwave. I complained that I didn't know how to operate it. So she gave instructions from the other room: "Place the cup of coffee in the oven. Close the door. Now press in the time you want and then press the start button." All went well until I went to enter the time. Instead of entering 40 seconds, I entered 4 minutes. *Oh,* I thought, *I'm in a mess now! The cup will melt away in 4 minutes! I have made an awful mistake!*

"Honey," I said, "I have really blown it! I have entered 4 minutes instead of 40 seconds."

"Well," she said, "look down at the bottom of the oven. There are several little buttons across there. One is a 'clear' button. Simply push 'clear,' " she said, "and it will clear everything out and you can start over again."

When I pressed the "clear" button, the mistake I made was gone. I thought, *What a wonderful illustration!* First John 1:9 is the Christian's "clear" button. "If we confess our sins, he is faithful and just to forgive us our sins, and to cleanse [clear] us from all unrighteousness."

That is hard to believe; but when we confess our sins, God not only forgives, He cleanses us. And we can begin again without worrying about our past mistakes. If we mess up again, we can push the "clear" button again. And every time we mess up we simply follow the instructions found in I John 1:9.

But I can hear someone asking,

V. "HOW MANY TIMES WILL GOD FORGIVE US?"

Just this week I received a call from a man who was concerned

about this very problem. He said, "You are the third preacher
I have called today, and I failed to get the other two on the phone.
I was afraid that I couldn't get you."

I assured him that I was more than happy to talk with him,
and he told how he was having a difficult time with a certain
sin in his life.

"I know it is wrong," he said, "and I have asked God to forgive
me; but I find myself doing the same thing over and over again."

I asked him to open his Bible to I John 1:9 and shared the verse
with him over the phone. I explained it just as I have in this
message, and we prayed together. I said, "Simply confess your
sin to God and accept the forgiveness and cleansing He offers."

"But," he said, "I have prayed about it and have gone to God
so many times that I'm afraid He is tired of me. How many times
will He forgive?" And then quickly answering his own question
he said, "Somewhere I read in the Bible 'seven times seventy.'"
Then, almost as if he were trying to comfort himself, he said,
"I don't think I have done it that many times!" The word
"faithful" means more than seven times seventy.

I quoted the verse again, emphasizing the word "faithful"; "If
we confess our sins, he is *FAITHFUL* and just to forgive us our
sins, and to cleanse us from all unrighteousness." I explained
that the word "faithful" meant every time.

A man who is faithful to his wife 364 days a year is not faithful.
Faithfulness is 365 days a year—every day of the year. And
"faithful" means every time.

We will never confess a sin to Christ that He does not forgive
and cleanse. Romans 5:20 states, "Where sin abounded, grace
did much more abound"—that is, where sin increased, grace increased all the more. Forgiveness and cleansing are always
available to those who confess their sins. There are no limits
on God's forgiveness. The shed blood of Jesus is adequate to cover
all our sins. This sounds too good to be true. That is the reason
many Christians live defeated, unhappy lives. They fail and fail
again. By and by they become discouraged, thinking God is

weary of hearing their confessions. But although we become weary of confessing the same sins over and over again, God never becomes weary of hearing our confessions.

Suppose I confessed the same sin at least 100 times and said, "Dear Lord, I know I have confessed this sin over and over again, and I know You get tired of hearing me." God would simply say, "What sin?"

I have already quoted Isaiah 43:25 which says, "I, even I, am he that blotteth out thy transgressions for mine own sake, *and will not remember thy sins.*" It sounds too good to be true; but when God forgives, God forgets. And when God forgets, He forgets! He has a divine forgetter, and no one can make Him remember our sins. If I confess a sin a hundred times or more and say, "Dear Lord, I know this is the 113th time I have been to You about this sin," He would interrupt and say, "No, this is the first time." You see, the other 112 times I confessed it, He forgave me, cleansed me, blotted it out, and forgot it.

> **His love has no limit, His grace has no measure,**
> **His pow'r has no boundary known unto men;**
> **For out of His infinite riches in Jesus,**
> **He giveth, and giveth, and giveth again!**

The sins you confessed yesterday will never again be a barrier between you and God. They will no longer interrupt your fellowship with Him unless you refuse to accept God's forgiveness and doubt the value of Christ's sacrificial death at Calvary.

When the believer gets hold of this blessed truth and learns to confess sin immediately, he can walk in unbroken fellowship with Christ. And unbroken fellowship means a happy, victorious Christian life.

Many reading these lines have gone days, weeks, even months, without prayer. Some have allowed sin to accumulate. In that case, the only thing to do is clear away the brush pile of sin, one stick at a time. Begin now to confess every known sin to Christ, then ask Him to help you remember those you have forgotten.

David prayed in Psalm 139:23,24, "Search me, O God, and know my heart: try me, and know my thoughts: And see if there be any wicked way in me. . . ." When God calls sins to mind, confess them immediately. And each time you confess a sin, accept the forgiveness and cleansing He promises. Whether you believe it or not, when you confess sin, it is forgiven and cleansed. That is the clear promise of God. But. . .

VI. WE MUST LEARN TO FORGIVE OURSELVES

The moment we confess our sins God forgives and cleanses us. The problem is, sometimes we won't forgive ourselves. Whether consciously or unconsciously, we want to pay for our sins. We just cannot accept the fact that God will forgive us and cleanse us. Somewhere we have gotten the idea that we must suffer. Several years ago two young sisters visited their grandparents. One day while out playing, they discovered a bicycle in the garage and asked if they could ride it. The grandmother agreed, but the girls could not agree which one should ride first, and an argument ensued. The older girl, being the largest, won and rode away on the bicycle. The younger sister screamed, "I hope it kills you!"

A few minutes later a car hit the little girl on the bike, and she was instantly killed. Her sister never forgot the words, "I hope it kills you!" She had made an awful mistake and somehow felt that she should pay. Her grades went down at school. She lost interest in everything. She spent many hours scolding herself for what she had done. Somehow she felt that she should never be happy again. To be happy, she thought, would be an indication that she was not truly sorry for her mistake. When she turned 19, she committed suicide. Why? Because she could not forgive herself. God is much more willing to forgive us than we are to forgive ourselves.

A mother sent her son to the store to pick up some items, but he never returned. An accident occurred not far from the house, and the boy was killed instantly. When I saw the mother, she said, "Oh, if I had not sent him to the store, he would still be alive!"

We did our best to comfort her, but she insisted, "No, if I had not sent him to the store, he would still be alive!" She felt totally responsible for his death and felt that if she forgave herself, it would be disrespect for her son.

When we sin or fail, we must not only confess our sin and accept the forgiveness and cleansing God offers on the basis of Christ's sacrifice; but we must go a step further and forgive ourselves.

Thousands of Christians are worrying over things that God has already forgiven and forgotten, and in Heaven they will be surprised to learn that God doesn't even know about the things they are worrying over.

If the death of Jesus Christ on the cross has paid the penalty for our sins and failures, why should we try to add our continual regret to His finished work? There is no reason we should be defeated. We are accepted in the Beloved; and if our fellowship is broken, it can be restored immediately by confession. The difference between the victorious and defeated believer is in what he does with his sins.

VII. ARE THERE NO CONSEQUENCES WHEN A CHRISTIAN SINS?

Yes. There are consequences when Christians fail to confess their sins and accept the forgiveness and cleansing God promises. **There is the loss of joy.** In Psalm 51:12 David prayed, "Restore unto me the joy of thy salvation." Earlier, in verse 7, he had said, "Purge me with hyssop, and I shall be clean: wash me, and I shall be whiter than snow." Because of unconfessed sin, David had lost the joy of salvation.

Unconfessed sin also results in chastening. Hebrews 12:6 says, "For whom the Lord loveth he chasteneth, and scourgeth every son whom he receiveth." Chastisement is the result of unconfessed sins. The Bible says in I Corinthians 11:31,32, "For if we would judge ourselves, we should not be judged. But when we are judged, we are chastened of the Lord, that we should not be condemned with the world." The purpose of self-judgment is to spot sin in our lives, confess it, and obtain forgiveness and cleansing. When we fail to do this, the Bible says we are judged of the Lord and chastened that we should not be condemned with the world.

But remember that chastisement is not payment for sin; it is child correction to make us better Christians. Hebrews 12:10 says, "For they [earthly fathers] verily for a few days chastened us after their own pleasure; but he for our profit, that we might be partakers of his holiness." Chastisement is for our profit. Verse 11 says, "...it yieldeth the peaceable fruit of righteousness unto them which are exercised thereby." **Unconfessed sin makes us ineffective soul winners.** In Psalm 51, after David asked for forgiveness and cleansing and the restoration of joy, he said in verse 13, "Then will I teach transgressors thy ways; and sinners shall be converted unto thee."

Because of unconfessed sin, David not only lost the joy of salvation, but he was not teaching transgressors the way and sinners were not being converted to Christ. Unconfessed sin makes us ineffective soul winners.

Sin unconfessed hinders our prayers. In Psalm 66:18, David said, "If I regard iniquity in my heart, the Lord will not hear me." And Isaiah 59:1,2 says, "Behold, the Lord's hand is not shortened, that it cannot save; neither his ear heavy, that it cannot hear: But your iniquities have separated between you and your God, and your sins have hid his face from you, that he will not hear." **Unconfessed sin in the believer's life stops the ears of God.**

Even when we confess our sins and obtain forgiveness and cleansing, and though God forgets our sins, that does not eliminate all the consequences. The guilt is gone, but the consequences remain. There are what I call the natural and spiritual consequences of sin. When we confess our sin, God forgives and cleanses us, and there are no spiritual consequences. Jesus took the spiritual consequences of our sins when He died on the cross. He paid it all. But even when sin is confessed, forgiven, cleansed, and forgotten, there still remain the natural consequences.

Recently I visited two young men in the county jail. They are facing trial for an awful crime. After making sure that both had trusted Christ as Saviour, I then talked about their sins. Sharing I John 1:9, I said, "If you confess your sin, God is faithful and just to forgive you and to cleanse you from all unrighteousness." I explained thoroughly the truths I have shared in this message, and they promised to confess their sins and claim the forgiveness and cleansing which God offers. I then shared with them Acts 24:16, "And herein do I exercise myself, to have always a conscience void of offence toward God, and toward men." I reminded them that first we should clear our conscience toward God by confessing our sins and then do everything in our power to have a conscience void of offence toward men as well. "Once you confess your sins and obtain forgiveness and cleansing," I said, "then you should go to those you have wronged and ask their forgiveness. Tell them that God has forgiven you and you want their forgiveness, too." They both agreed to do everything in their power not only to clear their consciences toward God but also toward men, and seemed very encouraged and happy despite their present surroundings. Then I further explained that sin has natural as well as spiritual consequences.

"It is very likely," I said, "that you will have to spend time in the State Penitentiary." I went on to explain that even though several years may be taken from their lives, they could still be a blessing in the prison by winning others to Christ and teaching them all they knew about the Bible.

Several days later I received a letter from one of the young men in which he said, "I really appreciate you for taking time to visit me, and every word you said helped me to realize a lot of things. I realize that things don't have to stop for me now and that I can be a real help to my fellow inmates, and I am going to try my best to do it."

Christmas Evans, a great preacher of yesterday, got into a fight before he was saved and lost an eye in that fight. Later God forgave and cleared him from all the guilt. But Christmas Evans was a one-eyed Christian as long as he lived. He never had to suffer the spiritual consequences of sin, but he did suffer the natural consequence—the loss of an eye.

Even though God forgives, **sin weakens our moral and spiritual resistance.** When a person takes something that is not rightfully his, it becomes much easier to steal the next time. The carnal mind reasons, *Well, I have already stolen once; I won't be any more of a thief if I steal again.* In years of counseling, I have discovered that once people commit a sin, it becomes easier to commit the same sin again.

I am thinking now of a sweet Christian lady who told how she got into sin before she was saved. She attended a party and drank until she was drunk. She said, "I woke up the next morning in bed with a man. It was the first time I had ever committed immorality. But after that," she continued, "it became easy. I figured I was already guilty and I wouldn't be any more guilty if I did it again." That is the natural consequence of sin. It weakens our moral and spiritual resistance. And if the Devil can get us to yield to temptation in some area, you can be sure he will attack us again and again in that same area because he knows it will be much easier to get us to yield the second time.

Christians can have forgiveness and cleansing, but there is no way to restore the lost years. Let's suppose a Christian gets away from Christ and neglects church, Bible reading, and prayer for three years. Then one day he decides to get right with God. He confesses his sins; and God forgives, cleanses, and forgets. The man has as good a standing with God as he has ever had or ever will have, but there is no way he can make up for those three years of lost Christian service.

Even though sin is confessed and forgiven, it sometimes

brings a reproach upon Christ and the Bible. The Bible says in Psalm 23:3, "He leadeth me in the paths of righteousness for his name's sake." Those who know Christ as Saviour should live righteous because God's name is at stake. We are Christians; we bear His name.

In his book, *When a Christian Sins*, Dr. Rice said, "One of the worst things that the sin of a Christian does is to bring a reproach on the cause of Christ and upon the name of Christ. How Jerusalem must have buzzed with gossip when Peter denied the Lord, cursed and swore and quit the ministry!

"When David committed his great sin, Nathan said, 'Howbeit, because by this deed thou hast given great occasion to the enemies of the Lord to blaspheme . . .' (II Sam. 12:14).

"The sins of the preacher who falls are blazoned on the front page of the newspapers. The sins of a simple lay Christian are held up in his own family and in his own community against Christ and the Gospel by those who are the enemies of God."

Dr. Rice goes on to tell the story of an atheistic publishing house that sent him a book mocking the Bible and the Christian religion. He said, "The book was full of cartoons and ribald stories about the incest of Lot, about the adultery and murder which David committed, about the shame of Samson and Delilah." Dr. Rice went on to explain that though these men had obtained forgiveness and were already received into Heaven, it did not stop the shameful reproach on Christ.

Yes, sin has its natural consequences; but once we confess our sins, they are forgiven, cleansed, and forgotten; and God will never hold them against us again.

We must not render the present ineffective by worrying over the past. We should confess sin as soon as we know we have committed it, accept God's forgiveness and cleansing, and then set out to be the best Christian we can. If we fail again, then confess again and try harder the next time. We must never let the Devil discourage us into believing that God is not willing and ready to forgive our sins and cleanse us from all unrighteousness.

The Believer and the Devil

C H A P T E R   F I V E

I. The Enemy We Face
II. The Exhortation to Fight
III. The Encouragement to Fight
IV. The Example to Follow

*"**S**ubmit yourselves therefore to God. Resist the devil, and he will flee from you."*—James 4:7.

"Be sober, be vigilant; because your adversary the devil, as a roaring lion, walketh about, seeking whom he may devour: Whom resist stedfast in the faith...."—I Pet. 5:8, 9.

Have you ever known a young person who was brought up in a fundamental, Bible-believing church, attended a Christian school, lived a separated, dedicated life, whose parents had family devotions every night, and yet when he was older became rebellious, yielded to temptation, and went out into sin?

More than once I have had parents ask, "Where did we go wrong? We never missed Sunday school. We never missed a preaching service. We tithed. We had family devotions. Our boy heard us read the Bible, and we prayed together. Now he seems to have no interest in spiritual things. How do you explain that?"

My answer is, "You taught him about God; you taught him about the Bible; you taught him about prayer, but you didn't teach him about his enemy."

Most battles are lost because the enemy is either unknown or underestimated.

The Bible warns in I Peter 5:8, "Be sober, be vigilant; because your adversary [opponent] the devil, as a roaring lion, walketh about, seeking whom he may devour."

If every believer in the world were in service for Christ, winning souls and working, we would fill every church building in America and evangelize the world in a few months!

You go out soul winning and ask a man, "Have you trusted Christ as your Saviour?" He drops his head and says, "Yes, I have. When I was eleven years old, I trusted Jesus in a revival meeting. And if anyone had told me I would be this far from God, I would not have believed it." What happened to that man?

I know preachers who were well respected, served God faithfully, won souls; now they are out of the ministry. What happened? They didn't know their enemy.

In most cases these Christians read the Bible, prayed and attended church; but they knew nothing about resisting the Devil. The promise in James 4:7, "Resist the devil, and he will flee from you," is just as true as John 3:16.

I. THE ENEMY WE FACE

We have an enemy named Satan who is as real as God Himself. The late Dr. Dallas Billington wrote a book entitled *God Is Real*. Someone should write one entitled *The Devil Is Real*.

Don't be like the boxer who, after the first round, went back to his corner and his trainer patted him on the back and said, "Go back and get him this next round; he hasn't laid a glove on you."

He went back and fought the second round, and his opponent almost knocked him out. He staggered back to the corner; his trainer patted him on the back and said, "Go back and get him this round; he hasn't laid a glove on you."

He went out the third round, was knocked down twice for the count of nine and saved by the bell. They dragged him back to his corner, his trainer patted him on the back and said, "Go back and get him this next round; he hasn't laid a glove on you." He said to his trainer, "I'm going back and get him this next round, but keep your eyes on that referee; somebody is beating the devil out of me!"

The Devil is never more successful in defeating us in our Christian lives than when he makes us think he doesn't exist. Billy Sunday said, "I know the Devil is real for two reasons. First, because the Bible says so; and, second, because I've done business with him." If the Devil was too subtle for our unfallen parents, Adam and Eve, then we must be careful not to underestimate him.

President Roosevelt had a dog he thought was a good fighter. One day while out for a walk, an old mangy dog jumped on the President's dog and almost killed it. The FBI agents rescued the dog. On the way back to the White House one of the agents said, "Mr. President, I thought that dog was a good fighter." Roosevelt replied, "He is a good fighter, but he is a poor judge of dogs!"

You may be a good fighter; but if you are a poor judge of your enemy, you will lose.

The Devil is powerful, but he is not omnipotent. He has limited power, only the power God allows him to have.

Satan has the power to take thoughts out of our mind. The Bible says, "When any one heareth the word of the kingdom, and understandeth it not, then cometh the wicked one, and catcheth away that which was sown in his heart [or mind]. This is he which received seed by the way side" (Matt. 13:19). A man hears the truth, and before the truth can take root in his heart, "then cometh the wicked one, and catcheth away that which was sown in his heart."

Why is it we have no problem remembering beer or cigarette

jingles but we have difficulty memorizing Scripture? The problem is, no one is trying to take the beer jingles out, but there is one trying to take the Bible verses out as fast as the seed is sown. We remember things we shouldn't remember and forget things we should remember. Satan has power to take out of one's mind the seed once it is sown. **He also has power to put thoughts into our mind.**

In Acts 5:1,2, Ananias and Sapphira lied about their possessions; and in the next verse Peter said to Ananias, "Why hath Satan filled thine heart [or mind] to lie to the Holy Ghost?"

The word "heart" in this verse has reference to the mind, the center of man.

When we talk about the "heart of the matter," we mean the "center of the matter." When we talk about the "heart of the earth," we mean the "center of the earth." When we talk about the "heart of the tree," we mean the "center of the tree." Most of the time when "heart" is used in the Bible, it has reference to the mind, not to the physical pump. "As he thinketh in his heart, so is he" (Prov. 23:7). You don't think in your heart; you think in your mind. The center of your being is your mind. That is the place of your emotions. This is the will and intellect, where decisions are made.

Peter said to Ananias, "Why hath Satan filled thine heart to lie to the Holy Ghost. . .thou hast not lied unto men, but unto God" (Acts 5:3,4). Now where did Ananias get the idea to sell those possessions and keep part of it and lie about it? From Satan. Satan put it in his mind or heart.

The Devil is subtle. He will put dumb, crazy thoughts in your mind and make you think you had those thoughts yourself. Then he will say to you through your thought process, "Saved people don't think like you are thinking," and have you doubting your salvation over thoughts he himself put in your mind. He is powerful but not all-powerful.

Temptation is always against scriptural principles. Temptation is a solicitation to do wrong, and wrong is anything contrary to the clear teachings of the Bible. Sometimes the Devil tries to get us to do the right thing in a wrong way. There is nothing wrong with sex within the bounds of marriage, but Satan would have us satisfy those desires outside marriage—do a right thing in a wrong way.

In the three temptations Jesus faced, the Devil did not try to get Him to do a wrong thing, but a right thing in a wrong way. "If thou be the Son of God, command this stone that it be made bread" (Luke 4:3). Jesus had been fasting forty days, and He was "afterward hungered." There is nothing wrong with a hungry man eating bread, but there is something wrong with Jesus' acting independently of God and commanding stones to be turned into bread.

Satan took Jesus up on a pinnacle of the Temple and said, "If thou be the Son of God, cast thyself down from hence: For it is written, He shall give his angels charge over thee, to keep thee: And in their hands they shall bear thee up, lest at any time thou dash thy foot against a stone" (Luke 4:9-11).

There is nothing wrong with trusting God to protect you if you fall, but there is something wrong with getting up in a window and jumping out in order to demonstrate your faith in God.

The Devil tried to get Jesus to live by chance, not by faith.

Satan took Jesus up into a high mountain, showed Him all the kingdoms of the world, and said to Him, "All these things will I give thee, if thou wilt fall down and worship me" (Matt. 4:9).

There is nothing wrong with Jesus' having all the kingdoms of the world. Someday He will have, when He is King of kings and Lord of lords and everything under Heaven is subject unto Him. Every knee will bow and every tongue will confess that Jesus Christ is Lord to the glory of God the Father. There *is* something wrong with Jesus' getting all the kingdoms of the world by bowing down and worshiping Satan.

The Devil wanted Jesus to take a shortcut, to enjoy the crown without going to the cross, glory without suffering. But Jesus, knowing that worship and service went together, answered, "It is written, Thou shalt worship the Lord thy God, and him only shalt thou serve."

The Devil is so subtle that it is almost frightening.

He is going to bug us until we die. He never gives up! He will be standing around when we press a dying pillow trying to get us to do something wrong. There is a real, live, walking, talking Devil going about as a roaring lion seeking whom he may devour. He has devoured many Christians! I don't mean they went to Hell, but that they are useless in God's work.

An old preacher wrote a book on the Devil. Since he couldn't sell the books, they were stored in his garage. One day when I went to see him, he told me about this book he had written on the Devil. "I want you to have a copy," he said. When we went to the garage for a copy, he discovered that rats had literally chewed the books to pieces. We went back in the house and he said to his wife, "Mom, the rats have chewed the Devil up!" "Who-o-o-o-o-o!" she shouted all through the house. "Glory to God! I'm glad he's gone."

Well, the rats didn't really chew him up. He is still around for us to contend with.

II. THE EXHORTATION TO FIGHT

The Bible exhorts us to fight. James 4:7 says, "Resist the devil, and he will flee from you." The word "resist" literally means "fight back."

The police officer goes to arrest a man, and the man resists arrest. What does that mean? It means he is doing everything in his power to keep the policeman from arresting him. He is fighting back.

When Satan attacks, the average Christian prays. Now there is nothing wrong with praying, but the promise is not, "Pray, and I will make the Devil flee from you." The promise is, "Resist the devil, and he will flee from you." Many Christians don't know what it is to have the Devil flee, because they have never resisted him. The average Christian never hears much about the enemy; and, as a result, most of his actions are God-ward. But God didn't promise, "Pray, and I will make the Devil flee from you." He did not say, "Tithe, and I will buy him off." He didn't say, "Go soul winning, and he won't bother you." What He did say was, "Resist the devil, and he will flee from you." "Resist" is the key word. If the Devil flees, we must resist.

One of Andrew Jackson's boyhood friends said, "I could throw Andrew nine times out of ten, but he wouldn't stay throwed."

Billy Bray, the Cornish miner, often did battle with the Devil. He was digging little shriveled-up potatoes in his garden. The Devil began to put thoughts into Billy's mind, "Billy, if God loved you, you would have big, nice potatoes instead of those little shriveled-up ones!" He kept bothering him until Billy shouted out loud, "You Devil, I've got your character at home in a Book, and it says in John 8:44 that you are a liar and the father of it. Besides that, when I served you, I didn't have any 'taters at all! Now git!"

Billy Bray did what we must learn to do: "Resist the devil, *and he will flee from you.*" Fight back.

Not a single verse in the Bible tells you to run from the Devil. There is a verse that says, "Flee also youthful lusts," but the Bible never says flee from the Devil. The Bible says to make the Devil flee from you.

Most Christians take only God-ward action. For instance, worrying over unpaid bills, they find it difficult to go to sleep. So they pray for help not to worry.

Now there is nothing wrong with praying, and we should pray about everything. But the problem is, those worries are put into the mind by Satan. He is saying, "You can't pay your bills. What are you going to do next week when the other bill comes due?"

We read in Philippians 4:6, "Be careful for nothing," or, "Don't worry about even one thing." Now the Devil says, "Worry." But God says, "Don't worry about even one thing." The only way to get rid of the worry is to take Satan-ward action. Resist the Devil, and he will flee from you. The moment you begin to worry, realize that this is the Devil telling you to do something that God has already told you not to do. God said don't worry about even one thing, and the Devil is putting the thought in your mind to worry about bills.

The way to get rid of the worry is to resist the Devil. And when he flees, so will the worry.

But how do you fight back? There is only one offensive weapon in the Christian's armor. You have a helmet of salvation, a shield of faith, a breastplate of righteousness; you are shod with the preparation of the Gospel; and you take the Sword of the Spirit which is the Word of God. The Sword is the only offensive weapon mentioned. And the Sword of the Spirit is just as sharp as it ever was.

Hebrews 4:12 says, "For the word of God is quick, and powerful, and sharper than any twoedged sword, piercing even to the dividing asunder of soul and spirit, and of the joints and marrow, and is a discerner of the thoughts and intents of the heart."

Later under the heading, "The Example to Follow," we will discuss in detail how the Christian can effectively use the Sword of the Spirit to resist the Devil. But first let me say a word about:

III. THE ENCOURAGEMENT TO FIGHT

First John 4:4 reads, "Greater is he that is in you, than he that is in the world." Here is an encouragement to fight. This verse is a statement of fact. It is not a magical formula that causes the Devil to flee when you quote it. Simply quoting, "Greater is he that is in you, than he that is in the world," will not insure victory over temptation. The statement of fact is an encouragement to fight because it is an assurance of victory. God is saying that you have within you a greater power than he that is in the world; and if you fight back, you can win!

Looking at a jet plane, I may say, "Greater is the thrust of those jet engines than the force of gravity." But saying it all day long will never cause that plane to leave the ground. I have stated a fact; but if that plane flies, its engines must be put into operation.

First John 4:4 is an encouragement to fight, but you must resist the Devil if you expect him to flee. The power in you is great enough for the victory, but the victory is not automatic. We must take action toward Satan.

We must learn how to use this power and how to resist the Devil. We must put James 4:7 into practice: "Resist the devil, and he will flee from you."

IV. THE EXAMPLE TO FOLLOW

There is a great example of this recorded in Matthew 4. Here we have the temptation of Jesus and a beautiful picture of His resisting the Devil. A careful study of this passage will show exactly how it is done.

The Devil doesn't fight fairly. He attacks at your weakest point. Dr. Bob Jones, Sr., once said, "When temptation and opportunity meet, we are in trouble."

Jesus had "fasted forty days and . . . he was afterward an hungered" (vs. 2). Then came the Devil saying, "If thou be the Son of God, command that these stones be made bread" (vs. 3).

If you ever had a bout with liquor before you were saved, he will tempt you with drink. He attacks where you are the most vulnerable. When Jesus was hungry, Satan said, "Command that these stones be made bread."

If you get discouraged in the ministry and want to leave your church, don't be surprised to get an offer for a very good job. If you and your wife can't get along and you are fighting and fussing and your relationship is poor, don't be surprised to have a beautiful woman about fifteen years younger show up and tell you, ugly as a scratch, that you are the most handsome thing that ever lived! If you are six months behind on your bills and are worrying yourself to death, don't be surprised to have someone offer you a get-rich-quick scheme!

Satan didn't attack when our Lord had just finished a good meal and say, "If you are the Son of God, command that these stones be made bread"; rather, it was after our Lord had fasted forty days and nights and was hungry.

Jesus responded, "It is written, Man shall not live by bread alone, but by every word that proceedeth out of the mouth of God." Jesus used the Sword of the Spirit, the Word of God, to counter the temptation.

The temptation amounts to, "The Devil said"; and the answer to the tempter and the way to resist the Devil is to tell him what God said, "It is written." Jesus used a verse from the Old Testament appropriate for the temptation.

To resist the Devil simply means to fight back with the only offensive weapon we have—the Sword of the Spirit, the Word of God.

But the Devil did not give up easily. Look at verses 5,6:

"Then the devil taketh him up into the holy city, and setteth him on a pinnacle of the temple, And saith unto him, If thou be the Son of God, cast thyself down: for it is written, He shall give his angels charge concerning thee: and in their hands they shall bear thee up, lest at any time thou dash thy foot against a stone."

Since the Lord had quoted Scripture, the Devil decided to try to get Jesus to yield to temptation by quoting Scripture back to Him. The only problem is, the Devil did not quote it exactly correctly. He was trying to get our Lord to live by chance and not by faith.

There is nothing wrong with trusting God, but there is something wrong with trying to demonstrate your faith by doing foolish things and tempting God.

In resisting the Devil, Jesus did the same thing He had done in the first temptation. In verse 7 He said to the Devil, "It is written again, Thou shalt not tempt the Lord thy God." Jesus continued using the Sword of the Spirit, quoting Scripture appropriate to combat the temptation. But the Devil still did not give up.

Verses 8 and 9:

"Again, the devil taketh him up into an exceeding high moun-
tain, and sheweth him all the kingdoms of the world, and the
glory of them; And saith unto him, All these things will I give
thee, if thou wilt fall down and worship me."

Again Jesus responded in verse 10 by quoting the Scripture:
"It is written, Thou shalt worship the Lord thy God, and him
only shalt thou serve." The Devil said nothing about service,
but the Lord knew that worship included service. What we worship, we serve. If we worship self, we will serve self. Nearly
everything we do will be selfish. If we worship the world, we
will serve the world.

I have known men to worship money and end up serving
money. Everything they did was for money. Money governed
their lives and conduct. It even determined their friendships.
What we worship, we serve.

And what we serve, we sacrifice for. Tell me what you are willing to make sacrifices for, and I will tell you what you serve
and worship. We cannot go to Sunday school and church on Sunday morning because it is too cold, but it is at least 15 degrees
colder the next Saturday, and we get up at 3:00 in the morning
to go deer hunting. Now I am not against deer hunting. I am
simply making a point. The same could be said for golfing,
fishing, or any other thing we are willing to sacrifice for.

In this third temptation, the Lord said in verse 10, "Get thee
hence, Satan," then, "For it is written, Thou shalt worship the
Lord thy God, and him only shalt thou serve." The next verse
continues: "Then the devil leaveth him, and, behold, angels came
and ministered unto him."

Now what does the Bible promise in James 4:7? "Resist the
devil, and he will flee from you." That is exactly what happened
in Matthew 4 when Jesus resisted the Devil by quoting an appropriate verse to combat the temptation. The Bible says, "Then
the devil leaveth him, and, behold, angels came and ministered

unto him." Luke 4:13 says, "He departed from him for a season."

James 4:7 is just as true as John 3:16. If we resist the Devil, he will flee from us. That is the promise in the Word of God, and God cannot lie.

Now do you see why we have trouble? When the Devil comes to tempt us, we call on God and ask Him to help us. But God never says, 'Pray, and I will make the Devil flee.' He says, "Resist the devil, and he will flee from you." We must do what the Bible says if we expect to get Bible results.

How can we put into practice what Jesus did? Let me give an illustration.

Suppose someone is having doubts about salvation. The Devil continues to put the thought in his mind that he is not saved. This person could pray all he wished to, but that would not solve his problem. If he has trusted Christ as Saviour, then the thing to do is resist the Devil. The moment the doubt comes, the person should realize that the doubt is from Satan and tell the Devil, "I know where that thought came from. You are trying to get me to doubt my salvation, but the Bible says in John 3:36, 'He that believeth on the Son hath everlasting life.' I know I am believing on the Son, and I know God meant what He said. Therefore, I know I have everlasting life."

John 3:36 is a good passage to quote to the Devil when he comes with his doubts. We could even say, "Get thee hence, Satan, for it is written, 'He that believeth on the Son hath everlasting life.' I know I am saved because God said so. Devil, take your doubts and leave with them!"

Does that mean the person will never doubt again? Of course not, for Luke 4:13 says, "He departed from him FOR A SEASON," not forever. He was only gone for a season. He never gives up. He will come back with the same doubts later. But when he does, simply repeat the same process.

John 3:36 is only one example of the Scriptures we could use. One could use John 3:16, John 5:24, or many other passages proving that we have everlasting life, based on the Word of God.

For every temptation, there is an appropriate verse. The Sword is sufficient.

Suppose the Devil puts a thought in your mind to commit immorality. As soon as the thought, temptation, or desire comes, then resist the Devil.

An appropriate verse for such a temptation is I Corinthians 6:19,20:

"What? know ye not that your body is the temple of the Holy Ghost which is in you, which ye have of God, and ye are not your own? For ye are bought with a price: therefore glorify God in your body, and in your spirit, which are God's."

When Satan tempts you to commit immorality, say, "Get thee hence, Satan, for it is written, 'Glorify God in your body, and in your spirit, which are God's.' "

We are to bring glory to God in our bodies, and we can say to the Devil, "To commit immorality does not glorify God in my body." It is important to note that Satan did not depart from Jesus until He said, "Get thee hence, Satan." In the first two temptations He simply quoted an appropriate verse to combat the temptation. In the third temptation Jesus said, "Get thee hence, Satan," and the Bible says, "He departed. . . . " The Devil will not leave until you tell him to.

I might say that the Devil is too powerful for us, but he is not too powerful for the indwelling presence of Christ. We must say, "In the name of Jesus, get thee hence," or "Depart."

If you knock on my door at night and say, "Let me in," I might not let you in. But if someone knocks on my door, shows me a policeman's badge and says, "In the name of the law, let me in," I don't have much choice. And when we say, "In the name of Jesus," the Devil doesn't have a choice. When he hears that name, he trembles. He still remembers Calvary. He knows that he is a defeated foe and that on the cross Jesus Christ bruised his head.

When I was in the sixth grade, I got into a fight with one of the roughest boys in school. He and I had been arguing all day, and he challenged me to meet him down the road under an old oak tree when school was out. Not willing to back down, I agreed. It was one of the worst decisions I ever made.

I will never forget it. Word got around, and that afternoon when school was out there must have been 50 or more boys and girls gathered to see the fight. I do not think I got in one punch. I was so humiliated that I did not want to go back to school the next day.

Ever since then, when that boy's name is mentioned, my ears perk up and I wonder if the person mentioning his name knows anything about the fight where I was soundly defeated and utterly humiliated!

Years after, when I was grown and pastoring a church in Decatur, Georgia, one of this boy's relatives joined the church. After the service she said to me, "Do you know So-and-So?" and called the boy's name. "He's my nephew." Though it was years later, I was still embarrassed and wondered if she knew of my defeat and humiliation.

When we mention the name of Jesus to the Devil, he remembers his defeat. And the Bible says the devils are subject to us through His name. Jesus said in Luke 10:20, "Notwithstanding in this rejoice not, that the spirits are subject unto you; but rather rejoice, because your names are written in heaven." If we resist the Devil by quoting an appropriate verse to combat the temptation and tell him to leave in the name of Jesus, he will depart. Oh, he may come back; and if he does, repeat the same process, even if he comes back five or six times the same day with the same temptation or the same doubt.

Now this may seem strange at first, but I can assure you that it works: first, because the Bible says so; and second, because I have put it into practice in my own life and have seen it work.

When my secretary first heard me talking to the Devil, she didn't understand it. She thought I had lost my marbles. I would yell out, "You dirty, lowdown, stinking rascal, get out of here!

I know where that dumb, crazy thought came from! You brought that right out of the back alley of Hell! You are trying to plant that in my mind. I'm not thinking about that junk because the Bible says, 'Whatsoever things are pure, whatsoever things are lovely, whatsoever things are of good report. . . think on these things' (Phil. 4:8)." I said, "Take those thoughts back to Hell. I'm going to sing 'Amazing Grace.'"

I once gave this Bible lesson on resisting the Devil to my congregation. The next week a dear lady came to me screaming, "It works! It works!"

"What works?" I asked.

"Resisting the Devil. It works!" Then she told the story of how she had been tempted and how she quoted an appropriate verse and commanded the Devil to leave in Jesus' name. "And as soon as I did it, the temptation was gone." The temptation was gone because the tempter had departed.

Dr. Tom Malone had been preaching in a little country church. Driving home after the service, the Devil got to putting thoughts into his mind. "He sat right there on the front seat of the car with me and said, 'You are crazy. You are killing yourself. You drove all those miles over there to preach to that little handful of people. That one man who got saved—how do you know he was saved? He probably just came down the aisle to make you feel good because you drove so far.'"

Dr. Malone said, "The Devil bugged me until I had about all I could take. So pulling over to the side of the road, I stopped the engine, got out, went around to the passenger side, opened the door, and said, 'Devil, this is my automobile. I pay the notes and the insurance on this car, and you have ridden with me as far as you are going to. Now, get out!' I slammed the door, got in on the other side and drove on home."

Friend, you are going to have to learn to open the door and say, "Get out!"

One could break sinful habits this way. Take, for instance, the habit of smoking. If you are one who "lights up," write the verses from I Corinthians 6:19, 20 on a 3 x 5 card and place it in your shirt pocket. Then every time you have a desire for a cigarette, reach into that shirt pocket where you usually keep cigarettes, and, instead of finding cigarettes, you will find the little 3 x 5 card. Pulling it out, you can simply say, "Devil, I know where this desire to smoke came from. But it says in I Corinthians 6:19, 20, 'What? know ye not that your body is the temple of the Holy Ghost which is in you, which ye have of God, and ye are not your own? For ye are bought with a price: therefore glorify God in your body, and in your spirit, which are God's.' Now, Devil, I'm not going to listen to you, but I'm going to do what the Bible says—glorify God in my body. I command you in Jesus' name to take your desire to smoke and leave with it!"

If James 4:7 is true, the Devil will flee. And when he flees, the desire to smoke will flee with him. But remember, when he departed from Jesus, he only departed for a season. He will come back later with that same desire. When he does, repeat the same process. As time goes by, the desires to smoke will get further and further apart until you have finally broken the habit.

Now if you are going to be successful in resisting the Devil, you must be familiar with your weapon—the Sword of the Spirit, which is the Word of God. Think of your worst temptation, the one you have the most often. Find an appropriate verse, and get ready to resist the Devil. Then find verses for every other temptation, and resist the Devil. He will flee from you.

The Word of God is not given to decorate coffee tables or bookshelves but to use. It is the Sword of the Spirit, and you are a soldier of Jesus Christ.

One final thought: the first part of James 4:7 says, "Draw nigh to God, and he will draw nigh to you." Before resisting the Devil, we should pray and get as close to God as we possibly can.

The Believer's Divine Commission

CHAPTER SIX

"**A**s my Father hath sent me, even so send I you."—John 20:21.

The most important statements ever uttered came from the lips of our Lord, and here is one of them: "...as my Father hath sent me, even so send I you." This indicates that whatever was required of Jesus in His coming to the earth is also required of believers. Whatever manner, whatever purpose, whatever sacrifice, whatever motivation that characterized Christ on His mission in the world must also characterize His servants in the world.

"...as my Father hath sent me, even so send I you" was addressed to Jesus' disciples corporately, but this likewise applies to all believers everywhere. As it was with our Saviour, so it must be with His servants.

"...as my Father hath sent me, even so send I you." What does that mean? In the first place, it means

I. UNDER SIMILAR MANDATE

"...as my Father hath sent me, even so send I you." Jesus

Christ was sent to the world by His Father. "And we have seen and do testify that the Father sent the Son to be the Saviour of the world" (I John 4:14). Galatians 4:4 says, "But when the fulness of the time was come, God sent forth his Son. . . ." And John 3:17, "For God sent not his Son into the world to condemn the world; but that the world through him might be saved."

Jesus Christ was under the mandate of the Father. According to the dictionary, a mandate is

"An authoritative command; an authorization to act given to a representative."

It was mandatory for Him to come. The Father sent Him. The New Testament tells us that Jesus was constantly aware of His task. "My meat is to do the will of him that sent me, and to finish his work" (John 4:34).

Just as the Father sent the Son into the world, so Christ sends us. And His mandate to us is clear: "Go ye into all the world, and preach the gospel to every creature." This Great Commission was not given to an institution but to individuals. It is every believer's responsibility to win souls. No church will stand at the judgment seat of Christ and be rewarded for soul winning. That reward goes to individuals.

Psalm 126:6 says, "*He* that goeth forth and weepeth [not, "the church that goeth forth and weepeth,"], shall doubtless come again with rejoicing, bringing *his* sheaves with *him.*" And Daniel 12:3 says, "And they that be wise shall shine as the brightness of the firmament; and they that turn many to righteousness as the stars for ever and ever" [not, "The church that turns many to righteousness"]. Soul winning is an individual, personal responsibility. Every believer is under mandate to win souls. Soul winning is not a matter of personal choice but of divine command. It is mandatory.

When a person is given a mandate by someone in a position of authority, he can only comply or refuse, obey or disobey, submit or rebel. The only alternative to soul winning is disobedience to Christ. If every believer would get busy about soul winning, then we could evangelize the world.

John Wesley used to say, "All at it, and always at it."

Our mandate is clear: "Go ye into all the world, and preach the gospel to every creature." The question is, Are we going to be obedient to our mandate as Christ was obedient to His? Or will we ignore it and let folks die and go to Hell and never hear a clear presentation of the Gospel?

Dr. Bob Jones, Sr., saw a plaque in an office which read:

> I'm one and only one. I cannot do everything, but I can do something. What I can do, I ought to do; and what I ought to do, by the grace of God, I will do.

Every one of us can do something. There is somebody we can win to Christ whom no one else can win.

"As my Father hath sent me, even so send I you" means

II. IN THE SAME MANNER

How did Jesus come to this world? He took on human flesh: "But made himself of no reputation, and took upon him the form of a servant, and was made in the likeness of men" (Phil. 2:7). Christ had to come as a human being in order to make contact with humanity. Jesus did not fulfill His mission from afar. Rather, He came down to where we were. He did not send salvation in a package, but brought it in a Person.

Thousands of people in every community are waiting for somebody to bring to them the simple message of salvation.

I recently had breakfast with a friend who told me how he and his daughters went from house to house passing out Christmas cards and wishing folks a Merry Christmas. On the card was the simple plan of salvation. He said, as he was walking away from one home, the man of the house came back to the door and yelled, "Wait a minute! You mean this is all there is to it?"

My friend smiled and said, "Yes."

The man replied, "Thank you, sir. Thank you."

I was pastor of Forrest Hills Baptist Church six years before

I led even one soul to Christ. My attitude was, *If they want to hear the Gospel, let them come to church on Sunday.* I never visited one home for the purpose of taking the Bible and showing someone how to be saved.

After attending a Sword of the Lord Conference on Revival and Soul Winning in 1961, I got so burdened for souls that I went out on Saturday and led my first three to Christ.

We must change our attitude about soul winning, and we must put more emphasis on Christians' going from house to house—out where the sinners are—and winning them to Christ. We are not to preach the Gospel AT the people but TO the people. It is not enough to stand on the shore and shout instructions to the drowning man. We must go in after him!

A young preacher walked into a smoke-filled bar in Florida. Going up to the meanest looking guy he could find, he asked, "Do you think a Christian ain't got no guts?"

The rough-looking guy looked down and said, "No."

The young Christian looked up and said, "Well, I'm a Christian, and I've got more guts than you have."

The rough guy looked down and said, "Yeah? Is that so? Prove it!" (A juke box was playing loudly in the room.)

The Christian said, "If you've got the guts to unplug that juke box, I've got the guts to climb up on that pool table and preach a sermon."

The rough man paused a few seconds, then he walked over and unplugged the juke box which had been playing very loudly. When it stopped playing, people began to look around to see what had happened.

In the meantime, the young fellow climbed up on the pool table, opened his Bible to John 3:16, and began to preach. Some of the men in the bar became angry and began to curse. "What's going on here? Who unplugged that juke box?"

By this time the rough-looking man was kind of proud of himself. So standing up straight he said, "I unplugged it! And that man on the pool table is going to preach a sermon!" Nobody argued with him and the young man preached his sermon and gave an invitation.

Now what I don't like about that story is that it didn't happen to me. I wish I had been the young fellow on the pool table.

"As my Father hath sent me, even so send I you" means, "In the Same Manner."

Today the emphasis is on the *gathered* church, but in the New Testament it was on the *scattered* church. "Therefore, they that were scattered abroad went every where preaching the word" (Acts 8:4).

I have known no greater joy than that of taking the Bible and leading men to Christ in airports, drugstores, restaurants and many other places. I even led one man to Christ while he was on top of a telephone pole. He worked for the telephone company. He could hook into wire a small, portable telephone.

One day my phone rang. The man on the other end said, "Oh, I've got the wrong number."

I said, "No, sir. The Lord had you call this number for a reason. What is your name?"

He told me.

Then I asked, "If you died today, do you know you would go to Heaven?"

He said, "No, I don't know that."

In a few minutes he prayed and trusted Christ as Saviour. After he prayed and I had led him to the assurance of salvation, he said, "Do you know where I am? I'm on top of a telephone pole!" I laughed, and he explained that he was trying to call the office to check out a phone and had gotten my number.

We must go where the sinners are: in every shopping center, to every ball park, service station, airport and every place we can. We need to change our WELCOME mat to a WE'LL GO mat.

"As my Father hath sent me, even so send I you" means

III. FOR THE SAME MISSION

In a broad sense the mission of Jesus was threefold. He came to reveal God. John 14:9 says, "He that hath seen me hath seen the Father . . . ." And we read in John 1:18, "No man hath seen God at any time; the only begotten Son, which is in the bosom of the Father, he hath declared him."

In some measure, every believer should reveal Christ.

It is said that when Missionary Adoniram Judson came back from the field, he was met by reporters who said, "Mr. Judson, they are writing you up as another Apostle Paul."

Judson replied, "I didn't want to be like Paul. I wanted to be like Jesus."

The late Dr. George W. Truett was walking down the street in Dallas, Texas, when he noticed a woman staring at him. When he passed, somehow he felt she was still staring. He looked back. Sure enough, she was still staring. "Pardon me, lady. Do you know me?"

"No. I have never seen you."

"Then do I know you?"

"Not as I know of," she replied.

Mr. Truett said, "If I don't know you, and you don't know me, why are you staring at me?"

The lady calmly replied, "Mister, you remind me more of Jesus than anybody I have ever seen."

It is our mission to reveal Christ, to be as much like Him as we possibly can be.

But Christ came not only to reveal God; He came also to seek and to save that which was lost.

If I could ask Jesus, "Lord, why did You come?" He would answer in the words of Luke 19:10: "The Son of man is come to seek and to save that which was lost."

If we could call the Apostle Paul down from Heaven and put to him the question, "Why did Jesus come?" he would answer in the words of I Timothy 1:15, "This is a faithful saying, and worthy of all acceptation, that Christ Jesus came into the world to save sinners . . . ."

In tracing the steps of Jesus through the New Testament, we

find time and time again that He took time out to win one person to Christ.

In John, chapter 4, He went out of His way by the well of Samaria to lead one fallen woman to salvation. And when the disciples talked about going to town for meat, He said, "I have meat to eat that ye know not of."

He stopped under a tree, called the tax collector Zacchaeus down and said, "To day I must abide at thy house." He came to redeem men.

Our mission in the world is the same as His. "As my Father hath sent me, even so send I you." Soul winning should be the business of every believer. We are left here for one purpose—to win men to Christ. So, "As my Father hath sent me, even so send I you" means, "For the Same Mission."

He came to reveal God. He came to redeem man. But He also came to rear the church. Matthew 16:18 says, "Upon this rock I will build my church; and the gates of hell shall not prevail against it."

The Great Commission in Matthew 28:19, 20 says:

"Go ye therefore, and teach all nations, baptizing them in the name of the Father, and of the Son, and of the Holy Ghost, Teaching them to observe all things whatsoever I have commanded you: and, lo, I am with you alway, even unto the end of the world."

Notice that once we teach them, then we are to baptize them. We are not only to win men to Christ, but we are to get them down the aisle of the local church for baptism. We are to win them, baptize them, then teach them how to win others and get them baptized. In so doing, we start a chain reaction; and eventually the world can be reached.

Somebody told the person who won you to Christ how to be saved. And somewhere, at sometime someone told that person how to be saved. It is like a long chain reaching back to the cross. The message came from one to another and on to another and another and another and another, until finally the message reached you.

Now the question is, Did the message stop with us, or did we pass it on?

I heard of a group of Christians who organized and called themselves the PIO. Someone heard about the group and said, "I have heard about the CIO but never about the PIO. What is the PIO?"

The Christian replied, "Pass It On! Pass It On!"

What happened to the Gospel when it came to you? Have you told anybody else about it? Have you won anyone to Christ?

I was pastor of the same church for twenty-one years, and what a wonderful and beautiful sight to see Christians coming down the aisle Sunday after Sunday bringing those whom they had won to Christ, to join the church and be baptized! I knew that there would be somebody forward every Sunday, and for fourteen years I saw converts down the aisle for baptism. Many of these were won to Christ in their homes and then brought to the church for baptism. The church grew until it became the largest in the state of Georgia, with over 7,900 members.

The last year I was in the pastorate, we had a two-week soul-winning marathon. Many of the people went soul winning every morning at 9:00 and again each evening at 6:00. Then at 7:30 p.m. they would bring back as many converts as they could for baptism. In fourteen days we led over 2,000 to Christ and baptized converts every night, baptizing over 200 in two weeks.

Jesus came to reveal God. He came to redeem men. He also came to rear the church. The only way to build a church is by getting people saved.

"As my Father hath sent me, even so send I you" means

IV. WITH THE SAME MESSAGE

As my Father sent me into the world with a message, so send I you into the world with the same message. The message is simple. It never changes. Men are sinners. They owe a sin debt.

Christ died on the cross to pay the sin debt in full. Men must believe that Jesus died and trust Him as Saviour.

When I first understood the plan of salvation, I was so excited I hardly knew what to do. I thought, *Everyone needs to understand this simple plan of salvation.* I am sure that at times my congregation must have grown tired of hearing the message over and over. And at times I worried that I might preach the message too often. But I am convinced that the songwriter was correct when she said,

> **I love to tell the story,**
> **For those who know it best**
> **Seem hungering and thirsting**
> **To hear it like the rest.**
> **And when, in scenes of glory,**
> **I sing the new, new song,**
> **'Twill be the old, old story**
> **That I have loved so long.**

I went from house to house with the same message: men are sinners; they owe a sin debt; Christ died to pay the debt in full; we must believe it and trust Jesus Christ as Saviour. I told it over and over—the same message at every house—and it worked. At times I thought, *Maybe I should change it and use something different.* But I reasoned, *If a man has a certain shotgun that he enjoys hunting with and he gets results, there is no need to change guns every time he goes hunting.* So I kept with the same message.

When I am at home I eat from the same plate almost every time. I sit in the same chair at the same table and in the same room. When I go to the den to relax, I sit in the same chair in the same room. I sleep in the same bed, and for twenty-seven years have been sleeping on the same side of the bed. I part my hair the same way I have always parted it. I have never changed. And as long as I have hair to part, I will probably part it in the same place! Truth never changes, so the message never changes.

The message is simple: "For God so loved the world, that he

gave his only begotten Son, that whosoever believeth in him should not perish, but have everlasting life." I intend to preach it until I die.

Charles Spurgeon once said, "I don't want to be famous for anything except preaching the old Gospel."

When Jesus preached a message, it was always simple. No one had to carry his dictionary when he went to hear Jesus preach. Listen! Good preaching is not complicating a simple matter, but it is simplifying a complicated matter.

Dr. Bob Jones, Sr., said, "Truth's most becoming garment is simplicity."

And Billy Sunday said, "Put the cookies on the lower shelf so everybody can reach them."

It is simple.

I was in revival meeting in Oklahoma. An old man for whom the church had been praying for years came the first part of the week and trusted Christ as Saviour. The last night of the meeting a young girl came, along with others. She was having some difficulty understanding, and I took time after the service to lead her to Christ. As I presented the plan of salvation as clearly as I could, the old man came and sat on the other side of her. In a moment he reached across and, interrupting, said, "Little girl, now you listen very carefully. It is so simple you will miss it."

With that he got up and walked away. In a moment the little girl trusted Christ as Saviour.

When Nicodemus asked how to be born again, Jesus said very simply, "As Moses lifted up the serpent in the wilderness, even so must the Son of man be lifted up; That whosoever believeth in him should not perish, but have eternal life" (John 3:14, 15).

"Nicodemus," He said, "you are saved by trusting Me, by relying on Me for your salvation."

"As my Father hath sent me, even so send I you" means "With the Same Message."

But it also means

V. BY THE SAME MOTIVE

The final test by which all service will be judged is motive. First Corinthians 13:3 says, "Though I bestow all my goods to feed the poor, and though I give my body to be burned, and have not charity, it profiteth me nothing."

Jesus was not compelled by external pressures of any kind when He came to this earth. He was motivated by love. Matthew 9:36 says, "When he saw the multitudes, he was moved with compassion on them, because they fainted, and were scattered abroad, as sheep having no shepherd."

Oh, how He loved sinners! In Matthew 23:37 we read how He looked over Jerusalem and said:

"O Jerusalem, Jerusalem, thou that killest the prophets, and stonest them which are sent unto thee, how often would I have gathered thy children together, even as a hen gathereth her chickens under her wings, and ye would not!"

Several years ago I was pondering ways to be a better preacher. I thought, *If I use more Bible verses when I preach, that will add more power to the sermon.* And then I decided that it would be good if I not only used Bible verses but gave the chapter and verse when I used them.

One day it occurred to me that if I could feel toward sinners like Jesus feels, I could preach with greater power. And I prayed: "Dear Lord Jesus, please let me feel toward sinners the way You feel toward them. And when I preach, let me feel toward the congregation the way You would feel were You here preaching."

Suddenly I realized that it might not be possible in this fleshly body to have as much compassion and love for sinners as Jesus has, so I modified my prayer: "Dear Lord, let me feel as much like You feel as I possibly can and still stay alive to preach."

Charles H. Gabriel wrote,

> **I stand amazed in the presence**
> **Of Jesus the Nazarene,**
> **And wonder how He could love me,**
> **A sinner, condemned, unclean.**

> **How marvelous! how wonderful!**
> **And my song shall ever be:**
> **How marvelous! how wonderful**
> **Is my Saviour's love for me!**

Jesus was motivated by love. But He was also motivated by an awareness that no one else could perform the mission on which He was sent. If Jesus Christ did not die on the cross to save sinners then sinners cannot be saved. When you find that word "must" in the Bible, it means there is no other way. And John 3:14 says, "As Moses lifted up the serpent in the wilderness, even so *must* the Son of man be lifted up." There is no other way. Jesus *must* die for sinners. He *must* pay the debt or sinners cannot be saved.

If Jesus Christ had failed, there was no back-up plan. And if we fail to tell men about Christ, God has no back-up plan. He did not say, "Go into all the world and preach the gospel to every creature; and if that will not work, try something else." He only has one plan and that is to go tell men how to be saved. And if we fail, we fail. God has no other plan. The only way He will reach this world is through Christians.

May God help us to be motivated by an awareness that no one else can perform the misssion that He has sent us to do. If this generation of saints does not tell this generation of sinners about Christ, then forever they will remain untold.

Jesus was not only motivated by His love for sinners and by an awareness that no one else could perform the mission on which He was sent, but He was also motivated by joy. Hebrews 12:2 says, "Jesus the author and finisher of our faith; who for the joy that was set before him endured the cross, despising the shame, and is set down at the right hand of the throne of God."

When Jesus Christ died on the cross, He was thinking about the joy that was set before Him. When they plucked His beard, He was thinking about the joy that was set before Him. When they scourged Him and stripped Him naked, He was thinking about the joy that was set before Him. That joy was the joy of sinners coming to Him, the joy of sinners being saved.

I have known no greater joy than that of winning souls to Christ. Psalm 126:6 says, "He that goeth forth and weepeth, bearing precious seed, shall doubtless come again with rejoicing, bringing his sheaves with him." And the previous verse says, "They that sow in tears shall reap in joy." Oh, the joy of leading men to Christ! There is no greater joy than the joy of taking a Bible and showing someone how to be saved and having him kneel and trust Christ as Saviour. First Thessalonians 2:19, 20 says, "For what is our hope, or joy, or crown of rejoicing: Are not even ye in the presence of our Lord Jesus Christ at his coming? For ye are our glory and joy."

In a recent meeting I gave a soul-winning lecture. After the service the folk went out soul winning. That evening a few minutes before time for the service to start, one of the men came running into the church screaming to the top of his voice, "It works! It works! It works!" In a few minutes he had everybody in the church excited. Oh, the joy he found in leading someone to Christ!

If I knew there were no Heaven or no Hell and that when men die that would be the end, I would still want to win souls to Christ simply for the joy of it.

A number of years ago, after I first started soul winning, I picked up a visitor's card and noticed that the people had visited the church three months earlier. It was after 9:00 at night. But I had a strong impression to visit the family. I found the street on the map, and in a few minutes I was parked in front of the house.

The man was loading furniture into a rented truck that was backed up to the front porch. I walked up, introduced myself, then I said, "I am sorry I have waited so long to visit with you. You came to visit us at church three months ago. And it looks like now I have waited too late. You are moving."

He dropped his head. "My wife and I have decided to call it quits, and I am taking my things and leaving tonight."

I hardly knew what to say, but reaching out to take his hand, I said, "Before you leave could I talk with you briefly?"

"I guess so," he said; and together we went to one of the back rooms of the house, and sitting on the bed I led the man to Christ. He cried like a baby.

I said, "You wait here. I'll go get your wife." I went to the living room and called his wife. She came back to join us. I explained to her that her husband had trusted Christ as Saviour. She seemed a little suspicious but listened.

I said, "Now I want to take the Bible and show you what I showed your husband." In a few minutes she, too, had trusted Christ as Saviour. They both were crying like babies. They looked at each other, then embraced.

Several relatives were in the front room, some from his side of the family and some from her side. I said, "Let's go back into the living room and tell the others what has happened."

Together we walked into the other part of the house, and I asked all the folks to gather around and listen. I said, "Mr. and Mrs. _____ have trusted Christ as Saviour. They love each other, and they want to set out to make a Christian home." The people looked as if they did not know how to respond. I said, "Now may I take the Bible and show you what I showed them a few minutes ago?"

They agreed, and I gave the plan of salvation to every one in the house. Then with heads bowed and eyes closed, I asked how many would trust Christ as Saviour. Several did; and we had an old-fashioned shouting, hallelujah time!

It was too late to make any more calls; so I asked, "May I help you unload the furniture and put it back in the house?"

He smiled and said, "If you would like to."

I said, "I would love it!" I took off my coat and tie; and for the next few minutes I would drag a piece of furniture back into the house and then shout awhile, drag in another piece, then shout awhile. Oh, the joy of leading men to Christ!

"As my Father hath sent me, even so send I you" means,

"Under Similar Mandate," "In the Same Manner," "On the Same Mission," "With the Same Message," and "By the Same Motive."

Giving—the Believer's Responsibility

CHAPTER SEVEN

In this message I want to talk very simply and scripturally about Christian giving. I call your attention to I Corinthians 16:1,2:

"Now concerning the collection for the saints, as I have given order to the churches of Galatia, even so do ye. Upon the first day of the week let every one of you lay by him in store, as God hath prospered him, that there be no gatherings when I come."

Notice the context in which these verses are found. In chapter 15 Paul deals with some great doctrinal subjects. For instance, in the first four verses you have the definition of the Gospel. Paul defines the Gospel as being the death, the burial and the resurrection of Jesus Christ. He goes on to talk about the great doctrine of the resurrection: "Behold, I shew you a mystery; We shall not all sleep, but we shall all be changed, In a moment, in the twinkling of an eye...." He then discusses the second coming of Christ and closes the chapter by saying, "...be ye stedfast, unmoveable, always abounding in the work of the Lord, forasmuch as ye know that your labour is not in vain in the Lord."

Now comes chapter 16, and Paul begins with, "NOW concerning the collection for the saints...." He has just taken them through the definition of the Gospel, the resurrection and the second coming. "NOW," he says, "let's talk about giving." "Upon the first day of the week let every one of you lay by him in store, as GOD HATH PROSPERED HIM...." So there's no doubt about it; God's way of financing His work is that His people GIVE to its support.

I do not believe that it is right for a church to have to sell vanilla flavoring, popsicles, hunkies and Teddy bears in order to pay the bills. Christians should support God's work with their tithes and offerings.

> There was a church in our town
> Which thought 'twas very wise:
> It tried to pay expenses
> By selling cakes and pies;
> But after years of trying
> That plan to raise the cash,
> The folks got tired of buying,
> And the whole thing went to smash.
>
> There was a church in our town,
> And it WAS wondrous wise:
> It always paid expenses
> By simply paying tithes.
> For when 'twas found the tithe did pay,
> It seemed so very plain;
> Forthwith they'd have no other way,
> Not even once again.

Now there are three things I want to cover in this sermon. First:

The Rule of Giving

How much should we give? Every real Christian should want to know what God Almighty expects of him in this matter of giving. And I think I can show you from the Bible in the next few minutes that our giving ought to begin with at least ten percent (or the tithe). Nobody should think of giving anything less than that.

Immediately someone says, "That was under the Law. That was in the Old Testament." And you're right. It is in the Old Testament, but that doesn't mean it is not binding on you. I say, "Thou shalt not kill." You say, "That's the Old Testament Law." Yes, but it is just as wrong to kill today as it was under the Law.

But let's go back before the Law. Abraham is the first man mentioned in the Bible who paid tithes (Gen. 14:18-20), and that was before the Law was given. He gave ten percent to Melchizedek, who was a type of Christ. Now, I want to ask you a question: What made Abraham decide to give ten percent when God had not instructed him anywhere in writing to do so? Did he just happen to decide, "I want to give ten percent"?

Let's leave him a minute and go a little bit further. The next fellow in the Old Testament you find tithing is Jacob. You'll find that in Genesis, chapter 28, verses 20-22. And look at this! Jacob is giving ten percent, or a tithe. Well, isn't that strange? Neither did he have any written instructions from God as to how much to give. This was before the Law. This was before the Bible said, "The tithe is the Lord's."

Isn't it strange that Abraham and Jacob both would decide on the same percent of their possessions to give back to the Lord! When there were a hundred different decisions they could have made—one percent, two percent, three percent, all the way up to one hundred percent—both decided on ten percent. How did both decide on the same percent?

I think they prayed about it. I can't conceive of a man like Abraham being the "father of the faithful" and not consulting God about what he ought to give. I believe he prayed about it. And I believe God gave him DEFINITE INSTRUCTIONS about what he ought to give. I also believe Jacob prayed, and God gave him instructions. That's the only way I can explain how both Abraham and Jacob gave the same amount. So, some tithed before the Law.

Now under the Law, the tithe was required. Leviticus 27:30 says, "And all the tithe of the land, whether of the seed of the land, or of the fruit of the tree, is the Lord's: it is holy unto the Lord."

I suppose the best-known passage on tithing is Malachi 3:6-10:

"For I am the Lord, I change not; therefore ye sons of Jacob are not consumed. Even from the days of your fathers ye are gone away from mine ordinances, and have not kept them. Return unto me, and I will return unto you, saith the Lord of hosts. But ye said, Wherein shall we return? Will a man rob God? yet ye have robbed me. But ye say, Wherein have we robbed thee? In tithes and offerings. Ye are cursed with a curse: for ye have robbed me, even this whole nation. Bring ye all the tithes into the storehouse, that there may be meat in mine house, and prove me now herewith, saith the Lord of hosts, if I will not open you the windows of heaven, and pour you out a blessing, that there shall not be room enough to receive it."

So we have tithing by Abraham and Jacob before the Law, and we have the tithe demanded under the Law.

Nearly everybody agrees that tithing is taught in the Old Testament, but what about the New Testament? Take the case of the Pharisees in the time of Jesus. Jesus condemned the Pharisees for many things, but there is one thing He *commended* them for: giving a tithe. Matthew 23:23 says, "Woe unto you, scribes and Pharisees, hypocrites! for ye pay tithe of mint and anise and cummin, and have omitted the weightier matters of the law, judgment, mercy, and faith: these ought ye to have done, and not to leave the other undone."

He condemned them for omitting the weightier matters. He condemned them because of their hypocrisy, likening them to whited sepulchres full of dead men's bones. He condemned them about many, many things; but He *commended* them on their tithing: ". . . these ought ye to have done, and not to leave the other undone."

Consider the parable of the Pharisee and the publican in Luke, chapter 18, beginning with verse 9. Jesus "spake this parable unto certain which trusted in themselves that they were righteous. . . . " Jesus is giving an illustration to men who trusted in themselves that they were righteous.

Jesus said, "All right, I want to tell you a story. There were two men, a Pharisee and a publican; and both of them went up to the Temple to pray." Now remember, Jesus is painting a picture of a good man; then He is showing a sinner standing over in the corner smiting himself on the breast and saying, "God be merciful to me a sinner."

Painting the virtues of the good man, Jesus said the Pharisee stood up and prayed, "I thank thee, that I am not as other men are, extortioners, unjust. . . . I fast twice in the week, I GIVE TITHES OF ALL THAT I POSSESS."

That man never really existed. But Jesus is giving an illustration and pointing out the virtues of a good man. The two virtues were fasting and TITHING. So you have Christ commending the Pharisees for their tithing. Here He is teaching that tithing is one of the virtues of a good man.

Proportionate giving is plainly taught in the New Testament. For instance, I Corinthians 16:2 says, "Upon the first day of the week let EVERY ONE OF YOU lay by him in store, as God hath PROSPERED him. . . . " That is proportionate giving: ". . . as God hath prospered. . . . "

In Acts, chapter 18, you will find that the church at Corinth began with converted Jews. If you said to a converted Jew, "Take a portion of your income and give it to the Lord's work," what portion do you think he would give? Remember, his father Abraham gave ten percent before the Law; Jacob gave ten percent before the Law, and they were commanded to give ten percent under the Law. So he has been accustomed to giving ten percent all his life. Now he is converted, and he is told to give a portion of his income to the Lord's work. Do you think he would give anything less than ten percent, or do you agree with me that he would BEGIN with at least ten percent?

All through the New Testament Jesus commended people for giving more than a tenth, but He never commended anyone for giving less than a tenth. The widow who gave all her living was commended by our Lord. The people at Corinth who gave abundantly were commended. He often commended for giving more, but He never commended for giving less.

What is the rule for New Testament giving? I think it ought to be at least ten percent. That's where it begins.

Someone asks, "But doesn't the New Testament repeal the tithe?" I don't think so. It repeals the observance of days and months; it repeals circumcision; it repeals the dietary laws—read Colossians, chapter 2—but never one time does it mention the tithe as being repealed.

Abraham gave ten percent. Jacob gave ten percent. The Law demanded ten percent. The Pharisees were commended for giving ten percent. Jesus, teaching on the Pharisee and the publican, said the good man gave ten percent. Proportionate giving is taught, and the tithe is not repealed; so every honest Bible student should agree that Christian giving ought to begin with ten percent.

But wait a minute. I wish you wouldn't think of it as MY giving God ten percent of MY money. As a matter of fact, I wish you wouldn't think of it as my giving God any percent of my money. You see, it is not a matter of how much of my money I give to God, but it is a matter of how much of God's money I keep for myself, because all of it belongs to God.

I read an amusing story of a black preacher who was celebrating his 82nd birthday, his golden wedding anniversary and his 42nd anniversary as pastor. He wrote a letter to God saying,

> Dear God,
>
> I'm celebrating my 82nd birthday, my golden wedding anniversary and my 42nd anniversary as pastor. Would You please send me $100 to help me celebrate?

The postmaster general got the letter, and the story goes that he read it in a cabinet meeting. They all had a big laugh about the letter. The postmaster decided to put $10 in an envelope and send it back to the preacher. The preacher got the ten-dollar bill.

A few weeks later they found another letter in the mail addressed to God, and this time it said,

Dear God,

I received Your letter, and I did have a good celebration; but the next time You send me any money, don't send it through Washington. They deducted ninety percent.

That's about the way we do—deduct ninety percent for ourselves and give God the other ten percent.

The Bible never hints that we ought to give ONLY a tenth. Many times we ought to give more. It all depends. I can think of many people now who give much more than ten percent, but I think it ought to begin there. That's the rule of giving.

Now let me say a word or two about

The Reward of Giving

Proverbs 11:25 tells us, "The liberal soul shall be made fat: and he that watereth shall be watered also himself."

Malachi 3:10 says, "Bring ye all the tithes into the storehouse...and prove me...if I will not open you the windows of heaven, and pour you out a blessing, that there shall not be room enough to receive it."

Proverbs 3:9,10 promises, "Honour the Lord with thy substance, and with the firstfruits of all thine increase: So shall thy barns be filled with plenty...."

And here is one of my favorite verses about giving: "Give, and it shall be given unto you; good measure, pressed down, and shaken together, and running over, shall men give into your bosom. For with the same measure that ye mete withal it shall be measured to you again" (Luke 6:38).

When I was a boy, my mother would sometimes send me to a neighbor's house to borrow a cup of flour or sugar. And I remember on grocery day my mother would say, "Now, I owe Mrs. Owens a cup of flour. Which cup did I use?"

I'd say, "That one with the broken handle."

"All of them have broken handles!"

I'd say, "Well, that big one over there."

So she'd get that cup. The difference was, when my mother sent back what she had borrowed, she would put on what she called good measure, and she would shake it down. The neighbor always got back more than we borrowed.

Now listen to what Jesus said: "If you give, it will be given back to you in the same measure that you mete." If you give in a teacup, He'll give in a teacup. If you give in a bushel basket, He'll give in a bushel basket. The only difference is, when He gives it back, it will be "good measure...." Did you ever buy anything in a bushel basket and have the fellow throw several handfuls on top for good measure? Well, that's what the Lord is talking about here.

Then He says, "...pressed down...." He fills the basket, throws some on top for good measure, then PRESSES it down.

Third thing: "...good measure, pressed down, and SHAKEN TOGETHER...." Did you ever pick a bushel of beans and then shake it down? Remember how much space was left after the shaking? That's what the Lord is talking about here. Jesus said, "I'm going to use the same measure you use. The only difference is, I'm going to give it back to you good measure, pressed down, shaken together, and running over. After I give good measure, press it down, and shake it together, I'm going to RUN IT OVER."

There is one further thought in this verse. "Give, and it shall be given unto you; good measure, pressed down, and shaken together, and running over, SHALL MEN GIVE INTO YOUR BOSOM...." What does He mean by that?

Back in those days men wore long, flowing, robe-like garments. When a man would buy grain, the merchant would give him good measure, pressed down, and shaken together and then give it into his bosom. In other words, he would open this man's robe or garment and push the container full of grain under the robe, somehow wrapping the robe around it. The buyer then would hold the robe over the container so as not to lose one single grain.

God Almighty not only promises to prosper those who give, but He promises to preserve that which He prospers you with.

Now I'm not the smartest person in the world, but I know that is a good deal. "Give, and it shall be given unto you; good measure, pressed down, shaken together, and running over," and you won't lose one grain of it.

I read a story about a retarded boy and an educated fellow. The intelligent one thought he would take advantage of the retarded boy; so he said, "Let's ask each other some riddles; and if I ask you a riddle that you can't answer, you give me a dollar; and if you ask me a riddle that I can't answer, I'll give you a dollar."

The retarded boy knew he was retarded and that the other fellow was pretty intelligent; so he said, "That wouldn't be quite fair since you're so much smarter than I am. I'll tell you what: I'll ask you a riddle, and if you can't answer it, you give me a dollar. Then you ask me a riddle; and if I can't answer it, I'll only give you half a dollar."

This intelligent fellow thought he would still make money, so he said, "All right, I'll do that."

The retarded boy said, "I'll ask the first riddle: What has four legs—two on the ground and two in the air—and thirteen eyes?"

This intelligent fellow thought and thought and thought. Finally he reached into his pocket and took out a dollar and said, "I don't know. Here's your dollar. What is it?"

The retarded boy replied, "I don't know either; here's your fifty cents."

Now I may not be very smart, but I know this matter of giving has its rewards. "Give, and it shall be given unto you; good measure, pressed down, and shaken together, and running over,

shall men give into your bosom. For with the same measure that
ye mete withal it shall be measured to you again." Proverbs
11:24 says, "There is [he] that scattereth, and yet
increaseth...."

John Bunyan used to say:

> There was a man in our town,
> Some folks did think him mad;
> The more he gave away,
> The more he had.

A merchant was in his shop one day when the preacher went
in to ask for some money on a certain project at the church. The
merchant gave him a check for $300. The preacher started out,
rejoicing over the check for $300; but as he went to leave, news
came that a ship had just sunk with thousands of dollars' worth
of uninsured goods on it that belonged to the merchant.

The merchant said, "Wait a minute. Come back. Give me back
that check."

"Well," thought the pastor, "I don't blame him! If I had just
lost that much money, I'd want it back, too."

The merchant took the check, tore it up, and wrote another
one for $1,000, saying, "Since I see I'm losing it so fast, I'd bet-
ter invest where I can't lose it."

You say, "That's impossible, investing money where you can't
lose it." You need to read the parable of the unjust steward in
Luke 16 and notice that expression where it says, "Make to
yourselves friends of the mammon of unrighteousness; that,
when ye fail, they may receive you into everlasting habitations."
The marginal rendering for "unrighteous mammon" is "riches."
Use your riches to make friends so that when ye fail (or die) they
will receive you into everlasting habitations.

Let me ask you something. Where is your everlasting habita-
tion? If you're saved, where are you going when you die? You're
going to Heaven. Now, what is the verse saying? I'll paraphrase
it. It says, "Use your money to win souls so that when you die
you will have a welcoming committee waiting for you in

Heaven." I'd like to have welcome me into Heaven a few souls who were won to Christ through money I had given.

We have seen the Rule of Giving and the Reward for Giving. Now let me share with you

The Reasons for Giving

First, let me take the negative side. Number one: you should not give out of embarrassment. I've always been careful about this. I'm not critical of those who raise money this way, but I've tried to be careful not to embarrass people in the matter of giving. I have been in some places where I was embarrassed for those present. I've been in churches where, when they were to receive the offering, the preacher said, "I'm not going to preach until we get so much money. Now, who'll give $100, or who will give $50?" and so on. He kept on pressuring until the folks were embarrassed.

I heard the story of a new church member who was pretty well off. They had a stewardship banquet; and when it came time to take pledges, instead of writing them on paper, they made their pledges openly.

They began to pledge. One fellow pledged $1,000, though he had no intention of paying it. Another fellow pledged $500 and another $400 and so on. This new fellow knew how poor these people were; and he thought, *I'll have to make a big pledge.* So he pledged several thousand dollars. He paid his pledge, but the others did not pay theirs. They really had no intention of paying, so the story goes.

This new member was pretty spiritual. He had a Scripture verse for everything. Months later somebody asked him about the stewardship banquet. "You've got a Scripture verse for everything. Do you have one for the way they treated you at that banquet?"

"Yes," he replied, "I was a stranger, and they TOOK ME IN." And how true it was!

I know of a church where they had the junior boys receive the

Sunday evening offering. This one little fellow started down the front row. The first man in the pew was a deacon. This junior boy stopped in front of him and proceeded to wait for the deacon to put something in the plate. The old deacon looked at him and motioned for him to go on, saying, "I gave mine this morning." When the little boy kept standing there, the deacon said again, "I dropped my envelope in the plate this morning." The little fellow just kept standing there. He wasn't going to leave until that deacon put something in the offering plate. After a few minutes, the deacon reached into his pocket and dropped some money in the offering plate. The pastor of that church said everybody in that building began to reach for pocketbooks and checkbooks because they knew what was coming. They had the largest offering they had ever received on Sunday night in that church. Why? Because they didn't want to be embarrassed.

But you ought not give because you are pressured into it or embarrassed.

I heard of a pastor who said, "We've got to have a new building. Everybody's going to have to sacrifice." One fellow said, "I'm raising a new calf, and when I get that calf fattened, I'm going to sell it and give the proceeds to the church." Every time they would ask him for money, he would say, "As soon as I sell the calf."

Well, one night he got to church a little bit late, and they were singing, "The Half Has Never Been Told." This man's conscience was hurting him so badly about the calf that he thought they were singing, "The calf has never been sold." So he went home and sold his calf and brought the proceeds to the church.

One pastor asked his congregation to give. They said they would pray about it. The next week when the ushers passed the offering plates, they found a sign in them which read—PAY NOW—PRAY LATER.

You don't have to pray about whether or not you ought to give. You may have to pray sometimes about WHERE you ought to give, and you ought to be careful because you're responsible to

God for where your money goes. I wouldn't give a dime to a liberal organization that didn't believe in the fundamentals of the Faith. If I'd given anything to that kind of organization, I'd try to get them to give it back.

You say, "My church is liberal. I can't give there." Well, you ought to get out and get in a church where you can give with a clear conscience.

You shouldn't give because of embarrassment. You shouldn't give because of pressure. You shouldn't give for a show. But you should give as a reminder that all belongs to God.

The Canadian Pacific Railroad owned a little spot of land that was being used by the public as a path to the railroad station. There was a law in Canada that, if a piece of property were used indefinitely by the public, it became the property of the city. So once a year it was necessary for the Canadian Pacific Railway to put a fence around the path and not allow the public to use it. They also put up a sign saying, "This is the property of the Canadian Pacific Railroad." After one day, they took the fence and sign down, and the public continued its use of the property 364 days a year; but that one day was a reminder that the Canadian Pacific Railroad was the owner.

When you give your tithe to the Lord, it ought to be a reminder that it ALL belongs to the Lord. The dollar belongs to the Lord. The billfold the dollar is in belongs to the Lord. The pants the billfold is in belong to the Lord. And the man in the pants also belongs to the Lord.

Our giving ought to be an expression of our love. God gave because He loved—John 3:16—and God's way of giving ought to be our way of giving. You can give without loving, but you can't love without giving.

You ought to give, too, because you believe in a work. If there is a good work that is winning souls and you believe in it, then help support it. I have the idea that, when people really love a work where souls are being saved, they want to have a part in it. And it doesn't take a lot of pressure to get them to give.

Then, too, you should give because of your influence. Folks are watching you. Your children see you.

A little boy was playing store with his dad. He gave his dad some item, and his dad gave him a nickel. The boy said, "Dad, we're not playing church. We're playing store." That dad had made the wrong impression on his son.

I want my children to know that I give. I want them to know I believe in God's work. I want to teach them to give. We should give because of our influence.

Let me tell you something that happened in our church a year or so ago. One of our members, Mrs. Montgomery, was very sick and in DeKalb General Hospital. I was to fly out on Monday for a speaking engagement. On the way to the airport, I stopped by and visited with Mrs. Montgomery. I read to her from the Bible and had prayer.

As I started to leave, she called me back and asked me to get her pocketbook out of the night stand. I handed her the pocketbook, and she took out an offering envelope that said, **My Weekly Gift to the Support of Forrest Hills Baptist Church.** "I won't be in church Sunday," she said, "but here is my tithe. Will you drop it into the offering plate for me?" She died that week; and the next Sunday, when I dropped that offering envelope in the plate, Mrs. Montgomery was in Heaven.

I tell you, it made me want to give more. It made an impression on me just to think that her tithe was in the offering several days after she had already gone to Heaven. What a testimony! What an influence!

You ought to give because of your influence.

And then, you ought to give CHEERFULLY. The Bible says, "God loveth a cheerful giver" (II Cor. 9:7). Somebody said that means a "hilarious giver." The cheerful or hilarious giver doesn't sit there with his face so long it would take $20.00 to get a shave and looking like he was weaned on dill pickle juice and had wild persimmons for breakfast, as he drops in a quarter and sings, "God be with you 'til we meet again."

No, a cheerful giver says, "Ha, ha, ha! Whee! Praise the Lord! Boy, they're going to receive an offering. Ha, ha, ha! Honey, hand me the checkbook. Whee! Hurry up and get that offering plate back here! Good night, ya'll are too slow with that thing." That's a cheerful giver! That's a hilarious giver! We don't see many like that.

I read the story about a dad who, wanting his son to learn how to give, gave him a quarter and a penny and instructed him to put whichever he wanted to in the offering plate.

After church, the dad, anxious to learn what his son had done when the offering was received, asked, "Son, which did you put in the offering, the quarter or the penny?"

"Well," the boy replied, "before they received the offering the pastor said, 'The Lord loves a cheerful giver.' I knew I could give the penny more cheerfully than the quarter, so I gave the penny." Now, that's not the kind of cheerful giving I'm talking about.

I close with this: There is something that God wants more than He wants your money. Second Corinthians, chapter 8, verse 5, says they "FIRST gave their own selves to the Lord...." God wants you more than He wants your money. If He gets you, He'll get your money. Give yourself to Christ.

Let me ask you several questions. Have you received Him as your Saviour? Have you trusted Him? Are you depending on Him for your salvation? If you are, have you made a complete surrender of yourself to Christ?

If you haven't trusted Christ as your Saviour, do it now. Tell Him in your own words:

Dear Lord Jesus, I know that I'm a sinner. I do believe You died for me. And the best I know how I do trust You as my Saviour. I depend on You from this minute on for my salvation.

If you have trusted Christ but have never learned the joy of giving at least a tithe to His work, resolve now that, beginning with your very next paycheck, God will get a minimum of ten percent.

"Upon the first day of the week let every one of you lay by him in store, as God hath prospered him...."—I Cor. 16:2.

Three Groups of Believers
C H A P T E R   E I G H T

Open your Bible to Matthew, chapter 26, beginning with verse 20.

"Now when the even was come, he sat down with the twelve. And as they did eat, he said, Verily I say unto you, that one of you shall betray me. And they were exceeding sorrowful, and began every one of them to say unto him, Lord, it is I? And he answered and said, He that dippeth his hand with me in the dish, the same shall betray me."—Vss. 20-23.

Now verses 33 to 43:

"Peter answered and said unto him, Though all men shall be offended because of thee, yet will I never be offended. Jesus said unto him, Verily I say unto thee, That this night, before the cock crow, thou shalt deny me thrice. Peter said unto him, Though I should die with thee, yet will I not deny thee. Likewise also said all the disciples.

"Then cometh Jesus with them unto a place called Gethsemane, and saith unto the disciples, Sit ye here, while I go and pray

yonder. And he took with him Peter and the two sons of Zebedee, and began to be sorrowful and very heavy. Then saith he unto them, My soul is exceeding sorrowful, even unto death: tarry ye here, and watch with me.

"And he went a little farther, and fell on his face, and prayed, saying, O my Father, if it be possible, let this cup pass from me: nevertheless not as I will, but as thou wilt. And he cometh unto the disciples, and findeth them asleep, and saith unto Peter, What, could ye not watch with me one hour? Watch and pray, that ye enter not into temptation: the spirit indeed is willing, but the flesh is weak. He went away again the second time, and prayed, saying, O my Father, if this cup may not pass away from me, except I drink it, thy will be done. And he came and found them asleep again: for their eyes were heavy."

And now verses 47 to 50:

"And while he yet spake, lo, Judas, one of the twelve, came, and with him a great multitude with swords and staves, from the chief priests and elders of the people. Now he that betrayed him gave them a sign, saying, Whomsoever I shall kiss, that same is he: hold him fast. And forthwith he came to Jesus, and said, Hail, master; and kissed him. And Jesus said unto him, Friend, wherefore art thou come? Then came they, and laid hands on Jesus, and took him."

I speak tonight on three groups. Somebody has said there are three groups in every church: those who make it happen, those who watch it happen, and those who wonder what is happening. I suppose there is some truth to that.

Somebody else has said there are three groups: the plus-plus crowd: "I can do it, and you can do it, and let's get it done"; the plus-minus crowd: "I can do it, and you can't do it, so get out of my way and I will do it"; the minus-minus crowd: "I can't do it, and you can't do it, and whoever brought it up to start with?" I suppose there is some truth to that.

I am not proposing to divide Christianity into three groups

altogether. Surely there are more groups than that. But I call your attention to three groups in this passage of Scripture.

The Lord was at the table at the Last Supper when He said, "One of you shall betray me."

The disciples began to inquire, "Lord, is it I?"

Jesus said, "He it is, to whom I shall give a sop." And He took it and gave it to Judas. And Judas went out to betray the Lord.

Jesus left and went to Gethsemane to pray. We suppose there were eleven with Him, since Judas had gone. When He got to the edge of the Garden, verse 36 says, "Then cometh Jesus with them unto a place called Gethsemane, and saith unto the disciples, Sit ye here, while I go and pray yonder." We suppose He said that to the eight, because the next verse says, "And he took with him Peter and the two sons of Zebedee"—James and John no doubt. He said to them, "Tarry ye here, and watch with me." And as the Gospels record, He went a little farther and prayed, "Not my will, but thine, be done."

Three groups are here: (1) If we exclude Judas, a group of eight who sat around the periphery, just on the edge; (2) the three who went a little deeper into the Garden with Jesus; (3) Jesus alone, praying to the Father, "If it be possible, let this cup pass from me: nevertheless not as I will, but as thou wilt."

I. DIFFERENCE IN POSITION

First, there was a difference in position of these three groups: (1) Jesus, alone in the Garden; (2) the other three, a little nearer Jesus than the eight; (3) the eight, just on the edge of the Garden. And a fourth, if you consider Judas outside the Garden gathering with the scribes and Pharisees getting ready to betray Jesus.

Actually that group of eight (the largest) was, in a sense, nearer Judas and his crowd than they were to Jesus. Though they were not against Jesus, it would not have taken too many steps for them to have joined in with Judas who was ready to betray Jesus, who hated Jesus. Just a few steps and they would have been with the modernists and the liberals and those who would crucify Christ. They were just on the edge, not many steps away. The other group was a little nearer to where Jesus was. Then, Jesus was alone. There was a difference in position.

II. DIFFERENCE IN SIZE

I would say that not only was there a difference in position but a difference in number. The eight who were just at the edge of the Garden, not too far from Judas, not too far from the Pharisees and the Sadducees who were ready to take Jesus and crucify Him, compose the largest group.

They don't hate Jesus, they are not against Him, but it wouldn't take too many steps for that crowd to join Judas and his crowd. I think that is true of every church and of Christendom as a whole.

But wait a minute! I think it is true of preachers, too. There are a lot of preachers in the world. I have read that America has 93% of the preachers of the world, and they are preaching to 7% of the population of the world.

With all the preachers we have in America, it seems we are still getting farther and farther behind. Somebody said that if you line up all the unsaved people in a single file, they will circle the globe thirty times and the line grows twenty miles every day. Somebody else said there are nine times as many unsaved people in the world today as was the entire population of the world when Jesus gave the Great Commission.

Now with all these preachers, why are we getting so little done?

I went to Haiti twice and spoke in little villages and little mountain huts. These people had never heard the name of Jesus. I could not believe it. Haiti is not very far from the United States of America.

And while I spoke to people who had never heard the name of Jesus, I read Pepsi-Cola signs and Coca-Cola signs. There you could buy V8 juice and Singer sewing machines. You could buy every brand of beer advertised in America. The beer crowd had gotten there, the soft drink crowd had gotten there, the sewing machine crowd had gotten there; but somehow we had not gotten there.

I may be wrong, but it seems to me, with all the preachers we have, we ought to be getting more done than we are. It seems to me, with all the churches we have with thousands of members, we ought to be evangelizing the world a lot faster than we are.

Some 345,000 babies will be born in the next twenty-four hours who will live, grow up, and die never hearing a clear presentation of the Gospel—345,000! If statistics are right, when you go to church next Sunday morning, there will be a million more lost people in the world than there were last Sunday morning.

That bothers me, because I am convinced that Jesus loves every one of those souls enough to come from Heaven to die for them on the cross. And I am convinced that Jesus does not want a single individual to die and go to Hell. He would have all men to be saved and come to the knowledge of the truth. And I was not happy when we had 113 conversions or decisions on Sunday at Forrest Hills Baptist Church, when the babies in Atlanta, Georgia, were being born faster than we were evangelizing our city. Atlanta, Georgia, alone could have several churches running 10,000 in Sunday school, and several running 5,000, and several running 2,000, and not scratch the surface of Atlanta. I am not happy about what we are accomplishing in Atlanta, or anywhere else. I am burdened about it because we are getting farther and farther behind. With as many preachers as we have, and as many preachers as our universities and colleges are turning out, it seems that more ought to be happening than what is happening.

But I learned something early in my ministry while reading biographies of great men. Not every preacher is as close to Jesus as other preachers. Not every Christian is as close to Jesus as other Christians. The largest crowd of Christians and the largest crowd of preachers are out on the periphery. They are just as close to Judas and the God-haters and the God-deniers and the liberals and the modernists, as they are to Jesus; and in just two or three steps they could join the other band.

Occasionally you pick up a book and read about a man who went all the way with Jesus and who could say, as Jesus said, "Not my will, but thine, be done." But only a few folks can say that and mean it sincerely. We might say, "Not my will," but we sort of choke up and our throat tightens up when we say, "Thine be done," because that could mean anything—selling the business and going to the mission field or giving up the presidency of a bank to work for the Sword of the Lord. That may mean giving up a good pilot's job to fly a plane to some mission field. It may mean sacrifice. It is hard to say, "Not my will, but thine, be done," so very few ever say that and mean it. But God blesses the few who do say it and mean it.

There is a difference in the crowd.

Someone asked Daniel Webster, when he was a boy, "Daniel, when you grow up, what do you want to be?"

Daniel said, "I would like to be a lawyer."

"Daniel, don't you know the profession is overrun?"

And Daniel Webster replied, "There is plenty of room at the top."

That is true in Christian circles. The closer you get to Jesus, the more elbow room you have. The closer you get to Jesus, the smaller the crowd, because not many people want to get down to business and really sacrifice and surrender and give everything to Jesus and say, "I will go anywhere, do anything, be anything. All I want, Jesus, is for You to tell me what it is."

Preachers think they have to live in a parsonage with three bedrooms and four baths and have a brand new car every year. They have to have a salary of $500 a week and a $1,500-a-year car allowance. God can't use that kind of fellow. As far as I am concerned, you are on the periphery. God can only use a man who is not looking for an easy way.

A fellow wrote David Livingstone: "I would like to join you. Is there an easy way to get to where you are?"

David Livingstone wrote back, "I don't want a man to join me who is looking for an easy way. I want one to join me who will make his own way if he has to."

That is the kind of man God can use. The largest crowd was out on the periphery.

The nearer you get to Jesus, the smaller the crowd gets, and I might say, the better the crowd gets.

A. Consider Jesus Alone in Gethsemane

Let us talk with Jesus just a moment. We walk up to Him and ask, "Jesus, how many disciples do You have?"

"I did have twelve."

"You did have twelve; but how many do You have now?"

"I have eleven now."

"What happened to the other one?"

"He has gone out to betray Me. He is getting a mob together, and he is going to betray Me with a kiss. Then they are going to take Me away and crucify Me."

"Well, where are the other eleven?"

"Eight of them are out here on the edge of the Garden, three of them are out there a little bit closer, and I am here alone."

"Jesus, do You mean You are praying all by Yourself? You have eleven disciples and not one is praying with You?"

That reminds me of some churches. The pastor has 6,700 members, and he can't get two to stand by him. Try to get a little bunch together, and every pastor knows what happens.

We had a great church in Decatur, with some of the sweetest, most dedicated Christians this side of Heaven. But I know by experience that most churches operate with just a handful of faithful people, when every believer ought to be involved in the work. Most organizations find it the same way. Every believer ought to be busy for God. There are too many out on the edge.

So you ask, "Jesus, where are Your eleven?"

"Eight are out there on the edge, and one left Me altogether; he joined the crowd outside, the mob that is coming to get Me. And these three here were praying, but they went to sleep; now I am praying alone."

It is sad that Jesus has to stand alone and pray alone, with nobody willing to go with Him.

I am not trying to be pious, but I believe I would go with Jesus to the last inch. I used to sit on my front porch as a country boy and play my guitar and sing, "I'll go with Him through the garden." I wept and cried then, and silently, under my breath, I would say, *Jesus, I am not only singing this; but Jesus, I mean this. I will go with You through the garden. I will go with You all the way.* I felt then that some day God Almighty would give me a chance to preach to somebody, somewhere. He knew I meant it when I said, *I will go with You, Lord, all the way, and count it an honor to go with You.*

B. Eight Disciples on the Border Away From the Praying Saviour

Let us leave Jesus and go to the eight right here on the edge of the Garden.

"Say, fellows, where is Jesus?"

"We don't know."

"Where are Peter, James and John?"

"We don't know; we haven't seen them."

"Well, where is Judas?"

"Judas? He left us. He has gone to betray Jesus."

"How do you know that?"

"Well, we were at the Supper awhile ago. Jesus said the one He gave the sop to would betray Him, and He gave it to Judas, so he has gone now to betray Jesus."

"You mean Judas is going to betray Jesus and you are doing nothing about it? Why aren't you up on your feet doing something instead of sitting here twiddling your thumbs while the enemies of Jesus are betraying Him!"

I wonder how many of us twiddle our thumbs. I mean, we don't stand for anything. Too many are weak, wishy-washy, potato-stringed backboned, rose-water squirting, take-it-easy, Caspar Milquetoast,   start-nowhere-and-end-up-at-the-same-place preachers—no backbone, won't stand for anything. I would get out of the ministry if I couldn't stand for God and the Bible and the fundamentals of the Faith. I would quit preaching and make an honest living. I would much rather be back at the Post Office. If I can't stand in my pulpit and preach the fundamentals of the Faith, and preach soul winning, and giving, and clean living, and men dressing like men, and women dressing like women, and separated living, I will quit being a pastor. I don't want to be one if I can't be the right kind.

"Where is Judas?"

"Oh, he has gone to betray Jesus."

"And you are letting him do it?"

"Well—yes."

"Why don't some of you try to stop him?"

"Well, uh-uh...."

You won't make a lot of friends that way, but I would rather know I stood for the defense of the Faith, die and face Jesus in Heaven and be able to say, "Jesus, I told them the virgin birth is a fundamental, the verbal inspiration is a fundamental, the resurrection is a fundamental, salvation by grace through faith in the finished work of Jesus is a fundamental, the second coming is a fundamental. They didn't believe me, but I told them and they know where I stand."

"Nobody is going to try to stop him?"

Well, why isn't Judas looking for Jesus among this group of eight? This is the largest bunch. This is the bunch he has been with. I will tell you why. He knows that bunch. He was with them when Jesus went up to the Mount of Transfiguration and took with Him Peter, James and John, and left behind those eight, and Judas.

And Judas remembered that when Jesus was on the Mount of Transfiguration a man came with a demon-possessed boy. He had hope in his heart. He had faith in Jesus' disciples, His servants. He thought they could help him, so he said, "Here is my demon-possessed boy. I want you to cast the demons out of him."

But those powerless disciples could not cast the demons out of that boy. Judas remembered that.

When Jesus came down from the Mount of Transfiguration, the man was still there with his son. Their powerlessness caused the father to lose faith in Jesus. Now he says to Jesus, "*If* Thou canst. . . . I brought this boy to Your disciples, and they could not cast the demons out; but *if* You can, will You do something about it?"

Jesus threw the *if* back on the man: "*If* thou canst believe, all things are possible to him that believeth."

Lukewarm believers on the periphery, with no power, have done more harm to the cause of Christianity than the Bob Ingersolls, the infidels, the atheists, the skeptics, the drunkards and the harlots all wrapped up in one bunch. The world expects us to be different. So, because of their powerlessness, this poor man even doubted that Jesus would be able to help him.

I don't think a man has ever lived who wanted to preach with power more than I. Several years ago I started praying a prayer which at first frightened me: "Dear Jesus, if You are not going to bless me, let me die." And I will be honest with you—the first time I prayed that prayer I thought I was going to die. I went up in a plane. I said, "Lord, let me modify that a little. I am ready to die, but if You are going to kill me because You are not going to bless me—if I am going to die in a plane crash—don't scare me to death in a storm. Let it blow up quick. Don't let me go all the way down to the ground and cut off a couple of limbs and lie there eight or ten hours suffering. I don't mind dying, but, Lord, let me die quick. I am a coward, Lord. I am not brave." And was I glad when the plane landed safely!

I was afraid while driving out to the place where I was going to preach. I kept thinking a trailer-truck may run over me because I had wholly committed myself—"Lord, bless me or kill me." But I meant it.

And the next time I got a little bolder. Now when I say it, God knows I mean it: I would rather die than not preach with power, not be a blessing, not help and not stir hearts. Powerless Christians have done more to harm Christianity than anything else.

Charles Finney went to a meeting in a small church. When some of the crowd said, "Mr. Finney, would you like for us to pray for your conversion?" Charles Finney said, "I guess not. It seems God wouldn't hear your prayer anyway. You have been praying for revival for years and haven't had one. So you need not pray for my conversion."

That is sad. Christians ought to get their prayers answered. You ought to be able to ask for something and get it. The Bible says you can. Read Dr. Rice's book, *Prayer—Asking and Receiving*. It will help you. You can get an answer to prayer. There is a difference in the three crowds in position. There is a difference in size.

III. DIFFERENCE IN RESPONSIBILITY

Let me hurriedly say that there is a difference in responsibility. I am a preacher. I like to think that I am normal and that every preacher has the same feelings I had when God called me to preach. I wanted to preach. I had the preacher's itch. I preached in my sleep. I would wake myself up preaching. I would have given anybody a thousand dollars to get me a place to preach.

I used to work for a loan company in Atlanta. In my little Hudson Jet I would chase bad accounts. What a job! I chased a lot of preachers. We had a rule of thumb at the loan company: Don't loan anybody money whose occupation starts with a "p"—preachers, painters, plumbers, etc. That is a rule of thumb and we really believed that. And most times, generally speaking, it was right. A lot of preachers wouldn't pay their bills. (I just threw that in for good measure.)

There is a difference in responsibility.

Notice what He said to that crowd out on the edge of the Garden, that crowd who represented the largest group. "Sit ye here" (vs. 36). All He said was, "Sit down and be still." He didn't

ask that crowd to pray. I wonder why. He knew them too well.
"You just sit here."

A. God's Preacher Has a Burden, a Vision

He said to Peter, James and John, "I want you to watch and
pray." Most preachers, when they are called to preach, have a
vision. I don't mean a vision like when you have eaten too much
onions and buttermilk before you go to bed. I mean you have
a dream.

As I drove that Hudson Jet, I would see hundreds of people,
big crowds. I would visualize preaching to them. I preached to
the steering wheel of that old Hudson Jet. I screamed and
hollered. I gave an invitation. And I would say, "That's right—
come right on. God bless you! Amen! Glad to see you coming."

I used to pray out loud. I would pray and talk. People would
look out their car windows and laugh at me.

One day I saw a fellow driving along with a telephone receiver
in his hand. He was talking to somebody, and I didn't laugh;
I thought he was a big shot. So I got an old telephone receiver,
tore it off the phone and tied it around the steering wheel. Then
when I started to pray I would pick up that receiver and start
praying into that.

Jesus said to that big crowd, "You just sit here."

Dr. Bob Jones, Sr., said, "It is true the Lord said, 'Where two
or three are gathered together in my name, there am I in the
midst of them'; however, the Lord did not necessarily mean that
He would not like larger crowds."

Somebody would come in every once in awhile and say, as he
looked at our auditorium which is 208 feet wide in the back,
"I bet you never thought you would ever pastor a church this
large." I say, facetiously, of course, "No. I just went to sleep one
night and woke up and bang—it was here!"

No, I had been thinking about that ever since God called me
to preach. I visualized that. I used to stand in a park in Atlanta
and see thousands of people in my mind's eye. I would preach

and give an invitation. I visualized people coming forward.

What am I saying? That every preacher whom God ever called to preach has a burden, a vision.

When we read about Moody, Spurgeon, Torrey, Sunday or somebody else, most of us think we will be the next Sunday, the next Moody, the next Spurgeon.

I wrote my dad when God called me to preach, "Dad, I want to be a giant for Jesus." I did have a vision. I did have a burden. But God does not give responsibility just on the vision alone. You can have a big vision, a big burden, an ambition and a desire; but the closer one gets to where Jesus is, the more responsibility He gives. So He said to that crowd, "You just sit here."

I heard about a man who hired a maid who turned out to be very slow. He said, "Don't you do anything fast?"

She said, "Yes, Suh, I gets tired fast."

There was another fellow who went to join the service.

They asked him, "What do you want to join? There are several branches. You can join the Air Force and travel by air; you can join the Navy and travel by water; or you can join the Infantry and travel on land."

He said, "Don't you have something called the Coast Guard? I might join that and just coast!"

A lot of Christians are like that. They only sit out there—never give a dollar, never win a soul, never witness, never get excited, never go on soul-winning visitation, never go to prayer meeting on Wednesday night, never get involved in any of God's work.

There are a lot of preachers sitting out there, too, waiting for some opening to come, hoping somebody will die and leave a big church and they will get called to it. Shame on you! You wouldn't know what to do with it. You couldn't run one of the Sunday school classes!

Preachers are running from one church to the other waiting for a better opportunity, waiting for someone else to call, a bigger salary, a bigger car. You are just sitting around waiting, like an old dog, to take over something somebody else built.

Why don't you get busy and build something yourself?

If I had waited for a pulpit committee to come to see me, I would still be at the Post Office. I had a burden, a vision. Nobody was going to call me to be a pastor. I was going to build a church. God wants people to try to build one. I had a vision, a burden. You had one, too. But God doesn't give responsibility to the fellow who just has the vision and burden.

B. These Were Commanded to "Watch and Pray"

He gave that group of three more responsibility. He said, "You watch and pray."

But He who represented the third group had the greatest responsibility of all—that of bearing the sins of the whole world and providing salvation for all men.

Do you want a lot of responsibility? If you can go as far as Jesus went and say as Jesus said, "Father...not my will, but thine, be done," then God is looking for you.

But you can't just say it; you have to mean it. I believe a lot of fellows say it who think they mean it but don't. Is there any reservation in your heart? Is there anything at all that you wouldn't do if God asked you to do it?

You preach along this line and people say, "If I make that kind of a surrender, if I yield like that, then if God asks me to sell my business and become a missionary, I will have to go to China." That is what it means. You are saying, "I don't really trust God. I think I know better than God does. He might ask me to do something that would not be the best thing for me."

Don't you know that whatever He asks of you will be the best thing that can happen to you? God is listening to what I am saying. God bears me record. Do you know what I want?—to do His will. I don't even have a preference. I say honestly and sincerely, everyone at Forrest Hills Baptist Church joined since I became pastor and I am the oldest member there. I started with 12 and they left after a little while. And 6,700 came to see why those 12 left.

I said I would resign my church just as quickly as I would take a drink of water, if I honestly knew that was God's will. I want His will more than I want to live.

Somebody said to the late Dr. Bob Jones, Sr., "Some are predestined for Heaven and some are predestined for Hell." Dr. Bob answered, "If it is God's will that I die and go to Hell, I don't want to go to Heaven. I would rather be in Hell in God's will than in Heaven out of His will, because if I were in Hell in God's will, then Hell would be Heaven."

I agree with that. If God wants me in Hell, I don't want to go to Heaven. I would rather be in Hell in God's will than to be in Heaven out of His will. But the truth of the matter is, He wills for all to be in Heaven (see II Pet. 3:9).

C. It May Mean Giving Up Things Dear to Us to Do God's Will

Can you say with Jesus, "Not my will, but thine, be done"? It made me quit my job. I got on my face in 1961 and said, "Lord, I will do anything You want me to do." But I didn't want to go to Bible college and seminary. I couldn't see going four years and then three more—seven years! I wanted to preach. I even said, "Lord, if You want me to, I will sell my house and give up my church and go to Bible school or Bible college." When I became willing, I learned I didn't have to do it. But He wanted me to be willing to do it. When I was willing to do His will, He said, "I will let you stay right where you are and keep building the church."

I got to the place where I could say, "Lord, if there is a place where nobody will go and preach, I will go; if there is a church nobody will take, I will take it; if there is a task nobody wants to do, I will do it; if there is a little place where nobody will stay, I will go there and stay. I will do anything, Jesus. And the only thing that will keep me from doing it is that I won't know what it is. You tell me and I will go." And I meant every word.

In 1961 I quit the Post Office. My church was paying me $75

a month. My house notes were $95.20 a month. I didn't know where the other $20.20 was coming from to pay the house notes. I had a wife and two children and a car. Everybody said I was crazy, that I was irresponsible, quitting a job with a wife and children and not knowing how I was going to make a living. If the church had given me all they took up every Sunday, I could not have lived off it. The offerings were about $60 a week.

"Not my will, but thine, be done." It may mean quitting that job.

One thing that bothers me is to see these preachers selling the *Book of Life*, insurance policies, automobiles, vanilla flavoring, running a Watkins' route, selling Amway on the side, and preaching a little bit. If there is a God in Heaven, why don't you just preach? If there is a God in Heaven, and if He wrote Philippians 4:19, why don't you just believe it and preach? You say, "I would starve." Then you ought to quit preaching. You are not worth being a preacher. Why don't you quit selling products and start building a church and winning people to Christ? You can win enough in one week to pay your salary if you get busy.

This is a true story that happened a short time ago. A fellow and his wife from Montgomery, Alabama, walked into my office. He said, "I am so burdened. Things are not happening in my ministry like I want to see them happen."

I counseled with him for hours. I gave him three tapes on soul winning and how to get people down the aisle once you have won them to Christ. He carried them home and listened to them. He called me on Monday and said, "Last Friday and Saturday I went out all day long and won twenty-five people to Christ! And Sunday morning when I gave the invitation—you won't believe this—all twenty-five came forward to join the church by baptism!"

I said, "That is wonderful!"

He said, "There is something better than that! A man in my church, fifty-two years old, whom I have been trying to win to

Christ, when I gave the invitation last Sunday and twenty-five people started coming down the aisle (it looked like everybody was coming), this fellow came running behind them. He thought the last train was going out for Heaven and he was going to miss it! He got saved and some others came and got saved!"

The next Tuesday this same man called me, shouting, "I did it again last Friday! I won twenty-five more, and they all came when I gave the invitation!"

Three weeks later he called me and said, "I did it again! We have had eighty-five conversions and additions for baptism in the last three weeks. I have never seen anything like it! Hallelujah! From now on I am not going to do anything but go soul winning. I am letting the deacons do everything else. Hallelujah!" and he hung up the phone.

I have been looking for smoke to come out from around the Montgomery area! He decided, "Not my will, but thine, be done."

I wish I had time to go into this a little further. It may mean quitting that job. If you get it like I got it, it will! I got to where I couldn't put the mail in the right boxes. I was so burdened for souls I almost quit in the middle of the route. I said, "Lord, if You will let me get the mail delivered today, I am through. I am quitting. I am going to be a preacher or nothing."

D. The Closer to Him You Get, the Smaller the Crowd Becomes

Someone asked me how I got to know Dr. Rice. At a Sword conference, I got my candle lit spiritually and I began winning souls. When you stand for the same thing, aim at the same thing, and are headed in the same direction, you meet each other.

"Hey, what is your name?"

"John R. Rice."

"What are you doing here?"

"I love Jesus and souls. I believe in the fundamentals of the Faith. I believe in evangelism. I believe in separation. And who are you? And what are you doing here?"

"I am Curtis Hutson. And you believe what I believe."

That is what happens when people believe alike.

Do you know why they met at the tomb that Easter morning? Not because they saw an invitation that said, "You meet Me at the tomb." They all met at the tomb because they all loved Jesus.

What brought Dr. Rice and me together? Our love for Jesus. That will make you stick, too. It may mean traveling with a smaller crowd. It may mean some persecution.

I thought, *Man! Everybody is going to love me now.* When I was in that little white frame building, a Primitive Baptist preacher, I believed what is to be will be even if it doesn't happen. Nobody ever cussed me. When I began winning people to Christ and got excited, went out knocking on doors, bought fifty buses and began running them all over Atlanta, advertising that we had 131 conversions or additions last Sunday, people began saying, "Well, I wonder how many of them are really saved?" I will tell you how many were saved—every single one of them, or they were liars. They were all dealt with personally and told how Jesus died to pay their sin debt, and they told us they were trusting Jesus. And if they trusted Jesus, they received everlasting life. Jesus said so and He can't lie.

A fellow got on the radio and said, "These churches that advertise as Georgia's largest Sunday school. . . ." What did he mean "these churches"? There is only one! Why didn't he just say Forrest Hills? He said, "I wonder how many were really saved?" We had 879 baptisms that year—he had 15!

I said, "If all yours were saved and only 50% of mine were saved, I would rather have my 50% than to have your 100%. I still have 400 and you have only 15. If only 10% of mine were saved and all of yours were saved, I would rather have my 10% than your 100%. I still have 87 and you have 15." The truth is, just as large a proportion of mine were saved as his.

Some people have the idea that in a big church people are not dealt with. You just don't know. The greatest, largest churches in America have the strictest standards. The counselors are trained more thoroughly.

Some fellow said, "Well, that big church is built around you." Sure it is. And that little rinky-dink failure is built around you. The Sword of the Lord was built around Dr. John R. Rice. And E. J. Daniels' evangelistic movement was built around E. J. Daniels. And the Bill Rice Ranch was built around Bill Rice. And that little fold you have over there in that storefront building is built around you.

It may mean some persecution. I have been called everything but a gentleman. I get nasty letters and nasty phone calls. But as long as they are kicking you in the back, you know you still have the lead. Amen! It may mean quitting that job. It may mean traveling in a smaller group. It may mean persecution. It may mean misunderstanding. It may mean sacrifice. Whatever it means we ought to be able to tell Jesus, *Not my will, but thine, be done.*

Oh, if every preacher in America could say that and mean it! Instead of making excuses for his failure, he should just admit that he is not totally, absolutely, unreservedly surrendered. Why not level with God and say, "Listen, God, I have been fiddling around long enough"?

I made up my mind when I read *Deeper Experiences of Famous Christians* and a few other books that I was either going to quit preaching or God was going to give me something that they had. I told God, "I am just not going to preach any more if I can't have a little bit of what they had a whole lot of."

I got up early Saturday morning and prayed all day long. I prayed all night. I was still in that little basement building in a little corner of a Sunday school room when the crowd started coming in Sunday morning. I had been there since Saturday morning.

The Devil said, "There are not but a few Dr. Jack Hyleses and Dr. Lee Robersons and Dr. John R. Rices."

I said to the Lord, "I don't want to be John R. Rice, nor Jack

Hyles, nor Lee Roberson. I want to be Curtis Hutson. I want to be on fire. Can't I have a little bit of the fire they have? If I can't, I will go back to carrying mail."

I thought He would never come through! I was so hungry for it I thought I would die if I didn't have it. And I got to the place where I was willing to say something similar to what Jesus said, "Not my will, but thine, be done. It makes no difference, Jesus. Whatever You want, I am ready now."

Which crowd are you in? Are you still out there on the edge of the garden just sitting? Or are you a little bit farther in? You have prayed a little bit but you fell asleep. Or have you gotten to the place in your Christian experience where you can say as Jesus did, "Not my will, but thine, be done"?

I have no way of knowing, but I have an idea that not many people ever get that far. They will serve Jesus if they can get the place they want. They will serve Jesus if they can get the position they want, if they can live in the state they want. But not many get that far with Jesus.

But those who do get that far with Jesus have the greatest responsibility. He says to that fellow, "I want to use you."

Why is it that out of the hundred largest Sunday schools in America, thirty-two of them are pastored by men who never went to Bible college? Because God was not looking for educated but surrendered men. God was not looking for ability, but for dependability.

God will use mightily the fellow who makes such a surrender and means it. The field is wide open.

I should never have been a preacher as far as human reasoning is concerned. I was an introvert. I heard Dr. Hyles talk about being a thumb-sucker. I never did suck my thumb, but I was so timid I wouldn't give oral book reports. I would rather take an "F." I never did fake a faint like he did, but if I had thought of it I would have! I was timid. I should not have been used of the Lord.

God has brought me farther than I ever ought to have been.

God wasn't looking for somebody who had a lot of ability; He was looking for somebody who would surrender.

Give Him what you have.

The Behavior of Believers

C H A P T E R N I N E

*"**B**ut, beloved, we are persuaded better things of you, and things that accompany salvation, though we thus speak."*—Heb. 6:9.

A recent Gallup Poll showed that one out of every three voting-age people in America professes to be born again. That is enough believers to evangelize the world and have a tremendous spiritual impact, if we were serious about our Christianity.

One problem with Christianity today is that we have too many average Christians. Far too many believers are like the man who when asked, "How long have you been a Christian?" replied, "I've been a Christian off and on for nearly forty years." Too many believers are off and on.

Henry Drummond said, "What the world needs is not more men, but a better brand." Billy Sunday made this statement: "What the church needs is not a lot of new members, but the old members made new."

Most churches are like an ailing lung with only a few cells doing the breathing.

If every professing Christian in America were a successful Christian in the biblical sense, we would make a mighty spiritual impact on this country.

Now, in this sermon I want to share with you seven steps to successful Christian living or things that accompany salvation.

The prerequisite for salvation is faith in the Lord Jesus Christ. The Bible says in John 3:36, "He that believeth on the Son hath everlasting life. . . ." The seven things I share in this sermon are not prerequisites to salvation, but things that accompany salvation.

I. CONFESS CHRIST PUBLICLY

First, there must be an open, public confession of Christ. Romans 10:10 says, "For with the heart man believeth unto righteousness; and with the mouth confession is made unto salvation." And Jesus said, "Whosoever therefore shall confess me before men, him will I confess also before my Father which is in heaven. But whosoever shall deny me before men, him will I also deny before my Father which is in heaven" (Matt. 10:32, 33).

While a public profession is not essential to salvation, it certainly accompanies it. Someone said, "Too many Christians are like an Arctic river; they are frozen at the mouth." We can stand up for anything and anybody; but when it comes to standing up for Christ, believers seem to have a spiritual inferiority complex.

Every person who has trusted Jesus Christ as Saviour should go forward in a church service and make his public profession of faith. He should tell the preacher that he has trusted Christ and now wants others to know about it. If you've recently trusted Christ as Saviour and have friends who have been praying for your salvation, call and tell them you've trusted Christ. If you have parents in a distant city who have long prayed for your conversion, call and tell them that you've become a Christian. Unfurl your flag and come out into the open. Don't be a secret disciple.

II. CHURCH MEMBERSHIP IN THE LOCAL CONGREGATION IS THE NEXT STEP

The second step to successful Christian living is church membership. Now, you don't join a church to become a Christian; but church membership accompanies salvation.

Billy Sunday used to say, "Getting into the church won't make a Christian out of you anymore than getting into the garage will make an automobile out of you." But while church membership has nothing to do with salvation, it has a lot to do with successful Christian living. Hebrews 10:25 says, "Not forsaking the assembling of ourselves together, as the manner of some is . . . ."

The Bible order is found in Acts 2:41, "Then they that gladly received his word were baptized: and the same day there were added unto them about three thousand souls." Note the order that God gives here: believe, be baptized, belong.

I have never in all my Christian experience seen a successful believer who did not belong to a local church somewhere and was not faithful to that church. Of the 117 times the word "church" appears in the New Testament, 95 times it means "the local congregation."

The Bible doesn't tell us exactly which church to join. For instance, the Bible doesn't say, "Thou shalt join the First Baptist of such and such a city." So in this case, we have a right to expect the Holy Spirit to lead us. The believer should visit a number of good, Bible-believing churches in his area and pray that God will lead him to the right church. While the Bible doesn't say exactly which church to join, it does give us an idea of what kind of church to join.

In the first place, it should be a fundamental church. I mean, the pastor should believe in the virign birth, the blood atonement, the literal, physical resurrection of Jesus, the verbal inspiration of the Bible, and the literal, visible second coming of Christ. He should not only believe in the fundamentals of the Faith, but he should stand without apology for these great, essential doctrines.

Second, it should be a church that separates from apostasy. No believer should belong to a church that supports modernism or gives money through a program to pay some liberal professor's salary who is teaching the next generation of preacher boys that the Bible is not the Word of God. Any believer who belongs to that kind of church should transfer his membership as soon as possible to a church that does believe in the fundamentals of the Faith and refuses to support modernism, liberalism and apostasy.

Third, it ought to be a soul-winning church. Remember, the whole purpose of the church is to win souls to Christ. That's what it is all about! Everything else is a means to an end. If I attended a church for several Sundays and never saw one conversion, I would not join it. If the pastor didn't have enough concern over the lost to win at least a few to Christ himself, then I wouldn't want to be a part of that kind of fellowship. Soul winning ought to be the main thing in the church. If it were necessary, I would drive a hundred miles one way and a hundred miles back to belong to the right kind of church.

Fourth, the pastor should be a good Bible teacher. I mean by this that every time you attend church, it should be a learning experience. We go to church to learn. Of course, many of the services should be evangelistic, but I speak now of the Bible-teaching hours, such as Sunday school, prayer meeting, etc. The church is where the believer learns. It's a place of fellowship with other believers, where we can join with others in winning souls in our own communities and help evangelize the world.

If I were to move to a new town tomorrow, I would join a church in that city just as soon as possible. Every believer should be a church member and should be faithful to that church with his presence, prayers and pocketbook.

III. CONCENTRATE DAILY ON THE STUDY OF GOD'S WORD

The third step in successful Christian living is studying the

Word of God. Again, learning the Bible is not a prerequisite to salvation but something that accompanies salvation. First Peter 2:2 says, "As newborn babes, desire the sincere milk of the word, that ye may grow thereby." I'm not sure, but perhaps the apostle means, "Just like newborn babes desire milk, newborn believers should desire the Word of God." I do know that when I accepted Christ as my Saviour, there came an immediate hunger for the Word of God. I could not learn enough. The more I learned, the more I wanted to know. Feeding on the Word of God is essential to Christian growth.

Someone said, "So far in the history of the world, there have not been enough mature people in the right place at the right time."

Speaking from my experience as a preacher, I would say, "So far in the history of the church, there have not been enough mature believers in the right place at the right time." If all the professing Christians in America were strong, mature Christians, we could shape the world for God and right.

I read in a health magazine that you are what you eat. I do know that you are spiritually what you eat spiritually. Therefore, believers should avoid filthy magazines and books and have a good diet from the Word of God.

Then, too, if the believer is to be "a workman that needeth not to be ashamed," it is essential he study the Word of God. Second Timothy 2:15 says, "Study to show thyself approved unto God, a workman that needeth not to be ashamed...." Believers need a working knowledge of the Bible to win souls to Christ. Then the study of the Bible has a cleansing effect upon the believer. In John 15:3 Jesus says, "Now ye are clean through the word which I have spoken unto you." And in John 17:17 He prays, "Sanctify them through thy truth: thy word is truth."

Someone asked his pastor, "Should I continue reading the Word of God when I don't remember a thing that I read?"

The wise, old pastor thought a moment, then replied, "Yes, keep reading the Word of God even though you cannot remember what you read. When you pour water through a sifter, the sifter does not retain the water, but the water keeps the sifter clean."

I remember seeing written in the front of someone's Bible this profound statement: "This Book will keep you from sin, and sin will keep you from this Book." That is more than a cliche; it is a fact! The believer should set aside some time everyday for Bible-reading.

D. L. Moody said, "When we pray, we talk to God. When we read the Bible, God talks to us. And we need to do most of the listening." No man can be a successful Christian without reading his Bible regularly.

IV. COMMUNE DAILY WITH GOD IN PRAYER

The fourth essential to successful Christian living is daily prayer. The so-called "Lord's Prayer" implies daily communion with God. "Give us this day our daily bread" (Matt. 6:11). It seems that prayer would have to be prayed again tomorrow and the next day and the next and so on. If God intended that we pray only once a week, the passage should read, "Give us this day our 'weekly' bread." Luke 18:1 says, ". . . men ought always to pray, and not to faint." First Thessalonians 5:17 says we are to "Pray without ceasing." And Psalm 5:3 says, "My voice shalt thou hear in the morning, O Lord; in the morning will I direct my prayer unto thee, and will look up."

There are many reasons why believers should commune daily with God in prayer. In the first place, it's God's appointed way for us to obtain things. Matthew 7:7 says, "Ask, and it shall be given you. . . ." And James 4:2 tells us, ". . . ye have not, because ye ask not." You would be surprised what you can get from God by simply asking. And don't be afraid to ask too much.

One of Napoleon's soldiers made an unbelievable request. The other soldiers laughed at him. "You'll never get it. You've asked for too much." But to their surprise, Napoleon called the soldier in and said, "You have honored me by the magnitude of your request. It shall be granted."

God likes for us to ask for big things. Psalm 81:10 says, ". . . open thy mouth wide, and I will fill it." Oh, the wonderful answers to prayers that I've experienced—the many things that God has given to me!

After resigning my job at the Post Office in 1961 and trusting God to provide our needs, I saw many wonderful answers to prayer. One night my wife and I were standing in our kitchen crying because we could not pay our bills. We stacked the bills on the kitchen stove and laid our hands on them and prayed that God would supply the need.

In the middle of the prayer we were interrupted by a knock on the door. It was past midnight. Here stood a couple crying. They handed us a check and said, "God woke us up and told us to bring you this money." When they left, we found the check was for the same amount as the bills!

Prayer is also God's way for the believer to receive forgiveness and cleansing. First John 1, verses 8 and 9, say, "If we say that we have no sin, we deceive ourselves, and the truth is not in us. If we confess our sins, he is faithful and just to forgive us our sins, and to cleanse us from all unrighteousness." I wish no believer ever sinned. I was naive enough when I first accepted Christ to believe that I would never sin again. And I think I even promised God that I would never sin again, but I have. But, thank God, there is a way to receive forgiveness and cleansing— "If we confess our sins."

When my son was a tiny tot, I had him ask the blessing at the table before one of our meals. He prayed for several things, then he prayed, "And, dear God, bless all my sins."

I chuckled and thought, *That's the attitude many Christians take.* Later, I explained that we didn't ask God to bless our sins— we confess them and ask God to forgive and cleanse them. The believer should pray daily because he needs forgiveness and cleansing every day.

Martin Luther said, "Keep short accounts with God," meaning don't let sin build up in your life. When you sin, immediately confess it and claim the forgiveness and cleansing which God offers.

A preacher friend of mine, on the way to church early one Sunday morning, stopped at a service station where he saw a little girl with her baby brother. The little boy was grimy dirty. Looking at him, the preacher said, "Son, how in the world did you get so dirty so early in the morning?"

The little boy's sister interrupted, "Preacher, he didn't get that dirty this morning. He went to bed like that last night."

How many believers go to bed night after night with sins unconfessed. You allow sin to build up in your life and lose fellowship with Christ. Communing daily with God in prayer is an absolute essential to successful Christian living.

It's the way to get wisdom. James 1:5 says, "If any of you lack wisdom, let him ask of God, that giveth to all men liberally, and upbraideth not; and it shall be given him." Here God says, "Ask for all the wisdom you want, and I'll give it liberally and will not scold you for asking." What an encouragement to pray!

There are a number of other reasons why the believer should pray daily, but these are some of the more important ones.

V. COMMUNICATE DAILY THE GOSPEL TO OTHERS

Witnessing is an essential to successful Christian living. No believer is a success who doesn't try to win others to Christ. The only reason God left you here after you became a Christian was to win others. John 15:16 says, "Ye have not chosen me, but I have chosen you, and ordained you, that ye should go and bring forth fruit, and that your fruit should remain...."

Keep in mind that the fruit of the Christian is other Christians. Proverbs 11:30 says, "The fruit of the righteous is a tree of life; and he that winneth souls is wise." God leaves Christians here to bear fruit, that is, to win souls. Jesus calls us out of the world, then sends us back into the world to get as many out as we possibly can, while we're still in the world.

God's program for world evangelization is that every believer win others. The Great Commission in Matthew 28 teaches that we're to win them, baptize them, then teach them how to win others to Christ. We have yet to evangelize the world. And the reason is simple—we haven't done it the way God said. Soul winning is every believer's business.

A lady returning from a trip said to her husband, "I had an unusual experience on the train today. A man came up to me and asked if I were a Christian."

"Why didn't you tell him it was none of his business?" her husband retorted.

"Oh," she said, "if you had heard him, you would have known that it was his business."

Every believer should keep handy a supply of gospel tracts. And when it is impossible to give a verbal witness, at least pass out a Bible tract.

In my meetings I try to get believers to commit themselves to speak to at least one person a day about Christ. It is not difficult. Everyone has opportunity to speak daily to numbers of people. Let's make it our business. Second Corinthians 5:20 tells us that we are "ambassadors for Christ." Witnessing and soul winning accompany salvation. You don't win people to Christ to qualify for Heaven. You do it as an act of obedience to a clear command of Scripture.

VI. CONQUER TEMPTATION AND SIN

When I was a young Christian, I got temptation and sin mixed up. I thought that temptation was sin. When I had some evil thought or was tempted to do something sinful, I thought, *I must not be a Christian.* These terrible thoughts came to my mind. I did not realize that Satan has power to put such thoughts into our minds, and then he subtly accuses us of having the thoughts and tries to discourage us.

Temptation is sin only when one yields to it. Temptation is a common experience for everyone. First Corinthians 10:13 says,

"There hath no temptation taken you but such as is common to man...."

If we succeed in the Christian life, we must learn to resist the Devil and say "No" to temptation. When Satan comes, use the words of Jesus in Luke 4:8, "Get thee behind me, Satan."

I read the story of a young preacher's wife who could not resist the temptation of buying beautiful dresses. She kept her husband broke. The young preacher said to her, "When you go shopping today and Satan tempts you to buy a new dress, you say, 'Get thee behind me, Satan!'"

She came home that night with another new dress. "What!" exclaimed the preacher, "another new dress! Didn't I tell you to tell Satan, 'Get thee behind me'?"

"Well, Honey, I tried on this beautiful new dress. And when I looked in the mirror, Satan said, 'You ought to buy that dress; it's beautiful on you.' Then, Honey, I did what you told me. I said, 'Get thee behind me, Satan!' And Satan got behind me and said, 'It looks good on you from this side, too.' So I just couldn't resist the temptation."

The successful Christian must deal thoroughly with sin. If we fail, we must honestly confess it and endeavor to forsake it, claiming God's forgiveness and cleansing. We must be honest about our sins.

One lady went to her pastor and implored, "Please pray for me! I have an awful cross to bear; it is a bad temper."

The pastor replied, "Nonsense! You don't have a cross to bear; you have a sin. Your husband has a cross to bear."

Let's not cover our sins by calling them something else. When the other fellow acts "that way," he's ugly; when you do it, it's nerves. When he's "set in his ways," he's obstinate; when you are, it's just firmness. When he doesn't like your friends, he's prejudiced; when you don't like his, you're simply showing good judgment of human nature. When he tries to be accommodating, he's "polishing the apple"; when you do it, you're using tact. When he takes time to do things, he's "slow as Christmas"; when you take ages, you're deliberate. When he picks flaws, he's "cranky"; when you do, you're discriminating.

Let's level with God about our sins. We'll never be successful believers until we do.

VII. CONTRIBUTE REGULARLY TO THE CAUSE OF CHRIST

I don't know a successful Christian who's stingy and greedy. Again, I must say that giving money is not a prerequisite to salvation. It is something that accompanies salvation.

Sixteen of the thirty-eight parables Jesus used were about stewardship. One of every six verses in the New Testament mentions the right or wrong use of possessions—man's relationship to material things.

First Corinthians 16:2 says, "Upon the first day of the week let every one of you lay by him in store, as God hath prospered him, that there be no gatherings when I come." When? "Upon the first day of the week." Who? ". . . let every one of you." How? ". . . as God hath prospered him." Why? ". . . that there be no gatherings when I come."

A good rule to follow is: Give God the first part of every day, the first day of every week and the first fruits of all your increase. God only has one way of financing His work and that's through the gifts and offerings of His people.

Every believer should have a regular habit of giving. Leviticus 27:30 says, ". . . the tithe . . . is the Lord's . . . ." The tithe is ten percent. At least ten percent of the believer's income should be given to the cause of Christ. That should be the minimum.

Many believers will want to give more and should give more. Christians who make more and have extra money should not stop at ten percent. God has given some men the ability to make money. Some dear Christian ladies have been left sizable amounts of money. Some have been left fortunes, and they'll never spend the money in their lifetime. These people should be very prayerful about what to do with the money God has placed in their hands. The believer is only a steward, not a possessor. God has put things in our hands to be used for His cause.

I want every dollar that I possibly can give to be used for winning souls. The believer should not only give while he's living, but should contact a Christian attorney and make out a will for his money to be used in God's service after his death. Of course, he will want to make this a matter of prayer and allow God to lead him as to what to do.

God knows where the money is most needed, and He is able to direct the believer in giving his money.

I have given you seven things that accompany salvation as a pattern for successful Christian living. These are not prerequisites for salvation but guidelines for the believer's behavior.

If one or more of these things are lacking in your life, I encourage you to confess that lack as sin and set out to be all that God wants you to be.

It is God's design and desire that every believer be a successful Christian.

The Believer and Criticism

C H A P T E R T E N

*"**J**udge not, that ye be not judged. For with what judgment ye judge, ye shall be judged: and with what measure ye mete, it shall be measured to you again. And why beholdest thou the mote [tiny speck] that is in thy brother's eye, but considerest not the beam [two-by-four] that is in thine own eye? Or how wilt thou say to thy brother, Let me pull out the mote out of thine eye; and, behold, a beam is in thine own eye? Thou hypocrite, first cast out the beam out of thine own eye; and then shalt thou see clearly to cast out the mote out of thy brother's eye. Give not that which is holy unto the dogs, neither cast ye your pearls before swine, lest they trample them under their feet, and turn again and rend you."* —Matt. 7:1-6.

There are actually three kinds of criticism in this passage.

Verse 1, "Judge not, that ye be not judged," I would classify as "destructive criticism." The cynical critic. This man is always trying to find something wrong with somebody, and his aim is to destroy.

Verse 4 is what I call "deluded criticism." Here one is trying to get a mote out of his brother's eye, while at the same time having a beam in his own eye. And, according to the words of Jesus, his vision is impaired; and he cannot see clearly to get the mote out of his brother's eye. It is all right to help your brother, but you don't want to knock his head off with a two-by-four hanging out of your own eye while trying to get a speck out of his eye.

Verse 6 I call "discriminating criticism." "Give not that which is holy unto the dogs, neither cast ye your pearls before swine, lest they trample them under their feet, and turn again and rend you."

Today it seems if you take any kind of a stand against anybody for anything, somebody is sure to rise up and say, "Judge not, that ye be not judged." People use verse 1 to try to keep you from taking a stand even against modernism and liberalism.

This verse does not teach that we cannot make any kind of judgment because verse 6 requires that we make at least four. If one "gives not that which is holy unto the dogs," he has to judge what is holy and who is a dog. If you do not "cast your pearls before swine," you have to make a judgment as to what is a pearl and who is a swine. So one has to make four judgments here. I call this "discriminating criticism."

I. THE RIGHT KIND OF CRITICISM

Second Corinthians 6:14 says, "Be ye not unequally yoked together with unbelievers...." First John 4:1 says, "Beloved, believe not every spirit, but try the spirits whether they are of God...."

I have a Bible command not to yoke up with an unbeliever. So I not only have a right, but I have a responsibility to make some kind of judgment about a man concerning the fundamentals of the Faith.

Now I am a fundamentalist and make no apologies for it. For many years I had no idea what modernism was. I read in my first copy of THE SWORD OF THE LORD that little heading, "Opposes Modernism, Worldliness and Formalism." I thought, *This man believes like I do. He is against modernism.* The only difference was, I thought modernism was having inside bathrooms in the church, giving the preacher a salary, going to Bible college to learn how to preach, having padded pews and carpeted aisles, and special singing in the church. I didn't know that modernism was a matter of belief.

When I first heard the word "fundamentalist," I thought a fundamentalist was somebody who screamed loud. Now some do scream loud; but a lot of wild animals scream loud, too. All four of my kids screamed loud before they knew what a fundamentalist was. If screaming loud made a man a fundamentalist, a lot of folks would be fundamentalists. But fundamentalism is not a matter of behavior; it is a matter of belief.

Some time ago while discussing fundamentalism with a preacher, he commented about an individual saying, "That man is a fundamentalist."

I asked, "How do you know he is a fundamentalist?"

"Because he wears his hair short."

I said, "Having short hair doesn't make a man a fundamentalist. I know some bald-headed modernists. It's not what's on your head that makes you a fundamentalist; it's what's in your head."

Now I'm for men having short hair. I think men ought to look like men and ladies like ladies. But fundamentalism is a matter of doctrinal belief. A fundamentalist is someone who believes in the fundamentals of the Faith. And a fundamental is a cardinal doctrine. It is an essential truth. It is something that you cannot deny and still have Christianity.

Let me illustrate.

I have a 1976 Buick. Everything in that automobile is not essential for the operation of the vehicle. For instance, the spare tire is not essential; it is not fundamental. I can drive the automobile without the spare tire. The stereo radio is not fundamental. I enjoy it, but I can drive without the stereo radio. The air-conditioner is not essential; it's not a fundamental. I can operate the automobile without it.

But wait a minute! The motor is fundamental! You take the motor out, and you may as well have a kiddie car, or a tricycle, or a skateboard. When you remove the motor, you've done away with the thing that makes the car operate. The motor is absolutely essential. You can't throw the motor out and still have an automobile that works. Gasoline is fundamental. You can't operate the automobile without gasoline; it won't run without it. The battery is fundamental. You take the battery out, and the motor is dead.

But now in Christianity there are fundamentals, essential truths, that we cannot deny and still have Christianity.

A. The Virgin Birth Is a Fundamental

If Jesus Christ is not the virgin-born Son of God, we don't have a Saviour. If He were born like we are born, then He inherited the same sin nature we inherited. Romans 5:12 says, "Wherefore, as by one man sin entered into the world [or into mankind]. . . ." Romans 5:19 says, "For as by one man's disobedience many were made sinners. . . ." If Jesus Christ is an offspring of man and not of God, then He inherited the same sin nature I inherited when I was born; and He owes the same sin debt I owe; and we do not have a sinless substitute to die in our place.

I say it reverently; but if Jesus Christ is not the virgin-born Son of God, we will all go to Hell, along with Jesus Christ. The virgin birth of Christ is a fundamental of the Faith. It is essential.

In John 8:21, 24 Jesus said,

". . . ye shall seek me, and shall die in your sins: whither I go, ye cannot come. . . . I said therefore unto you, that ye shall die in your sins: for if ye believe not that I am he, ye shall die in your sins."

B. The Physical Resurrection of Jesus From the Dead Is a Fundamental

If a man denies the resurrection of Christ, he is not saved. Romans 10:9 says, "That if thou shalt confess with thy mouth the Lord Jesus, and shalt believe in thine heart that God hath raised him from the dead, thou shalt be saved." The resurrection of Jesus Christ is a fundamental of the Faith.

That which separates Christianity from all other religions is the resurrection. Every religion has a founder who lived and died and is still in the tomb. But Christianity has a Founder who lived and died and was buried, and after three days and nights arose from the dead.

A little girl was talking about Christ. And a skeptic said, "Little girl, you keep talking about Christ this and Christ that. There are many christs. Which one are you talking about?"

The little girl replied, "I'm talking about the One who arose from the dead!"

The resurrection of Christ is the keystone in the arch. Destroy the resurrection and the whole arch will collapse.

C. The Substitutionary Death of Jesus Is a Fundamental

If Jesus Christ did not die on a cross in the sinner's place to pay the sinner's debt, then we don't have a plan of salvation. Deny the vicarious sufferings of Jesus Christ, and you have denied a fundamental of the Faith. Isaiah 53:6 says, ". . . the Lord hath laid on him the iniquity of us all." And II Corinthians 5:21 says, "For he hath made him to be sin for us, who knew no sin; that we might be made the righteousness of God in him."

The gospel story is simple. We are sinners. We owe a sin debt. Jesus Christ was not a sinner. He died on a cross and suffered Hell to pay our sin debt. And we are saved by trusting Him as our Saviour.

The dirtiest gang of thieves this side of Hell is a gang of religious thieves who are trying to climb up to Heaven some way other than the substitutionary death of Jesus Christ. Absolutely futile is any plan of salvation that by-passes the cross.

D. The Second Coming of Christ Is a Fundamental

There are twenty times as many references to the second coming of Christ in the Old Testament as there are to His first coming. Then in Paul's epistles, he speaks of baptism only thirteen times but of the second coming at least fifty times.

If Jesus Christ does not come again, then many, many verses in the Bible would be untrue. In John 14:3 Jesus said, "And if I go..., I will come again, and receive you unto myself; that where I am, there ye may be also." In Philippians 3:20, Paul said, "For our conversation is in heaven; from whence also we look for the Saviour, the Lord Jesus Christ." Jesus is coming again.

An old-fashioned preacher brought a wonderful sermon on the second coming; and, at the close of the service, one of these little, young, modernistic, potato-string backbone, rose-water squirting preachers, who start nowhere and end up in the same place, said to the old preacher, "I want you to know that I can't get that out of the New Testament."

The old-fashioned preacher smiled and said, "You sure can't, Buddy. It's in there to stay!" The second coming is a fundamental.

E. The Verbal Inspiration of the Bible Is a Fundamental

If the Bible is not the Word of God, then the foundations have been destroyed. It was from the Bible that I learned that Jesus Christ was virgin-born. It was from the Bible that I learned that Jesus Christ died on a cross for sinners. It was from the Bible that I learned that Jesus Christ was literally and physically raised from the dead. It was from the Bible that I learned that Jesus Christ is coming again.

Destroy the Bible, and you destroy all other doctrines. The

Bible is the Word of God." That's fundamental. Second Timothy 3:16 says, "All scripture is given by inspiration of God. . . ." And Matthew 4:4 says, "Man shall not live by bread alone, but by every word that proceedeth out of the mouth of God."

The modernists say, "The Bible contains the Word of God." But the fundamentalists say, "The Bible *IS* the Word of God."

Several years ago after mentioning in a sermon that the Bible is the Word of God, a man came to me and said, "Well, all the Bible is not the Word of God."

I asked, "What part is not God's Word?"

He turned to Genesis and read where the serpent said to Eve, "Ye shall not surely die." "Now," he said, "that's not God's Word. That's the Devil's word."

I replied, "That is God's Word. That's God saying that the Devil said to Eve, 'Ye shall not surely die.' It is God telling on the Devil. We wouldn't know the Devil said it if God hadn't told us. You listen, the Bible is the Word of God from Genesis to Revelation; and I believe every word of it."

> **The Holy Bible must have been**
> **Inspired of God and not of men.**
> **I could not, if I would, believe**
> **That good men wrote it to deceive.**
>
> **And bad men would not if they could,**
> **Proceed to write a book so good.**
> **And certainly no crazy man**
> **Could e'er conceive it's wondrous plan.**
>
> **And pray, what other kinds of men**
> **Then do these three groups comprehend?**
> **Hence it must be that God inspired**
> **The Word which souls of prophets fired.**
> **—*Author unknown.***

The virgin birth of Jesus, His vicarious suffering, His victorious resurrection, His visible second coming, and the verbal inspiration of the Bible are fundamentals of the Faith.

There are some things I would die for, some things I would

fight for that I would not die for, and some things I would fuss about that I wouldn't fight about. But when it comes to the spiritual realm, I would die for the fundamentals of the Faith.

Second Corinthians 6:14 says, "Be ye not unequally yoked together with unbelievers...." The test of our love is not willingness to fellowship with modernists and liberals but obedience to the commands of Scripture. Jesus said, "If a man love me, he will keep my words..." (John 14:23). Now we are not to be unequally yoked to an unbeliever.

An unbeliever, a modernist, a liberal, an infidel and an apostate—all are synonymous. The liberal or modernist is someone who deliberately rejects revealed truth. Though he knows the Bible says Jesus was born of a virgin, he denies it. It is one thing to be in error because of ignorance and another thing to deliberately reject revealed truth. A man can be in error because of ignorance and not be a modernist or a liberal.

There is not one preacher who has an excuse to stay yoked up with unbelievers. There is a right kind of criticism. There is a right kind of judgment. If you can't get the liberals and the modernists out of the movement, then get yourself out.

As long as we agree on the fundamentals, we ought to fellowship. But when someone denies one of the fundamentals of the Faith, if we are honest with the command of Scripture, we must separate from him.

Someone said, "In essentials unity, in nonessentials liberty, and in all things charity."

Now let's be honest. We don't all agree on everything with everybody we know everywhere in the world. I disagree with some things I've said. I have sermons I preached several years ago that I could not preach now. If a man reads and studies, he learns. If he is learning, he will change his mind about some things.

My old pastor didn't believe in a physical resurrection of the body, so for years I, too, thought there would be no resurrection—until I read the Bible and found that John 5:28 and 29 said,

"Marvel not at this: for the hour is coming, in the which all that are in the graves shall hear his voice, And shall come forth."

A preacher said to me not long ago, "Well, bless God; I'm the same as I was thirty-seven years ago!" Well, a man who hasn't changed in thirty-seven years is either perfect or stubborn; and I don't know any perfect people.

I've changed. For years I didn't believe in the second coming of Christ. I never heard a sermon on the second coming. The first time I heard "premillennial," I thought it was a breakfast cereal!

A man was visiting in the church service one Sunday night. We only had a small handful of people. When he came in, I noticed that he had a Bible in his hand—the only one who had ever come to church with a Bible. And he scared me. I thought he was a spy coming to check me out!

It so happened that Sunday night I was preaching my first seven-point sermon. I never had pointed my sermons before. I had just read Revelation, chapters 2 and 3, and noticed several times the expression, "To him that overcometh." That night I announced, "I'm preaching tonight on 'God's Promises to the Overcomers.'"

I said, "First, him that overcometh will I give a white stone. And on that stone I will write a new name, and no man will know it except he that received it and he that gave it." I waxed eloquent. I preached on the white stone, not having any idea what it meant. I said, "Hallelujah, it's a white stone! It's got my name on it, and nobody can steal it. Glory to God!" I preached until I got all I could out of the white stone.

Then I said, "Second, him that overcometh will I give to eat of the hidden manna." I said, "Bless God! I know not what manner of manna it is, but if it lasts until I get there, it must be good. It won't mildew or spoil until I get there. And it's hidden, and the Devil can't find it. Glory to God!" I preached on the manna till everybody got hungry for manna!

I preached all my points. Then when I came to the last promise, I ran into a stump—Revelation 3:21. I said, "And finally, him that overcometh will I grant to sit with me in my throne, even as I also overcame, and am set down with my Father in his throne." I didn't know what it meant. I said to myself, *Self, what are you going to tell them about that verse? Well, I'll tell them what He said.*

I looked out at my congregation and said, "According to this verse, Jesus is not on His throne. But someday He will sit on His throne; and we will sit with Him on His throne, just like He is now seated with the Father on the Father's throne." That guy with the Bible said, "Amen!"

I said to myself, *You said something good, if you just knew what it was!* Then I thought, *If I say it again, I might catch it this time.* So I got a little louder and a little faster and I said, "Bless God, according to this verse, Jesus is not on His throne. But hallelujah, someday He will reign on His throne; and we will reign with Him!" And that man said, "Amen!" again.

I thought, *There is something good in this verse, if I could just find it. That guy has found it.* I said the same thing several times till the man was embarrassed to "amen" me anymore. Then I concluded my sermon.

He came to me after the service and said, "God bless you, boy! I didn't know you were a premillennial preacher."

I said, "We're glad you came to church. I hope you'll come back."

He said, "If I had known you were premillennial, I would have joined this church and helped you."

I said, "Come back and see us." He wouldn't leave.

He said, "You are premillennial, aren't you?"

I dropped my head and said, "Sir, I am so embarrassed. I never heard that word. What is it?"

He said, "You're not postmillennial, are you?"

I said, "That is another word I never heard."

He said, "Well, you are not amillennial, are you?"

I said, "I never heard any of those *millennium* words."

He said, "Boy, do you believe what you preached tonight?"
I said, "Yes, Sir."

He said, "Then you are a premillennial preacher and don't
know it." I didn't know whether it was good or bad. I was so
embarrassed.

At my ordination I had been given a Scofield Bible by a group
of amillennial preachers. I reached up and took my Scofield
Bible off the pulpit and started to leave that night. When this
man saw it, he said, "Boy, let me see your Bible." I wasn't anxious for him to see it, but he insisted. After looking at it, he
asked, "How long have you had this Bible?"

I said, "Five or six years. Some preachers gave it to me at my
ordination."

He said, "You've been preaching out of this Bible six years?"
"Yes, I have."

"Why, you almost made me believe you didn't know what a
premillennialist was."

I had never read the Subject Index in that Scofield Bible. I
didn't even know how to use the Concordance. But I spent the
next few months trying to find out what the Scofield Bible had
to do with being a "premillennial" preacher. I was dumb. I didn't
know what the fundamentals were. The test of fellowship where
I came from wasn't, "Do you believe the fundamentals?" but,
"Do you wash feet?"

Listen, it is one thing to be in error because of ignorance but
another thing to deliberately reject revealed truth.

Now we may disagree on how many specials to have sung
before you preach; we may disagree on when to receive the offering; we may disagree on whether or not to have a bus, but
we ought to agree to disagree on the nonessentials and still love
each other. We are God's army. We can shake the world for
Christ if we don't kill each other fighting over nonessentials.
It seems as though everybody has a little pet thing to preach
about.

Man, if you believe in the fundamentals of the Faith, I am for
you whether you promote or don't promote.

I was recently in the Fairhaven Baptist Church with Dr. Roger Voegtlin, and there were 5,235 in attendance. There were over 500 conversions in the morning service. I'm for getting all you can get. If you are not for it but still believe in the fundamentals, I will fellowship with you. I will pray for you to get enlightened on some things, but I will fellowship with you.

If you believe in the virgin birth, the vicarious sufferings of Jesus, His victorious resurrection, the visible second coming and the verbal inspiration of the Bible, then I will shake hands with you.

You know, if we're not careful, we will give our loyalty to some fellowship or some church or some school or some movement or some group, before we give it to our Lord. Our first loyalty ought to be to Jesus Christ.

I am a Baptist, but I love all fundamentalists. I really believe John Wesley will be in Heaven. If he is there with his robe on, I'm going to try to get it tangled around his legs and baptize him in the River of Life!

I have an idea that Uncle Buddy Robinson will be in Heaven. Uncle Buddy was a tongue-tied Nazarene who was saved under the preaching of a Methodist preacher and got what he called "the second blessing" under a sanctified, second-blessing Presbyterian preacher. Uncle Buddy went across this country preaching on the second blessing. I heard the sermon on an old recording. I don't believe in the second blessing as Uncle Buddy taught it, but he almost convinced me!

Uncle Bud said, "The Lord touched that man who was blind and said, 'What do you see?'

"And the man said, 'I see men walking like trees.' "

Uncle Buddy said, "He needed the second blessing. So the Lord touched him a second time—the second blessing—and said, 'Now what do you see?' "

And Uncle Buddy said, "The man said, 'I see all men clearly.' "

Then he explained, "When I just had the first blessing, I saw the denominational bosses like big old trees. But when I got the second blessing, I saw all men clearly."

Uncle Bud preached on the second blessing so much that one man said, "Bud, you keep preaching about the second blessing. Why, I've had a thousand blessings!"

Uncle Buddy said, "If you've had that many, you wouldn't care if old Buddy had two, would you?"

Uncle Bud went to see the doctor one day and said, "Doctor, I can't hear out of this ear." The doctor gave him an examination and said, "Uncle Bud, it's not a thing but old age."

Buddy said, "I'll declare, I don't understand it. I can't hear a word out of this ear, and I can hear perfectly clear out of the other ear. And you say it's old age. And both ears were born at the same time."

Uncle Buddy had better be in Heaven! I want to see him.

Listen, we don't all agree on everything. But if we believe in the fundamentals of the Faith, then let's agree to disagree. Let's not be divisive over every little thing that comes along. I want to fellowship with you. You may not like me, but I'm going to like you. I'm going to pray for you.

The right kind of criticism is criticizing the modernists and unbelievers and separating from them.

Now I want you to notice something else:

II. THE WRONG KIND OF CRITICISM

Verse 4 says,

"Or how wilt thou say to thy brother, Let me pull out the mote out of thine eye; and, behold, a beam is in thine own eye?"

Now here are two brothers, and God called one of them a hypocrite. Here is a brother going around with a two-by-four hanging out of the side of his head who says to his brother, "Let me help you get that speck out of your eye."

I want to ask you something, Why did he see a speck in his brother's eye? I've been here all morning, and I haven't seen a speck in anybody's eye. Listen, if you see a speck in somebody's eye, you have to be looking for it. It is not glaring. It does not demand attention. You know why he saw that speck? He was looking for it. If you look for something wrong, you will find it. Nobody's perfect.

When I was a pastor, we saw hundreds saved and baptized every month. Occasionally somebody would find something wrong with a service. Maybe one of the ushers didn't come down the aisle quite far enough. Maybe somebody didn't speak to the individual. And that person would miss the blessings of all the conversions, the wonderful choir music, the beautiful baptisms, to make a big issue over something that did not amount to a "hill of beans." Such people are speck-hunters.

You always find what you are looking for. You remember that old poem:

> **Pussy cat, pussy cat,**
> **Where have you been?**
> **I've been to London**
> **To see the Queen.**
>
> **Pussy cat, pussy cat,**
> **What did you there?**
> **I spied a little mouse**
> **Under her chair.**

Well, ring-a-ding-ling! There is Westminster Abbey with its sainted dead, the London Tower and old Big Ben, the palace and the Queen. But the cat went over there—and what did he see? A mouse! Do you know why? He was looking for a mouse.

You always find what you are looking for. If you want to get a report on the landscape, don't send a buzzard out. He will fly over the landscape and never see the beautiful, placid lakes, the flowering trees, the lush, green meadows, the fleecy, white clouds, nor many other wonderful sights.

When he gets back, ask, "What did you see?" The buzzard will answer, "I saw a dead cow with maggots in it." When he says that, he exposes his nature. He is a buzzard.

I've met a few of them. Several were members of my church. They never saw anything good. They were speck-hunters.

He found the speck because he was looking for it. But why

do we look for the specks? Sometimes it is because we are jealous, and we've got to find something wrong with the other fellow who may be more successful than we are. Envy digs the mud that jealousy throws at success.

The preacher who will win souls must run the risk of criticism from the man who will do nothing.

Then sometimes we look for specks because we think we can build our own ministry by tearing the other fellow's down. But no man ever built his house by destroying another man's house. It is sad when a preacher tries to destroy another preacher in order to build himself up.

Sometimes we look for specks in our brother's eye because it makes us feel more comfortable. We know our own mistakes, and somehow we feel better if we can find mistakes in others.

Listen, if I were dying with cancer, it would not help my condition to find ten thousand other people dying with the same disease.

When we look for specks in our brother's eye, we are blinded to our own condition. Here is a man with a two-by-four in his eye. I mean he has a beam sticking out the side of his head, and he is trying to find a speck in his brother's eye. If it were not so pitiful, it would be funny.

Let's not be experts in finding the mote in our brother's eye. But let's be experts at finding the beam in our own eye.

There is a right kind of criticism. We should fight the liberals and modernists and take a separated stand against them. But if a man believes in the fundamentals of the Faith, we should agree to disagree on nonessentials and get along.

Dr. Bob Jones, Sr., once said, "If a hound dog came through town barking for Jesus, I would throw him a bone."

We are fundamentalists. We don't all agree on everything. But thank God, we agree on the fundamentals of the Faith. So let's find something good to say about each other.

Several years ago my boy brought home an old dog that looked like he had been run over by an automobile. He had axle grease all over him. He was skinned in two or three places. Fleas had congregated all over him. He was so skinny and weak he could hardly walk. Tony was petting him.

When I saw that dog, I screamed, "Son, get away from that dog! He looks like he has a disease. He's terrible!"

"But, Daddy, I want this dog!"

"Son, you don't need that dog. He has sores all over him, and he is covered with fleas."

"But look, Daddy, he wags his tail!"

That was about the poorest excuse for a dog I've ever seen, but my boy found something good about him.

Can't we find something good about each other? If we believe in the fundamentals of the Faith, let's not be speck-hunters.

God bless you.

Why Believers Have Trouble

CHAPTER ELEVEN

In John, chapter 16, in the latter part of verse 33, Jesus said,

"In the world ye shall have tribulation: but be of good cheer; I have overcome the world."

One of the first questions that I was asked after I was saved was, "Why is it that believers have trouble?" I don't claim to have all the answers, but I think I have learned something since I have been saved.

In John, chapter 13, our Lord is washing the disciples' feet. And in verse 6 Peter asked the question, "Lord, dost thou wash my feet?" Jesus answered, "What I do thou knowest not now; but thou shalt know hereafter."

Some things we know now; some things we will know hereafter. Some things I understand now that I didn't understand as a young Christian; yet there are many things that I don't understand now. I suppose there are many things that I will not understand until after I die and go to be with Christ. When I pass on and am with Jesus forever and ever, I will know everything then.

I have heard people say, "When I get to Heaven, there are a lot of questions I want to ask the Lord." When you get to Heaven, you won't have any questions to ask, because then you will know even as you are known, and you will be like your Lord. Everything will be answered then. "For now we see through a glass, darkly; but then face to face: now I know in part; but then shall I know even as also I am known."

I think this morning that I have a partial answer to the question, "Why do believers have trouble?" If you do not need this message now, you will sooner or later. So, make notes and keep them; after awhile you will need them.

I. TROUBLE IS CHASTENING

The first reason I give as to why believers have trouble is this: Trouble is sometimes the chastening of the Lord.

A fellow said to me in Tulsa, Oklahoma, "If I believed like you believe, I would go out and live it up."

I think I know what he meant. We believe in eternal security. We believe that when a man trusts Christ as Saviour, he is eternally saved, basing that on numerous passages in the Bible, such as John 3:36, "He that believeth on the Son hath everlasting life." That passage is sufficient to tell me that the life I have will never end. It is everlasting—not something I will lose tomorrow or the day after tomorrow. But since he knew that I believed in eternal security and that a man who was saved could never be lost, this supposed Christian, a minister, said to me, "If I believed like you believe, I would live it up." He meant, "I would go out and fulfill all the desires of the flesh. I would have a good time. I would live in sin."

I wondered as I walked away from the man, *Though he is a preacher, could he really be saved? Could a man with desires like this in his heart, an attitude like this, really have the nature of God within his bosom?* The Bible says when you are born again, God imparts to you the divine nature, the very nature of God, and with the new nature come new desires.

D. L. Moody said, "I drink all I want to. I curse all I want to. I go to all the shows I want to."

A fellow interrupted him, "Mr. Moody, I had no idea you did that."

Moody answered, "Yes, I do. I do."

"I am shocked. I am amazed! I didn't know you drank."

Moody answered, "I don't."

This astonished fellow said, "I didn't know you cursed."

Moody said, "I don't."

"But you said you drank all you want to, and you curse all you want to."

To that Moody replied, "I did say that, but I don't want to drink, and I don't want to curse, and I don't want to go to the movies."

You see, that is the difference. Man, when he is born again, will live like he wants to live in a certain sense. But God places a new nature in him, gives him new desires.

I doubt a man's salvation who has such an attitude that he would want to "live it up" if he believed in eternal security, though that man may be a preacher. By his own testimony he gives evidence that really he does not have the new nature, that his desires are basically wrong. On the other hand, I would not rule out the fact that a man could sin after he is saved.

Last Sunday night while speaking from this very platform, I talked about a man's being worldly and still being a believer, or being carnal and still being a believer. I said I had rather a man be a little carnal than be a modernist. Being carnal has to do with our conduct. Being a modernist has to do with our belief. I would rather a man have his basic, fundamental doctrines correct and be saved and be a little worldly than have his basic, fundamental doctrines wrong and live a good, moral life, because morality will never save a man.

A dear visiting preacher came to me after the service and asked, "Did I understand you right?" Rather than take a long time trying to explain it, I more or less turned him away without explaining what I meant by being a carnal believer.

Let me say just a word about that this morning. It is possible for a person who is saved to yield to the fleshly desires in his life. Paul said in I Corinthians, chapter 3, "And I, brethren, could not speak unto you as unto spiritual, but as unto carnal, even as unto babes in Christ" (vs. 1). Notice that he addressed carnal believers as brothers. Paul would never call an unsaved man a brother, because Paul knew that God was not the Father of all men. Paul did not believe—as the modernists do—in the universal brotherhood of man and the universal Fatherhood of God. Rather, he believed that we are the children of God by faith in Christ.

"Oh," you say, "chapter and verse?" In Galatians 3:26 Paul wrote, "For ye are all the children of God by faith in Christ Jesus." He knew that one became a child of God by trusting Christ. The only people who were real brothers were those who were sons of God by faith in Christ. He would not refer to a man as a brother who had never been saved. Yet Paul addresses the people at Corinth as brethren in I Corinthians 3, "I, *brethren*, could not speak unto you as unto spiritual, but as unto carnal." He recognized carnal believers as his brothers.

Now be honest this morning. Have you always followed the Holy Spirit's leadership? I mean one hundred percent of the time—Monday, Tuesday, Wednesday, Thursday, Friday, Saturday, Sunday—all the week through, every week of every month, every month of every year, since you have been saved? Can you say, "Everything I do is motivated by the Holy Spirit"? Or must you confess with this faltering preacher that there have been times when you have done things motivated by the flesh? If so, when you were motivated by the flesh, at that particular moment you were a carnal or fleshly believer.

Now, I think that answers the question as to whether or not a man can be carnal and yet be saved. He can. But a man cannot be carnal without being chastised.

Hebrews, chapter 12, verse 6 and following, says:

"For whom the Lord loveth he chasteneth, and scourgeth every son whom he receiveth. If ye endure chastening, God dealeth with you as with sons; for what son is he whom the father chasteneth not? But if ye be without chastisement, whereof all are partakers, then are ye bastards, and not sons."

If we are God's sons, then when we get out of line, He will chastise us. And in chastising He deals with us just like a father deals with a son. He does not deal with a sinning saint as a sinner but as a son.

Two "Cs" are always operating in the believer's life. Either he is **changed** after he is saved, that is, his conduct changes, or there is **chastisement**. And if you endure chastening, God deals with you as with sons. God chastises every believer who gets out of line to bring him back.

He goes on in the book of Hebrews to say that He chastises us to make us "partakers of his holiness."

While in a revival meeting in Tulsa, Oklahoma, every night the pastor said, "Let's pray for Brother So-and-So—a dear man who is very, very sick." Every day the pastor expected to hear that the man had gone to be with the Lord.

The pastor visited with the man, and the man said, "Pastor, I know why I am sick. God is whipping me. And when I die, you can tell the people that I knew that I was getting a whipping."

I wonder how many Christians in this congregation know why you, at one time or another in your life, had trouble? I can put my finger on certain incidents where I knew exactly what was happening. I knew why suffering came, why trouble came. It was the chastening of the Lord that I should not be condemned with the world.

First Corinthians, chapter 11 and verse 30, says, "For this cause many are weak and sickly among you, and many sleep." The Bible goes on to say, "For if we would judge ourselves, we should not be judged." Then it says, "But when we are judged, we are chastened of the Lord, that we should not be condemned with the world."

So if you are born again and get out into willful sin, you will be chastised by the Lord; not because He doesn't love you but because He does.

How many of you heard your earthly father say, "Now I am going to whip you, and I am going to do it because I love you"? We have all had that experience. If you haven't, you should have. Every parent should tell the child that he spanks or corrects him because he loves him.

My father used to say, "This hurts me as much as it does you." I used to think, *It may hurt you as much as it does me, but it doesn't hurt you in the same place!* You can't live like you want to live and get by with it. You can't live just any kind of a life, if you are saved, without trouble coming sooner or later. The Lord will bring you back.

If you claim to be saved this morning, and you live willfully, habitually, by preference, in continual sin, and you never are chastened of the Lord, then, Sir, you should check up and make dead sure that you are saved.

II. TROUBLE IS CONDITIONING

I move on to say that not only is trouble sometimes chastening from the Lord, but it is sometimes conditioning. In II Corinthians, chapter 1, verse 4, we read, "Who comforteth us in all our tribulation, that we may be able to comfort them which are in any trouble, by the comfort wherewith we ourselves are comforted of God." Oftentimes trouble in our lives is conditioning us to be a blessing to others. Trouble sometimes is a blessing in disguise.

I read the story of two young mothers. The first one lost her baby. After several years the other one lost a baby. The second young mother sent for the first young mother to comfort her. She said to her friend, "You lost your baby, and you know what I am experiencing. You know how my heart feels. Maybe you can help me." And the first young mother was able to comfort and help her because she had had the same experience.

You know, it is pretty difficult to share something with someone who knows nothing about what you are talking about.

I have preached the funeral of the mothers of many, many people. But before I lost my mother, I never knew how that person felt who was sitting on the pew in front of me. Now, since my mother has gone to be with the Lord, I can genuinely sympathize with him. I know how he feels, know the aching void in his heart, know the thoughts going through his mind, know what he is thinking, because I have had his experience.

When trouble comes, sometimes God is getting us ready so He can use us in some marvelous, miraculous way.

This week I found myself praying, *Dear Lord, whatever it takes to have the power of God on my life, whatever it takes for me to be a blessing to people, whatever it takes, Lord, send it. I want it.*

I found myself praying the prayer of A. J. Gordon: "Dear God, be thorough with me." Time is so short and the responsibility so great. The number of souls that are dying and going to Hell is beyond our imagination, and we are reaching so few for Christ.

As I flew from Tulsa back to Atlanta and looked down at the cities we crossed, I thought, *The answer for this country is to have in every one of these cities a Bible-believing, soul-winning church so people will know what the Bible teaches and learn how to help other people.* The world is full of people who are sad, despondent, depressed, and on the verge of a nervous breakdown. And the only answer is people who are equipped to help people. Sometimes God, in a way unknown to us, gets us ready to use in a marvelous way.

Dr. George W. Truett was a great preacher of yesteryear, the famous pastor of the First Baptist Church in Dallas, Texas. Men still preach his sermons, still use his illustrations. Dr. Truett, in an accident, shot his best friend while on a hunting trip. Somebody said that after that tragedy Dr. Truett never smiled again. I don't know—he may have never smiled again, but they also say he never preached like he preached after that experience.

Wasn't it Dr. B. R. Lakin who, after he received word from Florida that his only son had been killed in a tragic accident, stood on this platform and said that the revival he held after that accident was his greatest revival? A preacher said, "Dr. Lakin, you have never preached with the power that you preach with now."

Charles G. Finney's own pastor said to him, "I am sorry that I laid my hands on you at your ordination." It broke his heart, but Finney went on and turned the world upside down for God.

Spurgeon was censured and voted out of the Baptist Union in his country because he withdrew over the modernism there, and he died an independent Baptist. Now the same group that voted him out has his picture in the halls of their buildings. He was censured with only seven votes for him. His heart was broken. Spurgeon suffered often and doubtless his broken heart greatly increased his usefulness.

I am saying that God sometimes sends trouble in our lives to condition us to be used by Him. The songwriter had it right when he said,

> **It isn't raining rain to me,**
> **It's raining daffodils;**
> **In every little drop I see**
> **Wild flowers on the hill.**

It is not raining troubles to us; it is raining blessings in disguise.

A woman's son left home. They corresponded. Finally she received no letter. Someone wrote that her son was very ill. Soon she received a telegram that said, "If you want to see your son alive, you had better come." Before she could get to the train, another message came that he was dead and his body was being shipped home for burial.

After that, when mothers lost children, they would come as far as fifty miles just to receive the comfort that mother could give.

God bears me record, if I could be better used of God, if I could come out a better and more powerful preacher, one who could turn this city upside down for God, I would be willing to undergo any suffering, any affliction—anything God would send.

III. TROUBLE IS CONFORMING

Sometimes suffering is chastisement; sometimes it is conditioning, but always it is conforming.

Do I believe in predestination? Yes. Romans 8:29 says that we are predestined to be "conformed to the image of his Son." Ultimately God wants you to be exactly like His Son. And trouble is designed to bring about that conformity. Philippians, chapter 1, verse 6, in the Amplified Version, says, "I am convinced and sure of this very thing, that he which hath begun a good work in you will continue it until the day of Jesus Christ"—right up to the time of His return, developing, perfecting, bringing it to completion in you.

The King James Version reads, "He which hath begun a good work in you will perform it until the day of Jesus Christ." I am thrilled that God is working in my life to bring me into the image of His Son.

Won't it be a glorious morning when we are everything we ever longed to be! When I was pastor at Forrest Hills, I used to sit in my study and weep. My heart would break; and I would say, *Lord, this church deserves a better pastor. This church deserves better sermons.* When I go back over old sermon outlines I think, *Why did I preach that sorry sermon!* I listen to a tape and say, *Why didn't they get up and walk out at that one!* I long to preach the perfect sermon. In fifteen years I have never been satisfied with one sermon I have ever preached.

But there is coming a day when I will say, *For one time, I did it right!* I have never closed my eyes at the end of the day and thought, *This is the perfect day. I've done everything I ought to have done today. My prayer life was perfect. My Bible study was uninterrupted. I witnessed at every opportunity. I radiated Christ. I had the right disposition. My attitude toward others was right.*

I have never been able to look back over a day and say it was a perfect day.

No wonder the psalmist said in the last verse of Psalm 17, "I shall be satisfied, when I awake, with thy likeness. . . ." What he really said was, "I am not satisfied being the king in Israel." David said, "I am not satisfied being recognized as a man after God's own heart." He said, "I am not satisfied being recognized as the shepherd and the author of the Psalms."

David, will you ever be satisfied? "Oh, yes, I will be." When? "When I awake with His likeness." Do you mean that someday you are going to come out of the grave? "Yes, I will be resurrected out of the grave. And when I come out and awake on that glorious morning, then I'll be exactly like Jesus Christ. I will have His likeness and be satisfied."

Trouble is sometimes chastening. Trouble is sometimes conditioning. And trouble is always conforming.

Two children were killed. They were both buried the same day, in the same graveyard. Afterwards their mother had a nervous breakdown, and her aunt had to look after her as though she were a little child. She waited on her and tried to comfort and help her.

One day the aunt said, "I want you to know that God loves you. Though your children were killed, still God loves you."

That mother said to that aunt, "If God loves me, why did He make me like this?"

The aunt paused a minute before saying, "Darling, God has not made you. He *is* making you."

The pearl is a product of suffering. A little piece of foreign matter enters an oyster, then the oyster secretes a solution that covers the little piece of sand or glass or foreign object and then secretes more—layer after layer as time goes by. Finally you have a perfect pearl.

Trouble comes into our lives; but if trouble is rightly received and correctly responded to, it will make out of us a pearl—a pearl of a believer.

IV. TROUBLE IS FOR GOD'S GLORY

Trouble is not only chastening, conditioning, conforming; but trouble is also for the glory of God.

In John, chapter 9, there is an interesting story. A man had been blind from his mother's womb. The disciples asked, "Who did sin, this man, or his parents, that he was born blind?" Jesus answered, "Neither hath this man sinned, nor his parents: but that the works of God should be made manifest in him" (vs. 3).

In II Corinthians, chapter 12, Paul prayed three times, 'Lord, remove this thorn from my flesh. Take this trouble from my life.' But God did not answer his prayer. He never removed the thorn, never removed the trouble. But God said in verse 9, "My grace is sufficient for thee: for my strength is made perfect in weakness."

Sometimes trouble is for the glory of God. Surely it was so in the case of Job. Satan went up and had a talk with God. They discussed Job. Satan said to God, "Job doesn't serve You for naught. The reason Job is a good Christian is because he has a lovely family, a good wife. He has cattle and is wealthy. No wonder he serves You. It is easy to serve You when you've got a bank account and cattle and a family and everybody is healthy." Then Satan added, "If You will let me have Job, when I am through with him, he'll curse You." God said to Satan, "You can have Job, and you can do what you will to him, but you can't touch his life."

Day after day Satan stripped Job of all he had. He stripped him of all his wealth and all his cattle; all ten of his children were killed at the same time. When he stripped him of his wealth and his children, then Satan stripped him of his reputation so that his friends came to him and accused him of being a sinner, saying, "Job, the reason you are having this trouble is because you are a sinner. If you were living right, you wouldn't have this trouble." Yes, Job lost his reputation among his friends. He lost his wealth. He lost his children.

Finally Satan made another attack. Job broke out with boils

from the crown of his head to the soles of his feet. With everything gone and in despair, depressed and blue, his wife came out last of all and began to say, "Job, why don't you just curse God and die and get it over with?"

Job sat down in a pile of ashes, took a piece of broken pottery and scraped his sores. Yet he determined, "Though he slay me, yet will I trust in him" (13:15). Job still could say, "When he hath tried me, I shall come forth as gold" (23:10). I believe the angels of God looked down, clapped their hands and said, "Hurrah for Job!"

When the average believer has the least bit of trouble, he throws in the towel. He puts up the white flag. He says, "I'm through. I quit. This Christian life is not for me."

Not so with Job. Through all of his suffering he never one time denied God. Rather he said, "Though he slay me, yet will I trust in him." And when everything was gone Job still could say, "The Lord gave, and the Lord hath taken away; blessed be the name of the Lord." And when it was all over, God gave Job twice what he had before.

Somebody says, "I wish I had the patience of Job." You can have it, but not without the tribulation of Job, because "tribulation worketh patience" (Rom. 5:3). No one can have patience without tribulation.

I am saying that sometimes it is for the glory of God. If God can be glorified and exalted in anything that could come to me, I want it to come.

A doctor goes to school. He studies for many years. Finally he gets his medical degree and begins his practice. After many, many years of study and preparation, now he has an opportunity to show his skill. But without a patient, he can't show his skill. God had a patient in Job, and in Job God could show His skill.

Why do believers have trouble? Sometimes it is for chastening. Sometimes it is for conditioning. Always it is for conforming. Always it is for God's glory.

We may not always understand it. We read in Isaiah, chapter 50, verse 10, "Who is among you...that walketh in darkness, and hath no light? let him trust in the name of the Lord." Did you ever walk in darkness and have no light? The prophet said, "Let him trust in the name of the Lord."

Someone has said, "You can't always trace Him, but you can always trust Him."

> So I go on not knowing,
>   I would not if I might;
> I'd rather walk with Christ in the dark,
>   Than walk alone in the light.

How the Believer Can Know God's Will

CHAPTER TWELVE

"*I beseech you therefore, brethren, by the mercies of God, that ye present your bodies a living sacrifice, holy, acceptable unto God, which is your reasonable service. And be not conformed to this world: but be ye transformed by the renewing of your mind, that ye may prove what is that good, and acceptable, and perfect, will of God.*"—Rom. 12:1, 2.

Being a pastor for twenty-one years, people often came to me for advice. A question often asked was: "How can I know God's will for my life?"

I remember as a young preacher how I struggled to know the will of God. I had a desire to build a great soul-winning church. But I asked, *Is this desire a God-given desire? Or is this my own personal ambition for self-glory?* I had to determine what God wanted me to do.

So far as I'm concerned, the successful man is the man who finds God's will and does it.

Dr. Bob Jones, Sr., emphasized the importance of being in God's will when he answered a hyper-Calvinist: "If it's God's will for me to go to Hell, I don't want to go to Heaven. I had rather be in Hell in God's will than to be in Heaven out of God's will. If I were in Hell in God's will, Hell would be Heaven."

If it is so important to be in the will of God, how can we know His will? Romans 12:2 says, "... that ye may prove what is that good, and acceptable, and perfect, will of God."

It is possible to prove the will of God. Of course you do not prove it to God; He already knows it. If you prove it to anyone, you prove it to yourself. Let me make several suggestions as to how to ascertain the will of God for your life.

I. REALIZE THAT GOD HAS A VERY DEFINITE PURPOSE AND WILL FOR YOUR LIFE

The first thing in trying to ascertain God's will is to realize that He has a very definite plan and purpose for every believer. The Christian life is not like a piece of cotton blowing in the wind, being carried from one place to another with no definite purpose; but there is a course and goal for every believer.

Once we realize this, the Christian life becomes most exciting and takes on new meaning. No one ever gets down to serious business about seeking God's will until he is thoroughly convinced that such a will exists. There can be no enthusiasm about seeking something unless you know that it's there.

When I was a boy, I often went fishing. However, I was not a very good fisherman. I got discouraged easily, and had little patience. After a few minutes, I would conclude there were no fish in the lake; and, laying my fishing pole aside, I'd wander off in the woods to play.

After awhile I would hear someone yell, "Someone come and help me with this one! I've caught a big one!" You could feel the excitement. And running to the edge of the lake, I'd see a friend drag in a five-pound bass. All of a sudden fishing took on a new meaning. I became all excited about it. And in no time flat, I had baited the hook and was ready to fish. I was sure now there were fish in the lake.

When you consider the personal interest that God shows in

each of us, it is astonishing. Matthew 10:30 says that "the very hairs of your head are all numbered." Exodus 3:7 says that He knows our sorrows. Psalm 56:8 says He records our tears. Psalm 139:2 says, "Thou knowest my downsitting and mine uprising." And Psalm 139:2 through 6 says that all our thoughts and ways are known unto Him.

If God shows this much personal interest in each of us, we must believe He has a very definite plan and purpose for our lives; "...that ye may prove what is that good, and acceptable, and perfect, will of God."

II. WE MUST HAVE A RIGHT ATTITUDE TOWARD GOD'S WILL

"If any man will do his will, he shall know of the doctrine..." (John 7:17). No one ever discovers God's will out of curiosity. Rather, we must commit ourselves unreservedly to do God's will, even before we know what it is.

Often my wife asks, "Curtis, will you do something for me?"

I never recall saying, "Yes, I will." I always ask, "What is it?" I never commit myself to do something until I first know what it is. But we cannot approach God's will in such a manner.

I'm afraid some are guilty of saying, "Lord, let me know Your will so I can decide whether or not I will do it." But God says, "You decide that you will do it, and then I'll let you know what it is."

A young man asked me, "But what if I surrender to do God's will and He leads me to do something I don't want to do?"

I thought a moment, then I answered, "You're not really trusting Christ. What you're saying is that you know more about how to run your life than God does." I continued, "Young man, you will find no happier place to be than the place God wants you. And you will find no better thing to do than what He wants you to do."

We must sign our names to the bottom of a blank sheet of paper and say, "Now, dear Lord, You fill it out. I'll do anything You want me to do."

In 1961 I had a small church and was seeing very little results from my preaching. My heart hungered; I wanted more. I wanted to please God more than I wanted to live. I remember lying on my face in a basement building and praying, "Dear Lord, I don't know where You will lead me. But I want to do what You want me to do, no matter what it is. I'll go anywhere, do anything, be anything. The only thing that will keep me from doing what You want will be that I won't know what it is." Then I added, "Dear Lord, in that case, it won't be my fault; it will be Yours."

I meant that with all my heart. It's one thing to say it and another thing to mean it.

If there is anything you would not do for Christ that He wants, then you are not surrendered enough to know His will. "If any man will do his will, he shall know of the doctrine. . . ."

III. THERE MUST BE AN ABSOLUTE SURRENDER TO GOD

"I beseech you therefore, brethren, by the mercies of God, that ye present your bodies a living sacrifice, holy, acceptable unto God, which is your reasonable service. And be not conformed to this world: but be ye transformed by the renewing of your mind, that ye may prove what is that good, and acceptable, and perfect, will of God."—Rom. 12:1, 2.

Paul is really saying, "If you want to prove to yourself what is that good and acceptable and perfect will of God, then present your body a living sacrifice. Give yourself over to Christ. Yield yourself to Him. Place yourself as an instrument in God's hand."

To know God's will you must be available. You are only valuable to God as you are available to God.

Being available means being accessible—having every area of our lives open, willing to allow God to run every aspect.

Since I travel in revival meetings, I spend a lot of time in motels. In the mornings when I go to breakfast, I notice on many doorknobs little signs that say, "Do Not Disturb." The person on the inside is saying, "Do what you will out there, but don't come in here!"

I wonder how many believers have "Do Not Disturb" signs hanging on doorknobs in various areas of their lives.

We must be willing for God to come into every room of our lives and instruct us. The businessman must be willing for God to run his business or at least lay down the principles by which it is run.

Being available not only means being accessible; it also means being acceptable.

Romans 12:1 says, ". . . present your bodies a living sacrifice, holy, acceptable unto God." We cannot tolerate any known sin. Psalm 66:18 says, "If I regard iniquity in my heart, the Lord will not hear me." This means if I tolerate known sin in my life, I cannot ask for God's guidance. We must deal thoroughly with sin.

I have an idea that when some believers confess sin, they think they are telling on themselves. No, God already knows it; so you may as well confess and forsake it. Proverbs 28:13 says, "He that covereth his sins shall not prosper: but whoso confesseth and forsaketh them shall have mercy." Confess every known sin; and present your body a living sacrifice, holy, acceptable unto God.

Being available not only means being accessible and acceptable, but it also means being adaptable: ". . . that ye may prove what is that good, and acceptable, and perfect, will of God." If God has something He wants us to do, we must be willing to adapt.

I'm often asked, "How could you resign the largest church in the state of Georgia with over 7,900 members?" Some people assume that something had to be wrong. No—I just knew God had something else for me; so because of that, it wasn't difficult to make the decision. In fact, I made that decision in 1961, when I told the Lord I would do anything He wanted me to do, go anywhere He wanted me to go, and be anything He wanted me to be.

Of course I miss my friends and still have great love for them, but I'm happy in the will of God. And He has given me many wonderful new friends in the Sword of the Lord ministries.

If you are to prove to yourself what is that "good, and acceptable, and perfect, will of God," then you must present your body "a living sacrifice, holy, acceptable unto God, which is your reasonable service." One condition to an enlightened head is a surrendered heart.

IV. WHEN IN DOUBT, PLAY SAFE

". . . whatsoever is not of faith is sin," says Romans 14:23. And Romans 14:5 says, "Let every man be fully persuaded in his own mind." If it seems that God is leading along a certain route, and yet there is some doubt, it is always safe to give God the benefit of the doubt.

One Sunday morning a couple was getting ready for Sunday school. The man yelled through the house, "Honey, is this shirt dirty?"

She yelled back, "I don't know. What do you think?"

"Well, it looks like it might be all right."

His wife replied, "If it's doubtful, it's dirty!"

I have found it wise to have full assurance about a matter before moving. I'm the slave, and God is the Master. It is not the slave's business to guess at what the Master wants. The slave is to obey. It is the Master's part to give clear orders.

Finding God's will should not be like looking for a needle in a haystack. If God wants us to do a thing, He is able to make it plain to us. Sometimes when I have doubts about a matter and the Bible does not make it clear, I'll pray, "Dear Lord, I want to do Your will. But I'm not certain what it is. If You will make it clear, I'll gladly do it." And God always comes through! When in doubt, play safe.

V. DO YOU HAVE PEACE ABOUT THE MATTER?

"And let the peace of God rule in your heart" (Col. 3:15). One translation says, "Let the peace of God umpire." Another one says, "Let the peace of God decide things for you." Do you have peace about it?

When I purchased my second car, the experience taught me a lesson. I saw this beautiful, shiny Hudson Jet on a used car lot. I looked at it several times. It was clean inside and out. It cost a little more than I was able to afford, but I wanted it. Several times I almost made the purchase but felt uneasy about it. When I would make my mind up to tell the salesman I would take it, something inside felt uneasy; I had no peace about it. But I bought it anyway.

Would you believe that car was a lemon? I mean a REAL LEMON. I hadn't had it a week before the transmission came out, costing several hundred dollars. Was I sick! A few weeks later something else went wrong. I had nothing but trouble with that car until I sold it, or almost gave it away.

If you think God is leading you in a certain direction, then He will give you peace about it. And you will be wise not to make any decision until you have peace. Let the peace of God rule in your heart.

VI. WALK IN THE LIGHT YOU ALREADY HAVE

Never is there a time in the believer's life when we can see all God has planned, because the Christian life is a life of faith. However, God gives to everyone of us sufficient light to take the next step. Psalm 119:105 says, "Thy word is a lamp unto my feet, and a light unto my path."

Have you ever seen a miner's hat with a lamp in front? Suppose a miner is down in the mine, and the light shines twenty-five feet out in front of him. And suppose he says, *I'm not going to take another step until I can see the end of the tunnel.* Then he would never take another step. Unless he walks in the light he already has, he will never receive more light. But as he walks in the light, he will find a light moving out in front of him. And the more he walks, the more the light will move.

And so a believer keeps taking the next step, and the next step. . . .

I counsel with young men in Christian colleges who sometimes are worried about what they are going to do twenty years from now. Some are not sure whether God wants them to be a missionary, an evangelist, or a pastor.

I always advise: "Make yourself available to God in absolute surrender, and He will let His will be known. In the meantime, make the best grades you can. Stay here in school and study hard and pass that test next Friday."

Walk in the light you have, and God will give more light. When Peter was in prison, it was not until he walked right up to the iron gate that it became an open door (Acts 12:10).

Don't expect God to show you His will for next week until you know and do His will today. There are occasions when God lets us take the long look. Maybe some can see further down the road than others. But every believer has enough light to take the next step.

VII. LET YOUR DESIRES HELP DETERMINE GOD'S WILL

"For it is God which worketh in you both to will and to do of his good pleasure," says Philippians 2:13.

If our lives are surrendered to Christ, He will give us right desires. Psalm 37:4 says, "Delight thyself also in the Lord; and he shall give thee the *desires* of thine heart."

I have had to make decisions concerning important matters when it seemed I did not know what to do. I knew what I wanted to do, but I wasn't sure that it was right. I asked the Lord to make my desires and His will one; so when I had a desire to do a thing, I would not have to wrestle to know His will. I have read Philippians 2:13 over and over—"For it is God which worketh in you both *to will* and *to do* of his good pleasure." God not only gives the desire but the power to make that desire a realization. There is a sense of fulfillment and happiness in doing what God wants us to do.

VIII. THE HOLY SPIRIT IS ABLE TO GUIDE US

"For as many as are led by the Spirit of God, they are the sons of God" (Rom. 8:14). Many things are made plain to us from Scripture, so we need not ask God's will about them. God's will and God's Word are always one, never contradicting one another.

We know it is God's will to win souls, so we need not pray about that nor wait for any special leading of the Holy Spirit. Mark 16:15 commands, "Go ye into all the world, and preach the gospel to every creature." And in John 15:16 Jesus said, "Ye have not chosen me, but I have chosen you, and ordained you, that ye should go and bring forth fruit." For a Christian to refuse to win souls because he has no special leading of the Holy Spirit is a cover-up for plain disobedience to a clear command of Scripture.

Take the matter of the salvation of sinners. The Bible makes it plain in II Peter 3:9 that He is not willing that any perish, but that all should come to repentance.

We need not have a special leading to tithe. Leviticus 27:30 says, "The tithe. . .is the Lord's." We know that ten percent of our income belongs to the Lord. We may need to ask Him where we should give it, but we should not pray about whether we should give it since that is already settled in the Word.

Now there are some matters that are not settled in the Word. For instance, the Bible doesn't say which church to join. It doesn't say, "Thou shalt join the First Baptist Church of such and such a city." So we have a right to pray and ask God to lead us to the church of His choosing. We ought to go to church: "Not forsaking the assembling of ourselves together, as the manner of some is. . ." (Heb. 10:25). But the verse doesn't tell us in which church to assemble. So we have a right to pray about that matter. If the Bible gives clear instructions, we need not wait for a leading of the Holy Spirit.

The Bible doesn't tell the young man which girl to marry nor the young girl which boy to marry. They must ask the leading of the Holy Spirit. However, the Bible does say, "Be ye not unequally yoked together with unbelievers..." (II Cor. 6:14). There is a guideline. No Christian is to marry a non-Christian. But since there are many Christian girls, the boy can expect the Holy Spirit's leadership in choosing the right one. The Spirit of God never leads contrary to the Word of God.

A young lady said to me, "I'm in love with a certain fellow, and I'm going to marry him."

I asked, "Is he a Christian?"

"Oh, no."

"Then you shouldn't marry him."

But she said, "I've prayed about it, and I know it is God's will."

I said, "Dear lady, God never leads contrary to His Word; and II Corinthians 6:14 commands, 'Be ye not unequally yoked together with unbelievers....'"

But she disregarded my advice and married the fellow. I'm sad to say she has had a miserable life.

In closing let me say again that many things are already settled for us in the Word of God. But where the Bible is not specific, we have a right to expect God to show us His will.

God's will does not necessarily mean change. You may already be doing what God wants you to do.

Success is knowing God's will and doing it.

God's Chastening of the Believer

CHAPTER THIRTEEN

*"**A**nd ye have forgotten the exhortation which speaketh unto you as unto children, My son, despise not thou the chastening of the Lord, nor faint when thou art rebuked of him: For whom the Lord loveth he chasteneth, and scourgeth every son whom he receiveth. If ye endure chastening, God dealeth with you as with sons; for what son is he whom the father chasteneth not? But if ye be without chastisement, whereof all are partakers, then are ye bastards, and not sons. Furthermore we have had fathers of our flesh which corrected us, and we gave them reverence: shall we not much rather be in subjection unto the Father of spirits, and live? For they verily for a few days chastened us after their own pleasure; but he for our profit, that we might be partakers of his holiness. Now no chastening for the present seemeth to be joyous, but grievous: nevertheless afterward it yieldeth the peaceable fruit of righteousness unto them which are exercised thereby."* —Heb. 12:5-11.

There are now several hundred denominations, sects, cults or religious groups in America, all teaching something different. However, in the final analysis, there are only two plans of salvation taught by men. The first is, God saves a man; the second is, man saves himself. Those who believe that God saves a man teach salvation by grace through faith in Christ. Jesus Christ made full payment for man's sins, and all we need do is trust Him for salvation.

Those who teach that man saves himself say that he saves himself by performing works before salvation in order to earn it, or performing works after salvation in order to keep it.

Those who teach salvation by grace are sometimes accused of giving a license to sin. The accusers evidently are not familiar with the Bible teaching of chastisement.

There are but three possible plans God could have in dealing with believers who sin. First, He could punish them beyond this life by sending them to Hell. But that would contradict the clear promises of God, "He that believeth on the Son hath everlasting life" (John 3:36). And, "He that heareth my word, and believeth on him that sent me, hath everlasting life, and shall not come into condemnation; but is passed from death unto life" (John 5:24).

The second possible plan for dealing with those who sin after they are saved would be to let them continue in sin and neither punish them beyond this life by sending them to Hell, nor chasten them in this life. But the Christian who sinned and was not chastened would eventually develop into the most warped and fearful character imaginable.

The third possible plan in dealing with those who sin after they are saved is to chastise them in this life so they will not be condemned with the world. This is what the Bible teaches: "We are chastened of the Lord, that we should not be condemned with the world" (I Cor. 11:32).

In this message, I will seek to set forth some simple Bible truths about Christian chastening.

I. WHAT IS CHRISTIAN CHASTENING?

The word "chastening" is built upon the Greek word for "child." It means, "to deal with as a child" or to "child-train."

The word "son" or "child" occurs six times in this passage. "If ye endure chastening, God dealeth with you as with sons" (vs. 7). "For whom the Lord loveth he chasteneth, and scourgeth every son whom he receiveth" (vs. 6).

When a person trusts Jesus Christ as Saviour, he becomes a son of God by faith. "As many as received him, to them gave he power to become the sons of God, even to them that believe on his name" (John 1:12). And, "For ye are all the children of God by faith in Christ Jesus" (Gal. 3:26).

When one is saved, God no longer deals with him as a sinner. All God's dealings from that point on are as with a son. Chastisement is not payment for sin. If I chasten my son for breaking a window, the chastisement would not be payment for the window. After I had spanked him, it would still be necessary for me to take money out of my pocket and pay for the window to be replaced.

God has only one payment for sin: "The wages of sin is death" (Rom. 6:23). If the child of God had to pay for any sin, it would be necessary to go into Hell forever. That is the payment God demands. Payment was made for our sins 2,000 years ago at Calvary. And when Christ died on the cross, He paid in full everything the believing sinner owes. That does not mean a Christian can sin and get by. The Bible teaches that God chastens every son He receives. And Hebrews 12:8 says, "But if ye be without chastisement, whereof all are partakers, then are ye bastards, and not sons."

Just as our earthly fathers correct us in order to build character, just so our Heavenly Father child-trains us to make us into the believers He would have us be. Can you imagine what a child would become if the parents never chastened him? Says Proverbs 29:15, "A child left to himself bringeth his mother to shame." Christian chastisement is divine discipline that regulates character. It is child-training. Chastening of God's children is for correction; punishment of the unbeliever is to carry out the law's demand for justice.

II. WHO ARE CHASTENED?

The Bible teaches that every child of God is chastened:

"For whom the Lord loveth he chasteneth, and scourgeth every son whom he receiveth. If ye endure chastening, God dealeth with you as with sons; for what son is he whom the father chasteneth not? But if ye be without chastisement, whereof all are partakers, then are ye bastards, and not sons."—Heb. 12:6-8.

Verse 6 says, "...and scourgeth every son whom he receiveth." Verse 7 asks, "For what son is he whom the father chasteneth not?" And verse 8 plainly states, "Whereof all are partakers." Here it is plain that every child of God is chastened.

When I was a young Christian, I wondered why the wicked prospered while seemingly the best Christians I knew had troubles. I recall singing,

> **Tempted and tried we're oft made to wonder,**
> **Why it should be thus all the day long,**
> **While there are others living about us,**
> **Never molested tho' in the wrong.**

I was saved when I was eleven. Some other children in the neighborhood who were not Christians cursed, smoked and did other things I was careful not to do; but it seemed things went better for them than for me. As a youngster I honestly questioned God and I have said to Him, *It doesn't pay to be a Christian. I try to do right and I don't seem to get along as well as some of my playmates who curse, lie, steal and do nearly everything that is wrong.*

I now understand that there are two groups of children in the world: "Ye are of your father the devil" (John 8:44); and "As many as received him, to them gave he power to become the sons of God" (John 1:12). There are God's sons and the Devil's sons, and God doesn't whip the Devil's children, but God will chasten believers. He leads us "in paths of righteousness for his name's sake."

The unsaved are not chastened. If they refuse to accept Christ as Saviour, they will be punished beyond this life when they are sent to Hell. The Bible says, "Fret not thyself because of him who prospereth in his way, because of the man who bringeth wicked devices to pass. . . . For evildoers shall be cut off" (Ps. 37:7,9).

No child of God is so good that he can evade chastisement. No believer can get by with sin. Every sin that is not confessed and forgiven brings the chastening hand of God upon the believer. "He chasteneth . . . every son whom he receiveth."

III. WHEN ARE BELIEVERS CHASTENED?

Christians are chastened when they tolerate known sin in their lives. The Bible teaches that when we refuse to confess our sins in order to obtain forgiveness and cleansing, we are judged of the Lord and chastened.

"For if we would judge ourselves, we should not be judged. But when we are judged, we are chastened of the Lord, that we should not be condemned with the world."—I Cor. 11:31,32.

The believer who would live in blessed fellowship with Christ should constantly be examining himself. The purpose of this examination or judgment is to spot sin in our lives.

When we find sin, we are instructed to confess it that we may obtain forgiveness and cleansing. "If we confess our sins, he is faithful and just to forgive us our sins, and to cleanse us from all unrighteousness" (I John 1:9). When the sin is confessed, forgiven and cleansed, we continue in fellowship with Christ. "IF we walk in the light, as he is in the light, we have fellowship one with another, and the blood of Jesus Christ his Son cleanseth us from all sin" (I John 1:7).

One of two C's is always present in the believer's life: he is either changed or chastised. If the believer persists in sin, he may expect the chastening hand of God; and if one persists in sin, without chastening, the Bible makes it clear that he is not a believer. "But if ye be without chastisement, whereof all

are partakers, then are ye bastards, and not sons" (Heb. 12:8).
The man who sins willfully, habitually and by preference,
without chastisement, is illegitimate; he is not a son of God.

Several years ago I was conducting a revival in south Georgia.
During the week several members asked if I would visit a certain man in the neighborhood whom they thought was lost.
When I called on the man, he was sitting on the front porch in
a rocking chair.

We talked a few moments, then I said, "Sir, let me ask you
a question. If you die today, do you know you will go to Heaven?"

To my surprise, he answered, "Yes."

Thinking he misunderstood, I continued, "Are you a Christian? Have you been born again?"

"Yes, I have accepted Jesus Christ as my Saviour."

I couldn't believe what I was hearing. Everyone in the
neighborhood just knew he was unconverted. "All right," I continued, "let me read several verses from the Bible and have
prayer before I leave." With an open Bible, I presented clearly
the plan of salvation, then asked, "Now, do you understand that
you are a sinner?"

"Oh, yes," he said.

"And do you know Jesus Christ died to pay your sin debt?"

"Yes, I understand that."

"And will you trust Him completely as your Saviour?"

"Yes," he said, "I have already done that."

Since he insisted that he was a Christian, I turned to Hebrews
12 and read verses 5-8. "Now, according to these verses, if you
are a Christian, you will be chastised unless you honestly confess your sins and set out to live for Christ."

The dear man began to weep. "Chastised!" he said, and with
that he held up the nub of one arm. "I lost this arm in a hunting accident." Pointing to the home he said, "I have lost my wife.
I have lost my children. I have lost my health. Oh,"said he, "I
have been chastised!"

I said, "You will continue to be chastised until you get right with God. And the ultimate in Christian chastisement is premature death to the believer. 'To deliver such an one unto Satan for the destruction of the flesh, that the spirit may be saved in the day of the Lord Jesus' (I Cor. 5:5)."

In a few moments we were on our knees; and the dear man confessed his sins, claiming the forgiveness and cleansing that God promises in the Bible. He arose with a radiant face and that night was in church and came forward stating that he wanted to live for Christ and be a good Christian.

IV. HOW IS THE CHRISTIAN CHASTENED?

Chastisement for believers who sin takes various forms. **Sometimes God uses as a rod the loss of health.** All sickness is not chastisement. For instance, in John 9:2, we read, "And his disciples asked him, saying, Master, who did sin, this man, or his parents, that he was born blind?" And verse 3 continues, "Jesus answered, Neither hath this man sinned, nor his parents: but that the works of God should be made manifest in him." The blindness of this young man was not chastening for sin, as is clearly indicated.

On the other hand, the Bible speaks of those who are sick because of certain sins: "For this cause many are weak and sickly among you, and many sleep" (I Cor. 11:30). Here the Bible teaches that some were sick because they had committed sin in connection with the Lord's Supper. The expression, "for this cause," takes us back to verse 29: "For he that eateth and drinketh unworthily, eateth and drinketh damnation to himself, not discerning the Lord's body." They were weak and sickly because they had eaten and drunk unworthily, not discerning the Lord's body.

Says James 5:14-16,

"Is any sick among you? let him call for the elders of the church; and let them pray over him, anointing him with oil in the name of the Lord: And the prayer of faith shall save the sick, and the Lord shall raise him up; and if he have committed sins, they shall

be forgiven him. Confess your faults one to another, and pray one for another, that ye may be healed."

It seems that the sickness here was a result of sin. This is implied by the statement in verse 16, "Confess your faults one to another, and pray one for another, that ye may be healed." If the sins are confessed, then, of course, the person would be healed if the sickness was chastisement for unconfessed sins.

Again I say that all sickness is not chastening, but some sickness is for unconfessed sins in the believer's life.

Sometimes God uses as a rod the loss of property.

"I have also given you cleanness of teeth in all your cities, and want of bread in all your places: yet have ye not returned unto me, saith the Lord. And also I have withholden the rain from you, when there were yet three months to the harvest: and I caused it to rain upon one city, and caused it not to rain upon another city: one piece was rained upon, and the piece whereupon it rained not withered. So two or three cities wandered unto one city, to drink water; but they were not satisfied: yet have ye not returned unto me, saith the Lord. I have smitten you with blasting and mildew: when your gardens and your vineyards and your fig trees and your olive trees increased, the palmerworm devoured them: yet have ye not returned unto me, saith the Lord."—Amos 4:6-9.

Here the teaching is that Israel was hungry, that is, they had cleanness of teeth in all their cities and want of bread in all their places. And why were they without food? God said, "Because you have not returned unto Me." The palmerworm had devoured the olive trees, the gardens, the vineyards and the fig trees. There was no water to drink, and several cities wandered into one in search of water, yet they found none. Why? God said, "Ye have not returned unto Me."

The loss of property was chastisement from God because the children of Israel would not return unto Him.

In John 21, Jesus made Peter a business failure. Peter had

quit the ministry and gone back into the fishing business. Here was an experienced fisherman. If anyone could catch fish, he could. Yet he toiled all night and caught nothing.

God made him a failure because he had backslidden and left the ministry. When he said in John 21:3, "I go a fishing," he wasn't speaking of taking a fishing trip; he was leaving the ministry to go back to his old business. And God chastened him by making him a business failure. But three chapters later, in Acts, chapter 2, Peter preached a great sermon and 3,000 souls were saved. The chastening had corrected the child of God.

Sometimes God uses as a rod the loss of joy. Consider the case of David in Psalm 51. In verse 8 he said, "'Make me to hear joy and gladness; that the bones which thou hast broken may rejoice." In verse 12 he prayed, "Restore unto me the joy of thy salvation." This entire Psalm is the prayer of a sinning saint. David is praying for forgiveness and cleansing. In verse 2 he cries, "Wash me throughly from mine iniquity, and cleanse me from my sin."

Sometimes God uses as a rod the loss of loved ones, as in the case of David, "Howbeit, because by this deed thou hast given great occasion to the enemies of the Lord to blaspheme, the child also that is born unto thee shall surely die" (II Sam. 12:14). Here God made it plain that because of David's sin and because he had given occasion to the enemies of the Lord to blaspheme, the child would surely die.

In the case of Israel, God said, "I have sent among you the pestilence after the manner of Egypt: your young men have I slain with the sword" (Amos 4:10).

The loss of loved ones is not always the chastening hand of God, but many times it is.

Finally, God sometimes uses as a rod premature death to the believer. The ultimate in Christian chastisement is premature death to the believer.

"For this cause many are weak and sickly among you, and many sleep"—are dead.—I Cor. 11:30.

"If any man see his brother sin a sin which is not unto death, he shall ask, and he shall give him life for them that sin not unto death. There is a sin unto death: I do not say that he shall pray for it."—I John 5:16.

"To deliver such an one unto Satan for the destruction of the flesh, that the spirit may be saved in the day of the Lord Jesus."—I Cor. 5:5.

God the Father corrects and child-trains us; but if other forms of chastening fail to get the desired results, the Lord will allow the believer to die a premature death.

Someone suggested that He speaks, spanks and calls Home. He speaks to the conscience; and if the believer does not make necessary corrections, He spanks, using the rod of sickness, death of loved ones or possibly loss of property. If the spanking does not produce results, then God calls the believer Home: as in the case of Moses in Deuteronomy 32:48-52:

"And the Lord spake unto Moses that selfsame day, saying, Get thee up into this mountain Abarim, unto mount Nebo, which is in the land of Moab, that is over against Jericho; and behold the land of Canaan, which I give unto the children of Israel for a possession: And die in the mount whither thou goest up, and be gathered unto thy people; as Aaron thy brother died in mount Hor, and was gathered unto his people: Because ye trespassed against me among the children of Israel at the waters of Meribah-Kadesh, in the wilderness of Zin; because ye sanctified me not in the midst of the children of Israel. Yet thou shalt see the land before thee; but thou shall not go thither unto the land which I give the children of Israel."

I recall vividly a young father and husband who was saved under my ministry. This dear man attended church faithfully and was a good Christian, with one exception. There was a particular sin he seemingly could not overcome. He would do well for several weeks and then fall back into sin again. This happened over and over. I prayed with him numerous times.

The last time he came to see me, I said, "You had better get your house in order. The Lord has brought all kinds of chastisement upon you, with seemingly no results. I wouldn't be surprised if someone called and told me you were dead." I warned, "The ultimate chastisement is a premature death for the believer."

A few days later his wife called to say he had been found dead in a motel room, and she asked if I would preach his funeral. The doctors never explained his death. But in my heart I knew what happened. He had persisted in sin; and though God had often chastened, he never made the needed correction; so God called him Home.

V. WHAT ARE THE RESULTS OF CHRISTIAN CHASTENING?

God is not a purposeless God. He never does anything without purpose. His ultimate aim for every believer is Christlikeness. "For whom he did foreknow, he also did predestinate to be conformed to the image of his Son" (Rom. 8:29).

A visitor watched as a silversmith heated the silver in his crucible. Hotter and hotter grew the flames while the silversmith was closely scanning the crucible. The visitor interrupted, "Why are you watching the silver so closely? What are you looking for?"

In an instant the silversmith replied, "I'm looking for my face. When I see my own image in the silver, then I stop. The work is done."

God is looking for a face in every child of God—the face of His Son. He chastens us for our own profit that we might be partakers of His holiness. "For they [earthly fathers] verily for a few days chastened us after their own pleasure; but he for our profit, that we might be partakers of his holiness" (Heb. 12:10).

The holiness mentioned here is not inward holiness but outward holiness. We receive the divine nature the moment we are saved. "Whereby are given unto us exceeding great and precious promises: that by these ye might be partakers of the divine nature, having escaped the corruption that is in the world through lust" (II Pet. 1:4).

The holiness mentioned in Hebrews 12:10 is outward holiness. God wants us to be like Him. He chastens us that we might be partakers of His holiness. The chastisement is always for our profit. Here the Bible says that earthly fathers sometimes chasten us for their own pleasure, but He for our profit. God never enjoys chastising the believer, but He knows we will never be all that He wants us to be without it.

Verse 11 says, "No chastening for the present seemeth to be joyous, but grievous: nevertheless afterward it yieldeth the peaceable fruit of righteousness unto them which are exercised thereby." The chastening is for our good and God's glory, that we may be more and more like Him. He is purging from us, in child-training, all that dims the image of Christ in us.

James H. McConkey said:

> Child of God, do not be associating chastening only with the word chastise. Couple it also with that beautiful word "chastity," the jewel of perfect, spotless purity of heart and life. Thus, chasten. . . is to make chaste, to make pure spiritually, to purge, to cleanse, to purify. That is God's great purpose in all His child-training.

Chastening produces in the believer the peaceable fruit of righteousness. Verse 11 states, "afterward it yieldeth the peaceable fruit of righteousness unto them which are exercised thereby."

The poet has said,

> It isn't raining rain for me,
>   It's raining daffodils;
> In every dimpling drop I see
>   Wild flowers on the hills.
>
> A cloud of gray engulfs the day
>   And overwhelms the town;

**It isn't raining rain for me,
It's raining roses down.**

The child of God who is being chastened may think, *It is raining hard on me today—the testings, the disappointments, the bereavements.* But it isn't raining rain for you; it is raining blessings. And out of the chastisement will come the peaceable fruit of righteousness.

VI. WHAT SHOULD THE BELIEVER'S ATTITUDE BE TOWARD CHASTISEMENT?

First, may I say God does not expect us to enjoy chastening but to endure it for the sake of its reward. Verse 11 reads, "Now no chastening for the present seemeth to be joyous, but grievous: nevertheless afterward it yieldeth the peaceable fruit of righteousness unto them which are exercised thereby."

Verse 5 states, "Despise not thou the chastening of the Lord." That is, we are not to think lightly or scorn the chastening of the Lord. Do not esteem lightly God's child-training. Do not look down upon it. And, above all, don't allow your heart to grow hard and bitter against God because of it.

Again, verse 5 states, " . . . nor faint when thou art rebuked of him," that is, we are not to lose courage or give up. It is a mistake for the believer to throw in the towel when chastening comes. Rather, we are to bear up under it, not to faint. Chastening is good for us, and some day we will look back and thank God that His chastening was thorough.

If one feels he is fainting, what can he do? What do you do when you are about to faint physically? Nothing! You cease from your own doing, and in your faintness you lean upon the shoulder of some strong loved one or friend, and there you lie still and trust until your strength returns. So it is when we are chastened of the Lord. When it seems we can bear it no longer, we simply lean hard on Him.

In the closing months of his life, Hudson Taylor was so feeble he wrote,

> I am so weak I cannot work. I cannot read my Bible. I cannot even pray. I can only lie still in God's arms like a little child and trust.

He need not do anything else. Leaning on Jesus was enough.

The Bible says in Psalm 55:22, "Cast thy burden upon the Lord, and he shall sustain thee." In Hebrews 12:5-11, God gives us a threefold attitude toward child-training. First, we are not expected to enjoy chastening: "No chastening for the present seemeth to be joyous, but grievous" (vs. 11). Second, we are to despise not chastening: "My son, despise not thou the chastening of the Lord" (vs. 5). And third, we are to faint not: " . . . nor faint when thou art rebuked of him" (vs. 5).

The Fullness of the Spirit, the Believer's Need

CHAPTER FOURTEEN

PRAYER:

Our Heavenly Father, I want to be a blessing. I'm a little frightened to speak on such a tremendous theme. It would be wrong for me to speak on the fullness of the Holy Spirit and I myself lack that fullness. I pray tonight for the Holy Spirit to absolutely control me, to help me to think my thoughts after Thee and to say tonight exactly what ought to be said, and to say it in the exact manner in which it ought to be said.

Jesus, You know what I am thinking. I am hoping there will be a number in this room who, after hearing this sermon, will have a hunger, an unsatisfiable hunger, for the fullness of the Holy Spirit. And I am hoping that at the close they will understand how to be filled, and I pray many will come and say, "This is my day. I am tired of mediocrity. I am tired of the normal, average, everyday Christianity."

Help me, Lord, as I speak tonight. I want to do good. Help me now to be a blessing to the people. Amen.

I call your attention to two verses:

"And be not drunk with wine, wherein is excess; but be filled with the Spirit."—Eph. 5:18.

"Not by might, nor by power, but by my spirit, saith the Lord."—Zech. 4:6.

When God called me to preach, I was only twenty years old. I had never heard a sermon on the fullness of the Holy Spirit. I had great ambitions and dreams. There were some who thought that to be ambitious or to dream too big was sinful. So I didn't share my dreams with too many. But I did dream. The night I told a friend that God had called me to preach, I cried and talked until 2:30 in the morning.

The group I was with didn't believe in paying a preacher. They thought he should preach on the weekends and do something else during the week for his livelihood. But I told my friend, "Some day I will preach full time."

I dreamed big! I saw that day come. And in God's providence a number of wonderful things happened in my life. One was finding THE SWORD OF THE LORD in my mail truck and attending that Sword conference in 1961 at Antioch Baptist Church. In that conference I noticed something different about preachers.

Dr. John R. Rice, Dr. Jack Hyles and Dr. Tom Malone were preaching. I was younger then, and curious. I listened. It did something to my heart. I heard preaching that made sense. Dr. Rice preached on "How to Get Your Prayers Answered." I watched him. I knew there was something different about him. He was not the average, run-of-the-mill preacher.

I remember walking by the book table and looking at all the books. Dr. Rice had written nearly fifty hardbacked books. I glanced over them and thought, *I have never read that many books.* I heard him preach. I was moved by him. One thing came through to me as he preached—soul winning is the most important thing in the world! And you can't do it without being filled with the Holy Spirit.

I heard Dr. Jack Hyles preach. I wanted to see him. I wanted to meet him. He came in late and was in the men's room in the basement shaving when I first saw him. I didn't know who he was then. When he got up to preach a few minutes later, I thought, *That is the man I saw in the men's room shaving.*

He preached on "What Is Man, That Thou Art Mindful of Him?" He told the story of an old man who wanted to talk with him in his church, and he almost turned him away, but one of the secretaries insisted that he see him. My heart burned and hungered. I thought, *I don't love people. I preach on Sundays— it is kind of part-time activity. I enjoy the occasional pat on the back if I happen to say something worthy of being patted on the back for. But I don't love people. I have never led a soul to Christ in my life, and I have been pastoring six years!*

I looked at Dr. Hyles. I later memorized his sermon and went back and preached it to my small congregation. I thought, *If I preach that sermon to my congregation, it will have the same effect on them that it had on me.* So I preached it. Nobody moved. Nobody was affected. I wondered why they didn't respond like I had responded. I wondered why they were not hurting inside like I was hurting when I heard it. It was the same sermon, the same verses.

I heard Dr. Tom Malone speak on "Deacons" from Acts 6. When he finished giving the requirements for deacons, I left the church shaking my head and asking myself, *Have I ever seen a deacon? Would I know a deacon if I met one?* Driving home from the meeting I thought, *I don't even meet the qualifications for being a deacon, let alone a preacher.*

For some time I considered resigning my small church and joining a good soul-winning church. I heard about the Highland Park Baptist Church in Chattanooga, Tennessee, baptizing over 1,000 a year for numbers of years. I seriously considered commuting to Chattanooga every weekend to be in a good church and learn what it was all about. But God wouldn't let me.

I thought, *What is different about those men? There are thousands of preachers in America! What is different about them?*

Last night Dr. Lee Roberson gave us seven mountain peaks

in his life. He mentioned conversion, soul winning, second coming, etc. I kept waiting. I thought, *He is going to say it.* He got down to the sixth thing and he said, "The Spirit-filled life." He said, "I don't know when I first got hold of it, but the Spirit-filled life...."

One thing all great preachers have in common is that they are Spirit-filled. They may not all agree on everything; they might not all preach alike; their delivery may be different, but they are all filled with the Spirit.

One day I went to a bookstore. I roamed through the building, checking the books on the shelves; and I came across a dark blue book with gold letters on the front, *Deeper Experiences of Famous Christians,* by J. Gilchrist Lawson. I thumbed through the table of contents to see what it was all about. Many of the names I did not know then; I know now. I recognized the name of D. L. Moody. I had heard of him. I recognized the name Billy Sunday. I had heard of him. I didn't know A. J. Gordon, Savonarola and many of the others.

Something seemed to say to me, *You ought to read the book.* So I purchased it, rushed out of the building, hurried home, and read the book. I read it in secret. It was what the title implied. It was deeper experiences of famous Christians. As I read the experiences of Billy Bray, the shouting Cornish miner, I wished that Billy Bray were alive and I could sit on the front porch and talk with him. Billy shouted everywhere he went.

In *Deeper Experiences of Famous Christians,* we read this about Billy Bray:

> "I can't help praising God.... As I go along the street I lift up one foot, and it seems to say 'Glory!' and I lift up the other, and it seems to say 'Amen,' and so they keep on like that all the time I am walking...."
>
> When Billy lay dying, and the doctor told him that he was going to die, he said: "Glory! glory be to God! I shall soon be in Heaven." He then added, in his own peculiar way, "When I get up there, shall I give them your compliments, doctor, and tell them you will be coming, too?" This made a deep impression on the doctor. Billy's dying word was "Glory!"

Some little time before dying, he said: "What! me fear death! me lost! Why, my Saviour conquered death. If I were to go down to Hell I would shout glory! glory! to my blessed Jesus until I made the bottomless pit ring again, and the miserable old Satan would say, 'Billy, Billy, this is no place for thee: get thee back!' Then up to Heaven I should go, shouting glory! glory! praise the Lord!''

When I read that, I laughed and my heart hungered for something that I didn't have. I said, *Lord, where are the Billy Brays in Atlanta, Georgia? Where are the Billy Brays of my day? I don't even know them.*

Then I read about Christmas Evans, the one-eyed Christian who made a thirteen-point covenant with God. I read all thirteen points. In one point he said, "Oh, prosper me as Thou didst prosper Bunyan, Vassar, Powell, Howell Harris, Rowlands and Whitefield. The impediments in the way of my prosperity remove." And I said, *Lord, I would like to talk with this guy. Here is a man with ambition, who is unafraid to say, "Prosper my ministry and make something out of me." Most men I talk with about that don't understand me. I would like to talk with Christmas Evans.*

I kept reading more and more. I read where Savonarola sat on his platform in a trance for five hours. You could hear a pin drop for five solid hours.

I thought, *I have never preached in my life. I am ashamed to even call myself a preacher.*

I read where D. L. Moody told of two ladies who came to his meetings and kept saying, "Mr. Moody, we are praying for you, because you need the power of the Spirit." Mr. Moody said, "I need the power? Why, I thought I had power. I had the largest congregation in Chicago, and there were many conversions."

But one day walking down Wall Street in New York, Moody said, "The power of God came on me in such a fashion that I ran to borrow the room of a friend. I closed the door and in the room I prayed that God would stay His power, lest I die."

The difference between great preachers and mediocre preachers is not dress, mannerisms, voice, delivery, length of sermon or current jokes, but great preachers are Spirit-filled.

Ephesians 3:20 says, "Now unto him that is able to do exceeding abundantly above all that we ask or think, *according to the power that worketh in us.*"

It doesn't say, "Unto him that is able to do exceeding abundantly above all that we ask or think" according to personality or ability or education or according to who promotes you or what fellowship you are out of, but "according to the power that worketh in us."

A tongue-tied man like Uncle Buddy Robinson can have it. An eloquent man like Spurgeon can have it. A demonstrative man like Billy Bray can have it. A simple man like Moody can have it. A deep man like John R. Rice can have it. When it comes to being filled with the Holy Spirit, everybody can have it.

For years I never heard a sermon on the subject. I was afraid to talk about it. I was so afraid I would get out on a limb that I never bothered to climb the tree. But by and by I got to the place where I had to have it.

I. THE COMPARISON

Three times in the Bible a drunk man is compared to a Spirit-filled man. That is not by accident; that is by design. The Bible is not written by accident.

Ephesians 5:18, my text, "Be not drunk with wine...but be filled with the Spirit." A drunk man—a Spirit-filled man.

It is said of John the Baptist, "For he shall be great in the sight of the Lord, and shall drink neither wine nor strong drink: and he shall be filled with the Holy Ghost" (Luke 1:15).

In Acts 2, on the day of Pentecost, Peter said in verses 15 to 17:

"For these are not drunken, as ye suppose, seeing it is but the third hour of the day. But this is that which was spoken by the prophet Joel; And it shall come to pass in the last days, saith God, I will pour out my Spirit upon all flesh."

Why does the Bible compare the drunk man to a Spirit-filled

THE FULLNESS OF THE SPIRIT

man? I think there are some lessons here. A drunk man is con-
trolled by another power. A drunk man is a different person.
Spirit-filled men are different.

You let a fellow who is shy, timid and backward get drunk,
then suddenly he is talking out loud; and the more he drinks,
the louder he talks. He gets so talkative you would think he had
been vaccinated with a Victrola needle.

You let a shy, timid, backward Christian, who is too timid to
suck his thumb, get filled with the Holy Spirit and he will start
talking in front of crowds and not be embarrassed.

The fellow who would never sing in public gets drunk, and
suddenly he sings three or four hours and thinks everybody is
enjoying it. I have never seen an unhappy drunk in my life. They
may lose everything they have, but they are still happy. You
can't discourage a drunk man. You may as well wait until he
is sober, when he is a different man.

When the poor, inhibited creature, who is afraid of his own
shadow, gets drunk, he becomes as bold as a lion.

I had an uncle who used to drink. He had a brown Pontiac.
He once asked me to take a ride with him. We went down
Georgia 12 Highway, before there was an I-20. That speedometer
went as far as it would go—I think it registered 85 or 90. He
scared me to death. In Covington, Georgia, the State Patrol
sounded the siren and pulled us over. It didn't bother him—he
was drunk. He wasn't a bit nervous. He cussed a little.

The State Patrol said, "Let me see your license." He gave the
officer his license. The officer said, "You are speeding."

"Yeah, I know it."

The officer said, "You can pay me now or come to court."

"How much is it?"

"Ten dollars."

My uncle handed him a $20 bill. The patrolman started to
hand him $10 back and my uncle said, "Just keep it."

He said, "What do you mean, keep it?"

"I'm coming back through here in a few minutes and I don't
want you slowing me down!"

Now he wouldn't have talked like that had he not been drunk. Had he been sober, he would have been scared to death.

When the poor, inhibited creature, who is afraid of his own shadow, is filled with liquor, he becomes as bold as a lion and does things he would not otherwise do.

I used to work at a fire station in DeKalb County. One day a drunk came in with a tablet and pencil. He said, "What's your name?" I told him and he wrote it down. He asked another fellow, "What's your name?" He told him and he wrote it down. He asked another guy; he told him and he wrote it down. He made a long list of names. Then when he came to this big engine driver, about 6′5″ and asked, "Boy, what's your name?" that engine driver answered, "My name's Glen So-and-So." He wrote it down. Then the engine driver asked, "What do you want my name for?" The drunk never looked up but just kept writing and said, "I'm writin' down everybody's name on this paper that I'm going to whip. When I get my list up I'm going to whip every one of 'em."

That big engine driver reached down, picked him up, shook him and said, "I tell you right now, you are not about to whip me!" The drunk said, "Put me down and I'll just scratch your name off the list." Had he been sober, he wouldn't have done that.

When a man is drunk, he will attempt most anything. I read of one drunk who was up in a hotel room with a friend. He actually thought he could fly and leaped out of the window to fly around the block. He came to several days later, arms all bandaged up, legs stretched out and in casts with weights on them, his face skinned and stitches everywhere. His friend went to visit him and he said to his friend, "Why did you let me do that?" He said, "I thought you could fly." Both of them were drunk.

You get preachers drunk on the Holy Spirit and one will say, "I'm going to build the biggest church in the world." Another one will say, "I think you can do it." He may wind up in the hospital with a broken leg, but he is more apt to fly than the fellow who doesn't try.

A drunk man is talkative.

Too many Christians are like arctic rivers—frozen at the mouth, afraid to say, "Boo!" to the Devil.

The way a drunk man talks you would think his father was an auctioneer and his mother was a woman!

I was in the St. Louis airport and a drunk came in. He had a paper bag under one arm and a red cap on his head that said "Caterpillar" across the top. He looked wild-eyed at me and said, "Did you come in here on a flying saucer?" I said to this nut, "Yeah, I always fly on flying saucers. They are faster and more convenient." I figured that would shut him up. But he said, "Yeah, they fly good, but they sure do make you dizzy, don't they?"

I carried on the conversation with him. In a few minutes he looked into the mirror and saw that cap that said "Caterpillar" and it scared him. He said, "I'm a caterpillar! Yesterday I was a butterfly!" That drunk had no inhibitions. If I could have told him later what he did, he would have been embarrassed; but at the moment he didn't care.

"And be not drunk with wine, wherein is excess; but be filled with the Spirit."

II. THE COMMAND

"Be filled with the Spirit."

The same Bible, same book, same chapter, same verse, gives two commands. Let us take the first command—"Be not drunk with wine."

If I asked you tonight, "How many think it is wrong to get drunk?" everybody here would answer, "Yes, it is wrong to get drunk."

The command is, "Don't get drunk." Not a pastor here would allow a single choir member to sing in the choir who came to church drunk next Sunday morning. Not a preacher here tonight would lay hands on a man's head to ordain him if you knew he were a drunkard. Not one pastor would have a deacon serving if he knew he got drunk. And you are right to feel that way.

But the same Bible that says, "Be not drunk," says something else: "but be filled with the Spirit."

If I understand the Bible, then it is just as wrong not to be filled with the Holy Spirit as it is to get drunk. And yet we very seldom talk about the second command in that verse, while it is just as important as the first. The verb is in the imperative mood: it is a command, "Be filled." There is no command in the Bible to be sealed with the Holy Spirit. There is no command in the Bible to be indwelt by the Holy Spirit. Those things are positional. The moment I was saved I was sealed. "And grieve not the holy Spirit of God, whereby ye are sealed unto the day of redemption" (Eph. 4:30). The moment I was saved, the Holy Spirit came into me as a Person to take up His permanent abode. That happens automatically without any action on my part (I Cor. 6:19, 20). Every believer has the Holy Spirit; every believer is sealed with the Holy Spirit. That is why there is no command to be sealed or indwelt. But being filled with the Holy Spirit is not positional; it is a command. "Be filled with the Spirit."

The responsibility of the fullness of the Holy Spirit lies with each individual believer.

You come to my house, my wife fixes a big meal, and I say, "Sit down and be filled." Then if you leave without being filled, it is not my fault; it is yours.

It is a command. And I want you to notice to whom the command is given. Look at Ephesians 1:1. Ephesians is a letter to the church at Ephesus. Notice to whom it is written: ". . . to the saints which are at Ephesus, and to the faithful in Christ Jesus." The command is to every individual believer, not for preachers only.

Most people who experience the fullness of the Holy Spirit are saved for a number of years before they are filled with the Holy

Spirit. But there need not be a time lapse. The time lapse is brought about because of our ignorance concerning our responsibility to be filled with the Holy Spirit.

In my case I knew nothing about it. You don't have to wait five, ten or fifteen years to be filled with the Spirit.

The command is not only for the pastor and the deacon and the evangelist, but it is addressed to every Christian and every church member. It is to every single believer for all time and for every generation. It is not for a certain group; everybody can have it.

I want to say this: Most of what you think is trouble in your local congregation is only a symptom. Your people don't tithe. That is not the problem; that is a symptom. They don't win souls. That is not the problem; it is a symptom. Most of the trouble can be traced back to one thing: believers are not Spirit-filled.

In I Corinthians 3:1 Paul said, "And I, brethren, could not speak unto you as unto spiritual, but as unto carnal, even as unto babes in Christ." He goes on to say there is envying and strife and division among them. Why? Because they were not spiritual, were not Spirit-filled Christians.

You don't have problems with Spirit-filled Christians.

The command is to every individual believer.

III. THE CONDITIONS

I said you are not filled automatically. There are certain conditions. I don't have time to list them all. I will give you some that stand out clear to me from the Scriptures.

A. Thirsting

The first condition for the fullness of the Holy Spirit is thirsting.

Ray Hart sang a song a moment ago based on a verse from Isaiah that says, "I will pour water upon him that is thirsty." John 7:37-39 says:

"In the last day, that great day of the feast, Jesus stood and

cried, saying, If any man thirst, let him come unto me, and drink.
He that believeth on me, as the scripture hath said, out of his bel-
ly shall flow rivers of living water. (But this spake he of the Spirit,
which they that believe on him should receive....)."

Thirsting. Thirsting. Thirsting. I doubt seriously if anyone in
this building has ever been thirsty. You say, "I got thirsty today." No, you wanted water today. You see, the moment you
want water, it is in the faucet. You don't have to wait five
minutes to get it. But you go without water for a day, two days,
three days; go without water until your lips swell three times
their normal size and your tongue swells and begins to crack
and parch, go without water until you would give your
automobile and your house and everything you have in the bank
for one drop of water, then you are thirsty!

The prime reason many believers do not have the fullness of
the Holy Spirit is that they just absolutely are not thirsty
enough. If you can take it or leave it, you will leave it. You have
to get to the place where you say, "I have to have it or die! I
won't give up! I don't care what happens, I won't give up!"

Pardon the personal reference, but I got to the place where
I said, "Lord, if it means speaking in tongues, I am ready. I'll
join the Pentecostals. I'll get out of the Baptist church, but I don't
want to live without it. I've got to have it!"

Uncle Buddy Robinson is one of my favorite characters. He
was saved in a Methodist meeting, got what he called the second blessing in a Presbyterian meeting. Later he was thrown
out of the Methodist Church and died a Nazarene.

Uncle Buddy said, "I went to hear this Methodist preacher
preach and he preached on Heaven till I wanted to go there. Then
he preached on Hell till I thought I was going there. When he
gave the invitation that night I couldn't read my name in box-
car letters, but when I got up from the altar I could read my
title clear to mansions in the sky!"

Then Uncle Buddy said, "Awhile later this sanctified, second-
blessing Presbyterian preacher came through town preaching

on the second blessing. I went to hear him. When he preached, I wanted it so bad. I said, 'O God, give it to me!' But the Lord didn't give it to me. Then I said, 'O Lord, give it to me!' I threw away my deck of cards and my old pistol. I put my two mules on the altar. I put a bale of hay on the altar and I still didn't have it. I put my Presbyterian mother and my drunken brother both on the altar and I still didn't have it. Then I said, 'O God, give it to me!' And the Lord said, 'Buddy, there is too much between you and Me and the altar.' I said, 'O God, if You will give it to me, I'll give every neighbor I've got a jug of molasses.' And I can make the best molasses a man ever wallowed his biscuit in!"

He wanted it. He never gave up till he got it. He called it the second blessing. I don't even believe in the second blessing, but I have an old recording of Uncle Buddy preaching on the second blessing and all through the sermon I have to keep working not to believe it.

Uncle Buddy said, "This man in the Bible was blind and the Lord touched him. And He said to him, 'What do you see?' and the man said, 'I see men walking like trees.' He needed the second blessing. The Lord touched him the second time and said, 'Now, what do you see?' And the man said, 'I see all men clearly.' "

Uncle Buddy said, "When I just had the first blessing, I saw the denominational bosses like great big old trees. But when I got the second blessing, I saw all men clearly."

I thought, *Buddy, you are about to sell me on the second blessing. I can't call it what you call it, Bud, but I've got to get it.*

We argue over the right expression and die for a lack of the experience. Uncle Bud got it. He believed in complete sanctification with annihilation of the old sinful nature, which never happens; but I must say that he was closer to being sanctified than I was.

He went to New York City and they showed him all the sights. When he got back to his room that night, he prayed, "Dear Lord,

I thank You for all the sights of New York City, but I thank You most of all that I didn't see anything I wanted."

When I went to New York, I saw something I wanted.

One day Uncle Bud went to his doctor because he couldn't hear out of one ear. The doctor checked him out and said, "Bud, it isn't a thing in the world but old age."

Buddy said, "I don't understand it. I can't hear a word out of this ear and I hear perfectly clear out of this other ear, and you say it is old age. Both ears were born at the same time."

I thought, *Buddy, come back down here and let me talk to you. Sit down, Buddy, and tell me about this second blessing. I want it, Buddy, I want it.*

I was tired of basement buildings and outside toilets with nobody ever getting saved. I want something else!

The first condition is thirsting. Are you thirsty for it? My soul, I hope before this meeting is over someone gets thirsty for it!

B. Believing

The second condition is believing. Look at those verses again in John 7:37-39. Jesus stood that last day of the feast and said, "If any man thirst, let him come unto me, and drink." And he tells us in the next verse, "He that believeth on me, as the scripture hath said, out of his belly shall flow rivers of living water."

Underline two words: *thirsting* and *believing*. Believing. I didn't believe.

I heard Dr. Hyles tell about kneeling on his father's grave and praying until he was filled with the Holy Spirit.

I thought, *He is just talking. Surely he didn't have an experience like that. Well, maybe he did; but if he did, it is not for me, a poor country preacher, nobody to promote me, out of nobody's fellowship, out of nobody's school, left the crowd I was with . . . it's not for me. Oh, it's for Dr. Lee Roberson. It's for Dr. Jack Hyles. It is for Dr. John Rice and Moody and Torrey and Spurgeon and others I have read about, but not for me!* But down inside my heart kept saying, *Yes, it is for you, too! You can have it, too!*

If you are sitting here tonight saying, "I don't believe it," then you will never have it. But if you can leave here tonight saying, "If it is for Dr. Lee Roberson, if it is for Dr. John R. Rice, if it is for Dr. John Rawlings, if it was for Dr. J. Frank Norris, if it was for Gipsy Smith and Ira Sankey and R. A. Torrey, it is for me, too," then you can have it.

Don't you get tired of just swinging the ax handle with no head on it? Don't you get tired of going through the motions, knowing nothing is going to happen but thinking that the show must go on? If you did some Sunday mornings what you felt like doing, you would stand and announce, "Let's be dismissed. This place is as dead as a doornail. It is dead and empty and dry as last year's bird nest."

Spurgeon said, "When you meet together, pray that the power of the Holy Spirit will be there. If you pray and He is not there, dismiss the congregation and pray He will be there next Sunday."

C. Asking

The first condition is thirsting. The second condition is believing. Believe that it is for you and you can be filled with the Holy Spirit. The third condition is asking.

Luke 11:13, "If ye then, being evil, know how to give good gifts unto your children: how much more shall your heavenly Father give the Holy Spirit to them that ask him?"

Just keep on praying. Just keep on praying. Just keep on praying, till light breaks through.

James 4:2 says, "Ye have not, because ye ask not." Some of you will die and go to Heaven a mediocre preacher. You know I am telling the truth. You have no ambition. You are satisfied. You will die, go to Heaven, and say to Jesus, "I would have done more if You had given me the fullness of the Holy Spirit." And God is going to answer back, "Ye have not, because ye ask not. If you had asked, I would have given."

What an accusation against believers!

Acts 4:31 says, "And when they had prayed, the place was shaken where they were assembled together; and they were all filled with the Holy Ghost."

D. The Right Reason

I have time for one more important condition. We must want the fullness of the Holy Spirit for the right reason. There are some who want the fullness of the Holy Spirit, but for the wrong reason. They want to have an ecstatic experience. They want to feel something. They want their hair to stand on end. They want to feel lightheaded. Some want to talk in what they think is a heavenly language. But in Acts 2 there is no ecstatic, heavenly language. There were languages of people present on the day of Pentecost. People didn't speak in an ecstatic tongue that day. They spoke with "other tongues,"—plural, languages. And every man heard them in his own language. They marveled and said, "Behold, are not all these which speak Galileans? And how hear we every man in our own tongue [language], wherein we were born?"

You want to get it so you can feel good and be lightheaded and run around shouting. I'm not against shouting, but that is not the reason God wants you to be filled with the Spirit.

Then what is the reason? Acts 1:8:

"But ye shall receive power, after that the Holy Ghost is come upon you: and ye shall be witnesses unto me both in Jerusalem, and in all Judaea, and in Samaria, and unto the uttermost part of the earth."

You won't stop until you have reached the whole world with the Gospel! You will be fanatical about soul winning when you are filled with the Holy Spirit.

We want the blessing to end in ourselves. We want to hem it all up. We want to get in our little prayer groups and have these wonderful experiences. But it doesn't say you will have that. Rather, you will have power to be a witness.

The word "witness" is found 33 times in the book of Acts. Compare that with the number of times they spoke in tonuges, which was three times: in Acts 2, Acts 10 and Acts 19.

You must want it for the right reason. If you are not willing to make soul winning the main business of your life, then you will never be filled with the Holy Spirit. You have to want it for the right reason.

IV. THE CONSEQUENCES

Today I listed eighteen things from the Bible that the Holy Spirit does for us. I am not saying there are only eighteen. I am going to mention a few. The Holy Spirit strengthens the believer in the inner man (Eph. 3:16). The Holy Spirit leads the believer (Rom. 8:14).

You don't have to go around guessing what you ought to and ought not to do. When you are Spirit-filled you can make your decisions much quicker and better. You can have clear directions from God.

The Holy Spirit produces Christian graces in the believer's life—love, joy, peace, longsuffering, gentleness, goodness, faith, meekness and temperance.

The Holy Spirit helps the believer understand the Bible (I John 2:27). You need illumination. The Holy Spirit gives you that.

The Holy Spirit improves your memory. "The Comforter, which is the Holy Ghost, whom the Father will send in my name, he shall teach you all things, and bring all things to your remembrance, whatsoever I have said unto you" (John 14:26).

He improves the memory. He helps you to preach the Word effectively, like Dr. Rawlings did awhile ago.

He improves your preaching and makes it effective.

First Thessalonians 1:5 says, "For our gospel came not unto you in word only, but also in power, and in the Holy Ghost."

He guides the believer in prayer (Rom. 8:26). We don't know what to pray for as we ought "but the Spirit itself maketh intercession for us with groanings which cannot be uttered."

These are a few of the eighteen things I listed that the Holy

Spirit does in the believer's life. But I want to talk about the main one.

The consequence of the fullness of the Spirit—I don't mean this critically or to be mean, but I must tell our Pentecostal friends—is not speaking in tongues. Not one time does the Bible say when you are filled with the Holy Spirit that you will speak in tongues. The Bible does say in Acts 1:8 that we will be witnesses. Open your Bible to Luke 1:15. Speaking of John the Baptist the Bible says,

"For he shall be great in the sight of the Lord, and shall drink neither wine nor strong drink; and he shall be filled with the Holy Ghost, even from his mother's womb."

Notice the next verse:

"And many of the children of Israel shall he turn to the Lord their God."

He would get a lot of people saved.

A man stood in the balcony in one of Moody's meetings and said, "Mr. Moody, let me tell you about my mountaintop experience."

Moody asked, "How many souls have you led to Christ since you have been on the mountain?"

"Why," he said, "none."

Moody said, "Sit down, we don't want to hear about that kind of mountaintop experience!"

I don't see how anybody can read Acts 2 and get ecstatic utterances out of it. It says, "other tongues," "in his own language," "our own tongue." And I don't see how anyone can read Acts 2 and miss the latter part of the chapter where it says three thousand souls were saved.

Here is what happened on Pentecost. There were at least three thousand unconverted people gathered at that place. How do we know? Because three thousand got saved; there had to be that many, and there were probably many more.

Here were some men who knew the Gospel and who could present it and win people to Christ, but they had a problem—not knowing the languages of the people who needed to hear the Gospel. And God had a problem. He said, "There are three thousand people who need to get saved and those men who know how to tell them how to get saved can't speak their language." So in Acts 2 God leaped a language barrier and allowed men to speak in languages they had never spoken before, not to magnify the language but to magnify the importance of getting the Gospel to the lost and getting them saved.

It is foolish to magnify the language, which carried the message resulting in 3,000 conversions, and never talk about the message itself nor the conversions.

That is like my bringing you a million dollars in a brown paper bag, and your dumping out the million dollars and running through the house shouting over the brown paper bag. You are more interested in the vehicle that brought it to you than what came to you in the vehicle.

The important thing on Pentecost was the message and the three thousand saved. The tongues were secondary and incidental.

*"And be not drunk with wine, wherein is excess; but **be filled with the Spirit**."*—Eph. 5:18.

". . . and ye shall be witnesses unto me. . . ."

The comparison, the command, the conditions, the consequences.

How many tonight want to be filled with the Holy Spirit? Maybe you are not as thirsty as you ought to be, but there is some longing in your heart. You are not satisfied with mediocrity.

Let us have several preachers form a line across the front. When the choir starts singing, will you start moving? I want you to go to the nearest preacher and say, "I want the fullness of the Holy Spirit, and I don't intend to stop until I get it," then go back to your seat.

(As the choir sang, hundreds came forward and said, "I want to be filled with the Holy Spirit.")

What Every Believer Should Know About Speaking in Tongues

CHAPTER FIFTEEN

The Meaning of It;
The Motive Behind It;
The Method for It;
The Misunderstandings About It

*"**N**ow, brethren, if I come unto you speaking with tongues, what shall I profit you, except I shall speak to you either by revelation, or by knowledge, or by prophesying, or by doctrine? And even things without life giving sound, whether pipe or harp, except they give a distinction in the sounds, how shall it be known what is piped or harped? For if the trumpet give an uncertain sound, who shall prepare himself to the battle? So likewise ye, except ye utter by the tongue words easy to be understood, how shall it be known what is spoken? for ye shall speak into the air."*—I Cor. 14:6-9.

The subject of tongues is worth study because it is in the Bible, and we need to learn how it concerns this important subject for two great reasons.

First, the tongues, or charismatic, movement is experiencing rapid growth. Seeking for a deeper experience, well-meaning and sincere believers have been led into the movement. Due to a false understanding, thousands of believers seek for the experience of speaking in tongues instead of for the power and fullness of the Holy Spirit to win souls.

On the other hand, many more thousands are so repulsed by what seems to them fanaticism, that they turn entirely away from any study of the fullness of the Holy Spirit. So afraid they will get out on a limb, they never bother to climb the tree.

I want believers everywhere to be filled with the blessed Holy Spirit. There can be no great soul-winning churches, no revival, without the power of the Holy Spirit. Zechariah 4:6 states, "Not by might, nor by power, but by my spirit, saith the Lord of hosts."

Now there is a second great reason for studying the question of tongues. There is such widespread difference of opinion among sincere believers that the truth should be known. Every honest believer should approach the study of tongues with an open mind and without prejudice. Surely God must be grieved when those who love Him and believe the Bible think so harshly of one another and differ so radically on such an important subject as being filled with the Holy Spirit.

In this study I will not talk about experience; we will only see what the Bible says. If one's experience does not agree with the Bible, the experience is wrong, not the Bible. Experience is not the principle; the Bible is. And doctrine is not settled by one's experience but by what the Bible has to say.

Several years ago a popular weekly television program featured a detective. If I recall correctly, his name was Sergeant Friday. In every story a situation developed in which Sergeant Friday said to a witness whom he questioned, "Just the facts, Mister. Just state the facts." With God's help, I shall do just that. We will see what the Bible says concerning the meaning of it, the motive behind it, the method for it, and the misunderstandings about it.

I. THE MEANING OF IT

The word translated "tongues" in Acts 2:4 is the Greek word *glossa*. I have just counted 50 times in my Strong's Concordance where the word appears in the New Testament. Sixteen times it refers to a literal, human tongue—the physical organ in the mouth; once, in Acts 2:3, it is used of "cloven tongues like as of fire," and 33 times the word means "language." But not one time in all the Bible does "tongues" mean a heavenly language that only God understands. It never means something mysterious or unknown to mankind. In Acts 2 it was not a jabber but normal, human languages known and spoken by people present on the day of Pentecost; and the nationalities of those in whose language they were allowed to speak are given:

"And they were all amazed and marvelled, saying one to another, Behold, are not all these which speak Galileans? And how hear we every man in our own tongue, wherein we were born? Parthians, and Medes, and Elamites, and the dwellers in Mesopotamia, and in Judaea, and Cappadocia, in Pontus, and Asia, Phrygia, and Pamphylia, in Egypt, and in the parts of Libya about Cyrene, and strangers of Rome, Jews and proselytes, Cretes and Arabians, we do hear them speak in our tongues the wonderful works of God."—Acts 2:7-11.

Notice the language of this chapter. Verse 4 states, "They were all filled with the Holy Ghost, and began to speak with other tongues...." It does not say they spoke with the unknown tongue; they simply spoke with other languages.

Verses 7 and 8 say, "And they were all amazed and marvelled, saying one to another, Behold, are not all these which speak Galileans? And how hear we every man in our own tongue, wherein we were born?" Again the Bible does not say they spoke with some heavenly language and every man understood them because he was filled with the Holy Spirit. It simply says, "And how hear we every man in our own tongue, wherein we were born?"

Then verses 9 through 11 list the nationalities of people whose languages were being spoken.

There are only three places in the book of Acts where people spoke in tongues. Namely, at Pentecost—Acts 2:1-11; in Caesarea—Acts 10:44-46; and in Ephesus—Acts 19:1-6.

In Acts 10:46 we are told how Cornelius and his household were heard to "speak with tongues, and magnify God." And Peter responded by saying, "Can any man forbid water, that these should not be baptized, which have received the Holy Ghost as well as we?"

These were new converts, and Peter suggested baptism. The tongues spoken by Cornelius and his household were not miraculous tongues. It simply says that they spake with tongues and magnified God. Cornelius and his household were members of the Italian band from Rome, and their natural language was Latin. It is possible that in the centurion's household were soldiers, slaves, servants and government officials from many of the nations of the Roman world. Could it have been that in their heavenly ecstasy they reverted each to his mother tongue in praising God?

It is a psychological truth that in moments of extreme delight or peril a foreigner will exclaim in his native tongue rather than in the language he has more recently acquired. But be that as it may, the tongues referred to in Acts 10:46 were known languages, not an ecstatic utterance.

The third historical record of people speaking in tongues in the book of Acts is found in chapter 19:1-6. When Paul met these twelve men in Ephesus, he asked, "Have ye received the Holy Ghost since ye believed?" Their reply was that they had never heard of the Holy Spirit.

Now, how could followers of John the Baptist be ignorant of the Holy Spirit, when he preached the Holy Spirit (Matt. 3:11)? Evidently the true message of John the Baptist had been lost as it was passed from one disciple to another, then when these misled men heard a clear presentation of the Gospel, they were baptized (vs. 5). Verse 6 states, "And when Paul had laid his hands upon them, the Holy Ghost came on them; and they spake with tongues, and prophesied."

Here again the Bible does not say they spoke with heavenly languages or in some ecstatic utterance, but that they spoke with tongues, or languages. Ephesus, a great cosmopolitan city, was made up of people from different parts of the Roman world. The Bible does not indicate what languages were spoken. But it clearly indicates that more than one language was used: ". . . they spake with tongues" (plural). And verse 7 states, "And all the men were about twelve." It is possible that a dozen different languages were spoken, as these new Christians, filled with joy, prophesied.

Aside from these three instances in the book of Acts, tongues are mentioned in Paul's discussion of the gifts of the Spirit (I Cor. 12: 1-14 and in I Cor. 14). A study of I Corinthians 14 will reveal that the tongues mentioned are not so-called spiritual or heavenly languages. The languages used were normal, human languages. It was no jabber, no babble of sound unfamiliar to any human ear.

In that chapter it is referred to as "an *unknown* tongue," but *"unknown"* is in italics, which means it is a supplied word, placed there by Bible translators for the sake of understanding. The languages mentioned here are simply foreign languages unknown to those present. Verses 23 and 24 make this especially clear:

"If therefore the whole church be come together into one place, and all speak with tongues, and there come in those that are unlearned, or unbelievers, will they not say that ye are mad? But if all prophesy, and there come in one that believeth not, or one unlearned, he is convinced of all, he is judged of all."

Now, visualize the scene. A church service is in progress and people are speaking in numerous foreign languages. Some uneducated or unlearned person, as the Scripture calls him, happens to walk into the service. He hears a number of people speaking in various languages; it is mass confusion, so he concludes all are mad! But if the church members would speak words easy to understand, instead of speaking in foreign languages that the unlearned do not know, then the unbeliever and the unlearned would be convinced of all.

The use of the word "unlearned," in verses 23 and 24, shows that the languages referred to were not supernatural but could be learned by proper study. One can learn any foreign language if he studies it enough. If the languages used in I Corinthians 14 were a supernatural gift, then it would be available to the unlearned as well as the educated. If speaking in tongues means speaking in some mysterious language known only to God and not to any group of men, no matter how much learning and education a man has, he will not understand the heavenly language. But foreign languages, known and spoken by men, can be learned. The fact that these languages were the kind that unlearned men did not understand indicates they were known, normal, human languages.

Remember, then, that tongues in the Bible means languages and, in the case of I Corinthians 14, foreign languages, unknown by some who attended the church services.

II. THE MOTIVE BEHIND IT

I have already mentioned that there are only three places in the Bible where people spoke in tongues: Acts 2:1-11; 10:44-46; 19:1-6.

The central and most important Bible passage on the subject of tongues is Acts 2:1-11. First, it is important because it is the first time tongues are discussed in the New Testament. Second, it is important because speaking in tongues was on a larger scale in Acts 2 than in either of the other cases mentioned. Third, it is the most important passage because this is the only instance where we can be absolutely sure that speaking in tongues was a miraculous gift.

Acts 2:4 states:

"And they were all filled with the Holy Ghost, and began to speak with other tongues, as the Spirit gave them utterance."

Acts 10 and 19 simply say they spake with tongues. There is no hint here that speaking in tongues was a supernatural gift. Only in Acts 2:4 does the Bible say "as the Spirit gave them utterance."

Now, what was the motive behind this supernatural gift on the day of Pentecost? There were at least 3,000 unsaved people present. There could have been more, but according to verse 41, "Then they that gladly received his word were baptized: and the same day there were added unto them about three thousand souls."

On the day of Pentecost, God had a problem: 3,000 unsaved people were present. The Galileans knew the plan of salvation. They could present the Gospel clearly, but they could not speak in the languages of those who needed to hear the message. The problem God faced was language barrier. He wanted those 3,000 precious souls to be saved, but the men who knew how to present the Gospel could not speak in the languages of the unconverted. So God allowed them to speak in languages which they had not learned. They spoke in other languages supernaturally, in the words of Acts 2:4, ". . . as the Spirit gave them utterance."

Sixteen different nationalities are named as hearing in their own language the wonderful works of God. These Spirit-filled Christians at Pentecost witnessed for Jesus in sixteen different languages beginning with that of the Parthians and ending with that of the Cretes and Arabians:

"And they were all amazed and marvelled, saying one to another, Behold, are not all these which speak Galileans? And how hear we every man in our own tongue, wherein we were born? Parthians, and Medes, and Elamites, and the dwellers in Mesopotamia, and in Judaea, and Cappadocia, in Pontus, and Asia, Phrygia, and Pamphylia, in Egypt, and in the parts of Libya about Cyrene, and strangers of Rome, Jews and proselytes, Cretes

and Arabians, we do hear them speak in our tongues the wonderful works of God." —Acts 2:7-11.

When these precious unconverted people heard the Gospel, they trusted Jesus Christ as Saviour. And the Bible states in Acts 2:41, "Then they that gladly received his word were baptized: and the same day there were added unto them about three thousand souls."

The important thing on the day of Pentecost was not the speaking in tongues but the conversion of 3,000 sinners. And that places importance on soul winning, not on speaking in tongues. Tongues were secondary and incidental, only a means to an end, the end being soul winning.

That is certainly consistent with Acts 1:8, where Jesus said,

"But ye shall receive power, after that the Holy Ghost is come upon you: and ye shall be witnesses unto me both in Jerusalem, and in all Judaea, and in Samaria, and unto the uttermost part of the earth."

It is said of John the Baptist in Luke 1:15, 16,

"For he shall be great in the sight of the Lord, and shall drink neither wine nor strong drink; and he shall be filled with the Holy Ghost, even from his mother's womb. And many of the children of Israel shall he turn to the Lord their God."

To put the emphasis on speaking in tongues would be like having someone bring you a million dollars in a brown paper bag, and your dumping the money into the trash and getting excited over the paper bag. The paper bag was the instrument in which the money was delivered. The money is the important thing, not the bag.

The tongues on the day of Pentecost were the instrument through which the message was delivered that resulted in 3,000 souls saved. The salvation of 3,000 sinners was the important thing, not the tongues that delivered the message. Winning souls was the motive behind speaking with tongues in Acts, chapter 2.

III. THE METHOD FOR IT

Aside from the three instances recorded in the book of Acts, one other place in the New Testament mentions speaking in tongues. It is in Paul's discussion of the gifts of the Spirit in I Corinthians 12:1-14. Verse 10 lists, among other gifts, "divers kinds of tongues." The church at Corinth is the only New Testament church that spoke with tongues. It is never mentioned in connection with the churches in Macedonia, Achaia, Judaea, Samaria, Asia, Rome or any other place.

First Corinthians, chapter 14, does not contain a list of exhortations to speak in tongues but a long list of restrictions against the practice. Paul is not encouraging the believers at Corinth to exercise the gift but to refrain from its use. He is not giving a set of rules on how to speak in tongues, but rather laying down strict regulations to restrain its use in the church.

Before giving a number of these regulations found in I Corinthians 14, I should call attention to the fact that the tongues in I Corinthians 14 are different than those in Acts 2, Acts 10 and Acts 19.

In Acts 2 the disciples simply preached the Gospel in the languages of those present. They heard the Gospel, trusted Christ as Saviour and 3,000 were saved. The tongues used on the day of Pentecost were not unknown languages to the hearers.

The tongues mentioned in I Corinthians 14 were unknown to the congregation. They were foreign languages not known by the people in the church, thus they were unknown tongues.

Now, notice several regulations Paul lays down in regard to speaking in tongues.

First, no tongues or foreign languages were to be used in the church except when people present understood what was being said.

"If any man speak in an unknown tongue, let it be by two, or at the most by three, and that by course; and let one interpret. But if there be no interpreter, let him keep silence in the church; and let him speak to himself, and to God."—I Cor. 14:27, 28.

Second, there should never be more than two or three in any service speaking in other languages or tongues. "If any man speak in an unknown tongue, let it be by two, or at the most by three, and that by course; and let one interpret" (vs. 27).

Third, only one person was to speak at a time. Any time two or three were speaking at the same time it was clearly out of order. ". . . let it be by two, or at the most by three, and that by course" (I Cor. 14:27). If tongues were ever spoken in a service, it had to be "by course," never two speaking at the same time.

Fourth, any religious service where speaking in tongues caused confusion was clearly not of God: "For God is not the author of confusion, but of peace, as in all churches of the saints" (I Cor. 14:33).

Fifth, under no condition was a woman to speak in an unknown tongue in the church:

"Let your women keep silence in the churches; for it is not permitted unto them to speak; but they are commanded to be under obedience, as also saith the law. And if they will learn any thing, let them ask their husbands at home: for it is a shame for women to speak in the church."—I Cor. 14:34, 35.

That is a strange statement for the Apostle Paul to make, since in I Corinthians 11:3-10 he had just given instructions how women were to dress when they prayed or prophesied in the church. This is not to say that a woman could preach or be the pastor of a church, since I Timothy 2:12 states, "But I suffer not a woman to teach, nor to usurp authority over the man, but to be in silence." Now, in I Corinthians 14:34 and 35 he says they are not to speak at all but to keep silent.

Has he forgotten what he has just written? Is he stupid? Has he lost his mind? No, not at all. These verses forbidding women to speak in the church are found in the middle of this chapter on speaking in tongues. He is giving regulations on the use of tongues in the church and he says the women are to keep silent. They are not permitted to speak!

Dr. W. A. Criswell said:

> In front of the ancient city of Corinth was the deep blue sea.
> Behind the city of Corinth was the steep, high Acro-Corinthus,
> an Acropolis far more prominent than that in Athens on which
> was built the Parthenon. Crowning the imposing Acropolis at
> Corinth was a magnificent temple to Aphrodite (Latin,
> "Venus").
> The Greek goddess of love and beauty was worshiped with
> sexual orgies. The temple prostitutes who were used in these
> orgies of worship worked themselves up into ecstatic frenzies
> as they followed their heathen, immoral rituals.
> The sight of frenzied women speaking in unknown tongues
> in their dedication to immorality was a common one in the
> days of Graeco-Roman culture. Paul's abhorrence of such
> speaking is explicable and obvious. Paul assumes that even
> strangers walking by an assembly of God's people, seeing and
> hearing the women talking in unknown tongues, would im-
> mediately say: "What have we here; a little colony of
> Aphrodite? Let us go in and enjoy the sensual pleasure." "No,"
> said the apostle, "a thousand times no! When it comes to speak-
> ing in tongues, let your women keep silent in the churches.
> It is a shame [mark this word 'shame'] for women to speak in
> unknown tongues in the church."
> That interdiction still stands, unremoved. The hysterical,
> unseemly excess of tongue-speaking women in public worship
> is a reproach to the name of the Lord.

Sixth, Paul encourages the church to speak in a language
understood by the congregation:

*"I thank my God, I speak with tongues more than ye all: Yet
in the church I had rather speak five words with my understanding, that by my voice I might teach others also, than ten thousand words in an unknown tongue."*—I Cor. 14:18, 19.

These are tremendous odds—5 to 10,000! This would be enough
to stop the practice of tongues forever in the judgment of any
ordinary fair-minded person. The practice has no place in the
church.

Recently I wrote on the margin of my Bible five reasons why
tongues were not suited for public worship services.

1. It could not be generally understood and therefore required the services of an interpreter to be of any value.

2. It repelled unbelievers and did not edify believers who could not understand what was being said.

3. It led unbelievers to conclude that those who spoke in this unintelligible manner, when they could have used known languages, were out of their minds; they were mad.

4. It might lead the hearers to conclude that God is the author of confusion, since those who spoke in tongues claimed to do so by the power of the Holy Spirit.

5. It actually thwarted God's purpose which is that His witness should be understood by all.

Why use such a round-about way to get the truth to people? God never used such means nor did the apostles.

IV. THE MISUNDERSTANDINGS ABOUT IT

There are several misunderstandings regarding speaking in tongues. Some say it is the evidence of the fullness of the Holy Spirit. Others say tongues is a prayer language and they speak to God in tongues. Still others insist that speaking in tongues is a sign of spirituality. When one becomes spiritual enough, he will speak with tongues.

Is speaking in tongues the evidence of the fullness of the Holy Spirit? Let us see what the Bible says. There is not a single statement—either before or after Pentecost—in which the Bible speaks of the gift of tongues as the evidence or part of the evidence of being filled with the Holy Spirit. This is a doctrine not founded upon a single clear statement in the Word of God.

Pastor Donald Gee, a well-known writer of the Pentecostal movement, said in his booklet, *Speaking in Tongues, the Initial Evidence of the Baptism of the Holy Spirit*:

> The doctrine that speaking with other tongues is the initial evidence of the baptism of the Holy Spirit rests upon the accumulated evidence of the recorded cases in the book of Acts where this experience is received. Any doctrine on this point

must necessarily be confined within these limits for its basis, for the New Testament contains no plain, categorical statement anywhere as to what must be regarded as THE sign.

Those who teach that speaking in tongues is the evidence of the fullness of the Holy Spirit get such an idea from history, from books or from human experience, not from the Bible, since it says nothing about it.

There are good reasons to believe that speaking in tongues is not the evidence of the fullness of the Holy Spirit.

First, as I have mentioned, the Scripture nowhere says that speaking in tongues was the evidence.

Second, another evidence was promised. Acts 1:8 states, "But ye shall receive power, after that the Holy Ghost is come upon you: and ye shall be witnesses unto me both in Jerusalem, and in all Judaea, and in Samaria, and unto the uttermost part of the earth."

Here the Bible says that when they were filled with the Holy Spirit they would receive power to witness. That is exactly what happened in Acts, chapter 2. Filled with the Holy Spirit, they preached the Gospel and 3,000 souls were saved!

It is said of John the Baptist in Luke 1:15, 16:

"For he shall be great in the sight of the Lord, and shall drink neither wine nor strong drink; and he shall be filled with the Holy Ghost, even from his mother's womb. And many of the children of Israel shall he turn to the Lord their God."

Notice it says nothing about John the Baptist speaking in tongues. It does say, "And many of the children of Israel shall he turn to the Lord their God." When he is filled with the Holy Spirit, he will be a great soul winner. If there is an evidence of the fullness of the Holy Spirit, it is soul winning, not speaking with tongues.

Third, there are examples in the Bible of those who were filled with the Holy Spirit but did not speak in tongues: Jesus—Luke 3:22 and Acts 10:38; John the Baptist—Luke 1:15, 16; the converts at Samaria—Acts 8:14-17; the Apostle Paul—Acts 9:17.

The great soul winners of our day are men who have been filled with the Holy Spirit but never spoke in tongues.

Dr. John R. Rice, the founder and editor of THE SWORD OF THE LORD, was knowingly filled with the Holy Spirit but never spoke in tongues.

Dr. Jack Hyles, pastor of the largest Sunday school in America, was knowingly filled with the Holy Spirit but never spoke in tongues.

Dr. Lee Roberson, pastor of the largest church in the state of Tennessee, speaks about the fullness of the Holy Spirit in his own life but he never spoke in tongues.

Then there are the great evangelists and preachers of yesteryear who were filled with the Holy Spirit but never spoke in tongues—Dwight L. Moody, Charles G. Finney, R. A. Torrey, John Wesley, George Whitefield, Charles Haddon Spurgeon, Billy Sunday, J. Wilbur Chapman, George Truett, Gipsy Smith and many, many others.

Since God gave another evidence of the fullness of the Holy Spirit, it is wrong and foolish for anyone to believe that speaking in tongues is the evidence when God says nothing of the kind.

There is another misunderstanding regarding speaking in tongues. Some who speak in tongues say it is a prayer language, basing the teaching on I Corinthians 14:2, "He that speaketh in an unknown tongue speaketh not unto men, but unto God." A little study here will clarify your mind. This verse simply says if a man speaks in the church in a foreign language, which no one understands, then he is not speaking unto men but unto God. Then the verse goes on to explain, ". . . for no man understandeth him." The Scripture does not say and does not mean that the tongues mentioned here was a language known only to God. An unknown tongue is any foreign language unknown to you or unknown to the person who hears it spoken.

If I spoke in Chinese to an English-speaking audience who did not understand Chinese, I would not be speaking to men because they would not understand the language. I would be speaking to God, since He understands and knows all languages. What God has in mind here is simply foreign languages unknown to those present but not unknown to God.

Recently in a restaurant, I sat near several people who were speaking in a language unknown to me. As I enjoyed my meal, I wished I could understand what they were saying. But they were not speaking to me since the language spoken was unknown to me. However, the language they were speaking in was not unknown to God, and He heard and understood every word.

There is no such thing as a special prayer language. God understands one language as well as the other. He is omniscient. There is no language unknown to God. He hears every conversation.

Several years ago I led a lady to Christ who knew very little English. When I asked her to pray, she indicated that she could not speak the English language well enough to pray. I suggested she pray in her own native tongue, which she did. The tongue was unknown to me. I have absolutely no idea what she said, but I am sure God understood every word. And when she had finished praying, a glow came over her face as she reached out to shake my hand. The next Sunday I had the happy privilege of baptizing her, and she made a faithful church member. There is no such thing as a special prayer language.

There are those who believe that speaking in tongues is a sign of spirituality. This is another misunderstanding. Only one church in the Bible ever spoke with tongues—the church at Corinth. The Bible specifically says the church at Corinth was carnal and not spiritual.

"I have fed you with milk, and not with meat: for hitherto ye were not able to bear it, neither yet now are ye able. For ye are yet carnal: for whereas there is among you envying, and strife, and divisions, are ye not carnal, and walk as men?" —I Cor. 3:2, 3.

They were not able to eat strong meat and had to be fed on the milk of the Word. Some of them were puffed up and offended with Paul (I Cor. 4:18). There was fornication among them: a man living in sin with his stepmother and the church openly taking his part (I Cor. 5:1). Church members were going to law with one another before unbelievers (I Cor. 6:1-8). Some of the church members ate meat offered to idols (I Cor. 8). There were divisions and heresies at the Lord's Supper, and some came to the communion drunk (I Cor. 11:17-21). Some church members denied the resurrection (I Cor. 15:12).

The only church in the Bible where members spoke in tongues was carnal. So, speaking in tongues could not be a sign of spirituality.

Now, these closing words.

I would exhort every believer to be filled with the Holy Spirit. You may as well try to beat back the tide with a pitchfork as to try to do God's work without the fullness of the Holy Spirit.

When you are filled with the Holy Spirit, then spend your time winning souls to Christ. The whole purpose of the Holy Spirit's coming into the world was to "reprove the world of sin, and of righteousness, and of judgment" (John 16:8). What does it matter if you speak with the tongues of men and of angels and never lead a soul to Christ! What difference would it make if you could speak a dozen languages—whether by human wisdom or by a miracle—if you never gave anyone the plan of salvation or told a sinner how to be saved?

Be filled with the Holy Spirit and win souls.

The Second Coming
of Christ, the
Believer's Hope

CHAPTER SIXTEEN

The Promise of His Coming
The Person of His Coming
The Program of His Coming
The Preparations for His Coming

*"**B**ut I would not have you to be ignorant, brethren, concerning them which are asleep, that ye sorrow not, even as others which have no hope. For if we believe that Jesus died and rose again, even so them also which sleep in Jesus will God bring with him. For this we say unto you by the word of the Lord, that we which are alive and remain unto the coming of the Lord shall not prevent them which are asleep. For the Lord himself shall descend from heaven with a shout, with the voice of the archangel, and with the trump of God: and the dead in Christ shall rise first: Then we which are alive and remain shall be caught up together with them in the clouds, to meet the Lord in the air: and so shall we ever be with the Lord. Wherefore comfort one another with these words."*—I Thess. 4:13-18.

Several years ago a preacher preaching on the radio brought

a series of prophetic messages. During that series he kept referring to his prophetic messages.

One day a lady, recognizing him on the street, ran to him and said, "O Brother _____, I really do enjoy those '*pathetic*' messages you have been bringing."

Some *prophetic* messages may indeed be *pathetic*, especially when we make the mistake of date-setting and try to pinpoint the very hour of Christ's return.

It is difficult, if not impossible, to get correct every detail of Bible prophecy. At best, we only get a general view of the landscape.

For instance, when I return from a revival meeting, my wife asks me about that church. I tell her, it was a brick church.

"What kind of brick?"

"I don't know. All I remember is red brick. I don't recall whether they were common brick or scratched surface."

"Were there any trees in the yard?"

"Yes, a number of trees."

"How many?"

"I don't remember."

"What kind of trees?"

"I don't remember that. I know there were several large ones."

You see, I got a general view of the landscape but not all the details. I had a good idea what the church looked like, but I could not be exact about all the details.

So it is with Bible prophecy. And one makes a mistake when he tries to pinpoint **everything.**

It is a mistake to try to set an exact date when the Lord will return.

Several years ago, I heard a preacher say the Lord would return before 1980 and if He didn't he would quit the ministry. I do not know if he quit the ministry since the Lord has not come, but I know he was wrong to set a date.

I have heard others name the Antichrist, and so far no one has been correct. If I understand the Bible, the Antichrist will not be revealed unto after the rapture of the church; therefore, his identity will not be known until after the first phase of the second coming of Christ (II Thess. 2:3-8).

While we may not know every detail, we do know the Lord is coming; and we have a general view of the landscape. I will say more about that in "The Program of His Coming."

In this message I will cover four thoughts: "The Promise of His Coming," "The Person of His Coming," "The Program of His Coming," and "the Preparations for His Coming."

I. THE PROMISE OF HIS COMING

There are twenty times as many references in the Old Testament to the second coming of Christ as there are to His first coming. In all of Paul's epistles he refers to baptism only thirteen times, while he speaks of the second coming more than fifty times. Among the last words Jesus uttered before He left this world were:

*"Let not your heart be troubled; ye believe in God, believe also in me. In my Father's house are many mansions: if it were not so, I would have told you. I go to prepare a place for you. And if I go and prepare a place for you, I **will come again,** and receive you unto myself; that where I am there ye may be also."*—John 14:1-3.

At His ascension in Acts 1:10 the Bible states, ". . . two men stood by them in white apparel." And verse 11 records their statement: "Ye men of Galilee, why stand ye gazing up into heaven? this same Jesus, which is taken up from you into heaven, shall so come in like manner as ye have seen him go into heaven."

It is believed that these men in white apparel were angels, and that they said, "This same Jesus. . . shall so come in like manner as ye have seen him go into heaven." How did He leave? Visibly. He will return visibly. He left in a body; He will return in a body. He left from the Mount of Olives; He will return to the Mount of Olives (Acts 1:12; Zech. 14:4).

Philippians 3:20 says, "Our conversation is in heaven; from whence also we look for the Saviour, the Lord Jesus Christ." Hebrews 9:28 states, ". . . and unto them that look for him shall he appear the second time without sin unto salvation."

The Bible is filled with promises of Jesus' coming. In Revelation 22—once in verse 7, once in verse 12, and again in verse 20—Jesus says, "Behold, I come quickly," "Behold, I come quickly," "Surely I come quickly." And the Bible closes with the Apostle John saying, "Even so, come, Lord Jesus. The grace of our Lord Jesus Christ be with you all. Amen" (Rev. 22:20, 21).

Friends, one verse in every thirty in the New Testament refers to the second coming.

A Bible-believing preacher brought a tremendous sermon on the second coming. When he had finished, one of these modernistic, potato-string-backbone, rosewater-squirting preachers, who start nowhere and end up in the same place, said to him, "I want you to know that I can't get that out of the New Testament."

The wise old preacher replied, "You surely can't, Buddy. It's in there to stay!"

Yes, the promise of the second coming of Christ is in the Bible to stay. There are 259 chapters in the New Testament and over 300 references to the second coming of Christ.

Now let me say a word about

II. THE PERSON OF HIS COMING

I mention this because there are different ideas concerning the second coming. Some say it is death. And at some funerals preachers imply that Jesus came for the individual. But when one dies, the opposite is true. The deceased goes to be with Christ. Second Corinthians 5:8 states, ". . . to be absent from the body, and to be present with the Lord." Paul said in Philippians 1:23, "I am in a strait betwixt two, having a desire to depart, and to be with Christ; which is far better." So the second coming is not the death of the believer.

When the Christian dies, his soul and spirit leave his body

and go immediately to be with Christ: absent from the body, present with the Lord (II Cor. 5:8).

Others spiritualize the second coming and say it is when Jesus comes into your heart, that is, when you are saved. I knew a dear preacher who believed and taught that. He told me when I got saved Jesus came into my heart, and that was the second coming. This teaching is not consistent with Scripture. In I Thessalonians 4:16 the Bible describes the coming of Christ for His own: "For the Lord himself shall descend from heaven with a shout, with the voice of the archangel, and with the trump of God: and the dead in Christ shall rise first."

When Jesus Christ came into my heart, there was no shout, no voice of the archangel, no trump of God; and there was certainly no resurrection of the Christian dead. The second coming is different from Jesus' coming into one's heart. When a man accepts Jesus Christ as Saviour, Jesus does not literally, physically return to the earth. When one is saved, the Holy Spirit comes into that person to take up His permanent residence. Jesus dwells in us in the Person of the Holy Spirit, but He Himself is in Heaven seated on the right hand of the Father. "To him that overcometh will I grant to sit with me in my throne, even as I also overcame, and am set down with my Father in his throne" (Rev. 3:21).

Friends, Jesus is now in Heaven, seated at the right hand of the Father. He is in our hearts in the Person of the Holy Spirit. Romans 8:9 says, "Now if any man have not the Spirit of Christ, he is none of his." First Corinthians 6:19 says, "What? know ye not that your body is the temple of the Holy Ghost which is in you, which ye have of God, and ye are not your own?" The Holy Spirit indwells the believer. So the second coming of Christ is not death; it is not the new birth.

The second coming of Christ means the literal, physical, bodily return of Jesus Himself. Notice what He said in John 14:3, "And if I go and prepare a place for you, I will come again." He says in that same passage, "If it were not so, I would have told you."

When I hear these modernistic preachers deny the second coming, I mumble to myself, *If it were not so, He would have told us.* Friend, Jesus Himself is coming!

In Acts 1:11 the angels said, "...this same Jesus"—not a spirit, not an angel, but—"this same Jesus, which is taken up from you into heaven, shall so come in like manner as ye have seen him go into heaven."

It will be the same Christ who lived on this earth two thousand years ago. It will be the same Christ who healed the sick, unstopped the deaf ears, raised the dead, was crucified, buried, and rose again. That same Jesus is coming again. His coming will be personal, bodily and literal.

The Bible says in I Thessalonians 4:16, "For the Lord *himself* shall descend from heaven."

III. THE PROGRAM OF HIS COMING

Now let me give you a bird's-eye view of the program of His coming.

When I first began to study the second coming, I noticed some verses that seemed contradictory. I say "seemed" because there are no contradictions in the Bible; for it is the inspired, inerrant, infallible Word of God. I give you two such verses. Revelation 1:7 says, "Behold, he cometh with clouds; and every eye shall see him." But Revelation 16:15 says, "Behold, I come as a thief. Blessed is he that watcheth, and keepeth his garments...." Is He coming in the clouds and every eye see Him, as the Bible says in Revelation 1:7? Or will He come as a thief? When a thief comes, every eye doesn't see him.

Recently several homes have been burglarized in our neighborhood, but no one has seen the burglar. Every eye doesn't see a thief. He slips in unexpectedly, gathers quickly what he came for, then leaves.

Revelation 16:15 states that Jesus is coming as a thief. Then Revelation 1:7 says, "Behold, he cometh with clouds; and every eye shall see him."

Another seeming contradiction is I Thessalonians 3:13, "To the end he may stablish your hearts unblameable in holiness before God, even our Father, at the coming of our Lord Jesus Christ with all his saints." In the next chapter He talks about bringing some of the saints with Him and says others (resurrected saints) will be caught up together with them, to meet the Lord in the air. How is He coming with all His saints if some saints are going to be caught up to meet Him in the air?

These verses can be understood when you understand the program of His coming. His coming is in two phases. He first comes for His own (I Thess. 4:13-18). He later comes with His own to fulfill His promise to David and to Abraham. He will sit on David's throne in Jerusalem and rule the nations with a rod of iron.

The first phase of His coming is called the rapture of the church. The second phase we call the revelation.

When Jesus Christ comes for the church, He will come as a thief. He will gather His own—the born-again believers from all over the world—and be gone.

When He comes with His own, at the revelation, then every eye shall see Him. "Behold, he cometh with clouds, and every eye shall see him" (Rev. 1:7).

Now here is the program: He first comes for His own. That is the rapture of the church. Later He comes back with His own to fulfill His promise to Abraham and to David. He will sit down on David's throne and rule the nations with a rod of iron. That is the revelation. He first comes for us (the rapture of the church); He later comes with us (the revelation).

A. The Rapture of the Church

The word "rapture" is not in the Bible. However, it does describe a Bible experience. First Thessalonians 4:13-18 gives us a description of the rapture:

"But I would not have you to be ignorant, brethren, concerning them which are asleep, that ye sorrow not, even as others

which have no hope. For if we believe that Jesus died and rose again, even so them also which sleep in Jesus will God bring with him. For this we say unto you by the word of the Lord, that we which are alive and remain unto the coming of the Lord shall not prevent [precede] them which are asleep."

The living Christians will not go ahead of those who are asleep, that is, those who are dead. Verse 16 gives the order.

"For the Lord himself shall descend from heaven with a shout, with the voice of the archangel, and with the trump of God: and the dead in Christ shall rise first. . . . "

When Jesus comes for His own at the rapture of the church, there will be a shout, the voice of the archangel, then there will be the sounding of the trumpet, and the dead in Christ shall rise first.

"Then we which are alive and remain shall be caught up together with them [those who have been resurrected] in the clouds, to meet the Lord in the air: and so shall we ever be with the Lord. Wherefore comfort one another with these words."

Jesus Christ could come for His own at any moment. There are no signs that precede His coming. The Bible does not say to watch for signs; but we are to watch for the Saviour, the Son.

For instance, Philippians 3:20 states, "Our conversation [citizenship] is in heaven; from whence also we look for the Saviour." Not looking for signs but for the Saviour.

Titus 2:13, "Looking for that blessed hope, and the glorious appearing of the great God and our Saviour Jesus Christ." Not looking for signs; looking for the Saviour.

Hebrews 9:28, ". . . and unto them that look for him shall he appear the second time without sin unto salvation." We are not told to look for signs but for the Son, the Saviour.

There are no signs that precede Christ's coming for His own. His coming is imminent and has been since New Testament times. The Apostle Paul thought Jesus Christ would come in his lifetime and said in I Thessalonians 4:17, "Then *WE* which are alive and remain...." Paul thought he would be living when Jesus came.

Every Bible-believing Christian expects to be alive when Jesus comes.

This week in my office sat an 84-year-old man who had driven over 300 miles to visit with me. As he sat there, suddenly his eyes closed and opened. The color left his cheeks. I thought he had a heart attack and was probably going to die in my office. In a moment he revived, smiled, and said, "I thought I would be alive at the rapture, but I believe the Lord is calling me Home."

He wouldn't let me call a doctor. His daughter-in-law drove him home that afternoon; and early the next morning his son called to say, "I am glad you visited with Father yesterday. He went to be with the Lord last night."

Here was an 84-year-old man who thought he would be alive when Jesus came.

Since Dr. Rice has gone on to be with Christ, I have had a hundred letters or more stating, "I never thought Dr. Rice would die. I thought he would be living when Jesus came." Well, to be honest, I thought so, too.

Paul thought Jesus would come in his lifetime. Said he, "*WE* which are alive and remain."

The coming of Christ for His own is imminent. It could happen any second. No signs have to be fulfilled. He could have come day before yesterday. He could have come last year. He could have come in Paul's time. **He may come today!** We are to live in constant expectancy of His coming.

While talking to five preachers, Robert Murray McCheyne, a great preacher of yesteryear, looked at one and asked, "Do you think Jesus will come today?"

His friend answered, "I think not."

To another he said, "Do you think Jesus will come today?"

He, too, replied, "I think not."

To the third he asked, "Do you think Jesus will come today?"

Again he heard, "I think not."

To the fourth he continued, "Do you think Christ will come today?"

This friend replied, "I think not."

Finally he asked the last one, "What about you; do you think Christ will come today?"

His reply was the same, "I think not."

Then McCheyne turned to Matthew 24:44 and read without comment, "Therefore be ye also ready: for in such an hour as ye think not the Son of man cometh."

Jesus Christ could come today; and when He comes for His own, the trumpet will sound, there will be the shout of the voice of the archangel, the dead in Christ will be raised first, then we which are alive and remain shall be caught up together with them in the clouds to meet the Lord in the air!

This does not mean that every believer will be given a cloud on which to ride. The expression "caught up in the clouds" means clouds of people. Revelation 1:7 says, "Behold, he cometh with clouds." And Hebrews 12:1 states, "Wherefore seeing we also are compassed about with so great a cloud of witnesses. . . ."

Did you ever notice birds migrating south? As they pass over, there seemingly are thousands of them. They are often referred to as a great cloud of birds!

Friends, when Jesus comes and the dead are raised and believers are changed in a moment, in the twinkling of an eye, a great cloud of believers will be leaving Murfreesboro, Tennessee; a great cloud of believers will leave Chicago, Illinois; a great cloud of believers will be leaving New York City, Atlanta, Georgia, and on and on and on. From all over the world **great clouds** of believers will be caught up. The trumpet will sound; the Christian dead will be raised, and we which are alive and remain will be caught up together with them in clouds to meet the Lord in the air.

When Jesus comes, the Christian dead will be raised and the living saints will be changed. Paul said in I Corinthians 15:

51, 52, "Behold, I shew you a mystery; We shall not all sleep
[we won't all be dead], but we shall all be changed, In a moment,
in the twinkling of an eye. . . ." those who are asleep will be
resurrected, and the living saints will be changed "in a moment,
in the twinkling of an eye."

I am told that the word "moment" comes from the same word
from which we get our word "atom," and means a space of time
so small that it cannot be divided again. Say, friends, that is
quick!

I have been told that the twinkle of an eye is much faster than
the blinking or closing of the eye. We shall be changed "in a
moment, in the twinkling of an eye."

Continuing in I Corinthians 15, the Bible says, ". . .then shall
be brought to pass the saying that is written, Death is swallowed
up in victory. O death, where is thy sting? O grave, where is
thy victory?" (vss. 54, 55).

The saints who are changed in a moment, in the twinkling
of an eye, will shout as they are caught away, "O death, where
is thy sting?" they never feel the sting of death. They are alive
when Jesus comes. The dead in Christ who are resurrected will
shout, "O grave, where is thy victory?" Some will have been
in the grave for thousands of years, but the grave will lose its
hold. It will not be victorious over the child of God.

Jesus said in John 11:25, 26, "I am the resurrection, and the
life: he that believeth in me, though he were dead, yet shall he
live: And whosoever liveth and believeth in me shall never die."
Two groups: "He that believeth in me, though he were dead,
yet shall he live"—the resurrection of the saints who die and
go on to be with Christ before the second coming; and "he that
liveth and believeth in me shall never die"—the person who is
alive at Jesus' coming and has trusted Him as Saviour.

Here are the events on God's prophetic calendar. He comes
for His own—the rapture of the church. The Antichrist is revealed on earth and has a successful reign for seven years, called
"the seventieth week" of Daniel, "the day of Jacob's trouble,"

or "the tribulation period." While the tribulation period is taking place on earth, the saints will be judged at the judgment seat of Christ. They will later be married to the Lamb, described in the Bible as "the marriage of the Lamb" (Rev. 19:7-9). At the close of the tribulation period, the saints, along with Christ, will come back to this earth; and Jesus will sit down on David's throne and rule the nations with a rod of iron.

B. The Revelation

Now I share with you the covenant God made with Abraham, which has to do with land and people. The covenant He made with David has to do with the throne. "The Lord hath sworn in truth unto David; he will not turn from it; Of the fruit of thy body will I set upon thy throne" (Ps. 132:11).

Some say that is a spiritual throne, but David never had a spiritual throne. This king in Israel had an actual, literal, physical throne. And when Jesus Christ comes again with His saints, at the close of the tribulation period, He will sit down on a literal, physical throne in Jerusalem—David's throne.

Notice the language of the promise, "The Lord hath sworn in truth unto David. . . ." Now, that is strong. But catch the rest of it, ". . . he will not turn from it." It makes no difference what anyone says or thinks, God has made the promise that "he will not turn from it; Of the fruit of thy body will I set upon thy throne."

He also made a promise to Abraham:

"Now the Lord had said unto Abram, Get thee out of thy country, and from thy kindred, and from thy father's house, unto a land that I will shew thee: And I will make of thee a great nation, and I will bless thee, and make thy name great; and thou shalt be a blessing: And I will bless them that bless thee, and curse him that curseth thee: and in thee shall all families of the earth be blessed."—Gen. 12:1-3.

Here God called Abram and his descendants to form a great

nation through which He would bless the land. Later He confirmed this covenant in Genesis 13:14, 15,

"And the Lord said unto Abram, after that Lot was separated from him, Lift up now thine eyes, and look from the place where thou art northward, and southward, and eastward, and westward: For all the land which thou seest, to thee will I give it, and to thy seed for ever."

Notice several things in this covenant. First, He said, "I will make of thee a great nation"—the nation Israel. Second, "I will bless thee." He spoke of temporal and spiritual blessing. Third, "I will...make thy name great." Abraham's name is one of the universal names. Fourth, He said, "And thou shalt be a blessing."

In Galatians 3:13, 14 the Bible says,

"Christ hath redeemed us from the curse of the law, being made a curse for us: for it is written, Cursed is every one that hangeth on a tree: That the blessing of Abraham might come on the Gentiles through Jesus Christ; that we might receive the promise of the Spirit through faith."

God goes on to say, "I will bless them that bless thee." Then He promises, "I will...curse him that curseth thee," and adds, "In thee shall all families of the earth be blessed" (Gen. 12:3).

God has not yet completely fulfilled His promise to Abraham.

After the Six-Day War, many Bible students thought Jesus would come in the next few days, or weeks. I heard preachers talk about how near the coming of Christ was. One went so far as to set a specific date.

Now wait a minute. I think His coming is imminent. It could happen today. But people did not understand the covenant God made with Abraham.

Notice several things regarding this covenant.

Abraham and his descendants were to have all the land of Canaan. To Abraham He promised: "For ALL THE LAND which thou seest, to thee will I give it, and to thy seed for ever." After the Six-Day War the Jews did not have all the land. The boundaries of the land are given (Gen. 15:18; Ezek. 47:19; 48:1). On the west side, the river of Egypt; to the east, the river Euphrates; north to Hamath; and to Kadesh on the south. The Jews never occupied all that land and they do not have it today. And that promise to Abraham will not be fulfilled until they have all this land. And all Jews will be back in the land when the promise is fulfilled to Abraham. All Jews are not back today.

So, they did not have all the land that was promised; and they were not all back. And when the Bible speaks of the regathering of Israel, it talks about giving them a new heart. So they were not all converted. The Bible talks about a nation's being born in a day. All the nation of Israel will be saved. That has not yet come to pass.

Now wait! They will not be saved as a nation. But each individual who makes up the nation will trust Christ as Saviour. They will look upon Him whom they have pierced. They will recognize that they have rejected the true Messiah. Then they will trust Him as Saviour, and a whole nation will be born in a day.

After the Six-Day War they did not have all the land.

They were not all back.

And they were not all converted as the Bible promises.

God also promised to give the land to Abraham himself. ". . . *to thee* will I give it, and to thy seed for ever" (Gen. 13:15). Abraham was not back in the land after the Six-Day War. When that promise is fulfilled, Abraham himself will be back in the land.

Christ was to be in the land with Abraham. Again, notice the expression in Genesis 13:15, ". . . to thee will I give it, and to *thy seed.*" Galatians 3:16 states, "Now to Abraham and his seed were the promises made. He saith not, And to seeds, as of many; but as of one, And to thy seed, *which is Christ.*"

So there are five things that will be true when God fulfills His promise to Abraham.

1. The Jews will have all the land—every inch of it—that God promised.

2. All the Jews will be back in the land.

3. They will all be converted.

4. Abraham himself will be in the land.

5. Christ will be in the land with Abraham.

The covenant God made to Abraham is not yet fulfilled and will not be until Jesus Christ comes again at the close of the tribulation. Then He will gather the nation of Israel and fulfill His promise to Abraham and His covenant to David.

The regathering of the nation Israel is repeatedly connected with the conversion of the entire remnant of the nation and the beginning of the reign of Christ (Isa. 11:1-12; Ezek. 34:12-14; Jer. 23:3-6; 33:14-17; Matt. 24:29-31).

Notice the order in Matthew 24:29-31:

"Immediately after the tribulation of those days shall the sun be darkened, and the moon shall not give her light, and the stars shall fall from heaven, and the powers of the heavens shall be shaken: And then shall appear the sign of the Son of man in heaven: and then shall all the tribes of the earth mourn, and they shall see the Son of man coming in the clouds of heaven with power and great glory."

Revelation 1:7 says, "Behold, he cometh with clouds; and every eye shall see him." We are talking now about the revelation, not about the time when He comes as a thief in the night for His own, but when He comes with clouds and every eye shall see Him.

"And he shall send his angels with a great sound of a trumpet, and they shall gather together his elect from the four winds, from one end of heaven to the other."

First, we have the tribulation: "Immediately after the tribulation of those days" (vs. 29).

Second, we have the second coming of Christ, the revelation. "Then . . . they shall see the Son of man coming in the clouds of heaven with power and great glory" (vs. 30).

Third, we have the regathering of the Jews: "And he shall send his angels with a great sound of a trumpet, and they shall gather together his elect from the four winds, from one end of heaven to the other" (vs. 31).

Now, the promise God made to Abraham will be fulfilled after the tribulation period, when Jesus comes to reign. The Jews will be regathered to the Land. They will all be saved—a nation will be born in a day. They will have all the land. Abraham himself will be there. And Christ will be there with Abraham.

Jesus Christ is coming back to the earth literally and visibly, to fulfill not only His promise to Abraham but also His promise to David. "The Lord hath sworn in truth unto David; he will not turn from it; Of the fruit of thy body will I set upon thy throne" (Ps. 132:11).

This reign of Christ is described as the millennial reign, because it is a thousand years.

"And I saw thrones, and they sat upon them, and judgment was given unto them: and I saw the souls of them that were beheaded for the witness of Jesus, and for the word of God, and which had not worshipped the beast, neither his image, neither had received his mark upon their foreheads, or in their hands; and they lived [they had been martyred, now they live, they were resurrected] *and reigned with Christ a thousand years. But the rest of the dead lived not again* [the unsaved dead were not resurrected] *until the thousand years were finished.* [A thousand years between the resurrection of the saved and the unsaved.] *This is the first resurrection* [of the saved]. *Blessed and holy is he that hath part in the first resurrection: on such the second death hath no power, but they shall be priests of God and of Christ, and shall reign with him a thousand years. And when the thousand years are expired, Satan shall be loosed out of his prison, And shall go out to deceive the nations which are in the four quarters of the earth."*—Rev. 20:4-8.

We call this thousand-year reign of Christ the millennial reign. We say we believe in the premillennial return of Christ, that is, we believe Christ is coming for His own before He comes back with His own to reign for a thousand years. That is premillennial.

I believe unfilled prophecy should be taken literally because prophecy that has been fulfilled thus far was literally fulfilled.

For instance, in Isaiah 9:6, 7, the Bible says, "For unto us a child is born." That was literally fulfilled. "Unto us a son is given." That was literally fulfilled. The Bible goes on to say, "And his name shall be called Wonderful, Counsellor, The mighty God, The everlasting Father, The Prince of Peace. Of the increase of his government and peace there shall be no end, upon the throne of David, and upon his kingdom, to order it, and to establish it with judgment and with justice from henceforth even for ever. The zeal of the Lord of hosts will perform this."

Why should we take the first few expressions in this passage literally and not take literally the latter few expressions? If the Child was born and the prophecy was literally fulfilled, then why are we not to believe that the remaining part of the prophecy will be literally fulfilled?

Yes, Jesus is actually, literally, physically going to return to the earth. He will sit down on David's throne. The Great Society which has been dreamed about for years will then be a realization rather than a dream. The curse brought on nature because of sin will then be removed. Wars will be no more. Righteousness will prevail on the entire planet. And happiness will be universal.

Several things will happen when Christ comes to reign:

1. The curse that has been on the earth because of sin will be removed.

"For we know that the whole creation groaneth and travaileth in pain together until now. And not only they, but ourselves also, which have the first fruits of the Spirit, even we ourselves groan within ourselves, waiting for the adoption, to wit, the redemption of our body."—Rom. 8:22, 23.

When Adam sinned, the ground was cursed, man was cursed,

and the animal kingdom was cursed. When Jesus comes to reign, the curse on the ground will be lifted.

"The wilderness and the solitary place shall be glad for them; and the desert shall rejoice, and blossom as the rose. It shall blossom abundantly, and rejoice even with joy and singing: the glory of Lebanon shall be given unto it, the excellency of Carmel and Sharon, they shall see the glory of the Lord, and the excellency of our God."—Isa. 35:1, 2.

Here the Bible teaches that the curse will be lifted from the ground.

2. The curse will also be lifted from animal nature.

"The wolf also shall dwell with the lamb, and the leopard shall lie down with the kid; and the calf and the young lion and the fatling together; and a little child shall lead them. And the cow and the bear shall feed; their young ones shall lie down together: and the lion shall eat straw like the ox. And the sucking child shall play on the hole of the asp [a very poisonous snake]*, and the weaned child shall put his hand on the cockatrice' den. They shall not hurt nor destroy in all my holy mountain: for the earth shall be full of the knowledge of the Lord, as the waters cover the sea."*—Isa. 11:6-9.

Try putting a leopard and a kid together today and see what happens! But during the reign of Christ, the leopard and kid shall lie down together. The wolf and the lamb shall dwell together. And "the calf and the young lion and the fatling together." Notice this: "and a little child shall lead them"— the wolf, the lamb, the leopard, the kid, the bear, the young lion and the fatling. Wild animals, such as lions and tigers, will be like house cats during the millennial reign of Christ.

3. During Christ's reign "the earth shall be full of the knowledge of the Lord, as the waters cover the sea."

When I was a little boy in a country church, I recall singing:

> **The kingdom is coming, O tell me the story,**
> **God's banner exalted shall be!**

The earth shall be full of His knowledge and glory,
As waters that cover the sea.

But I had no idea what it meant. When Jesus Christ comes to reign, the earth will be filled with the knowledge of the Lord.

4. The curse will be lifted from human bodies. Isaiah 35:5, 6:

"Then the eyes of the blind shall be opened, and the ears of the deaf shall be unstopped. Then shall the lame man leap as a hart, and the tongue of the dumb sing: for in the wilderness shall waters break out, and streams in the desert."

According to Isaiah 65:20, men will live to be a thousand years old. "There shall be no more thence an infant of days, nor an old man that hath not filled his days: for **the child shall die a hundred years old.**" If a man dies at a hundred years old, he will be considered still a child! Man's life span will certainly be increased.

5. During the millennial reign of Christ there will be no more poverty.

"And they shall build houses, and inhabit them; and they shall plant vineyards, and eat the fruit of them. They shall not build, and another inhabit; they shall not plant, and another eat: for as the days of a tree are the days of my people, and mine elect [Israel] *shall long enjoy the work of their hands."*—Isa. 65:21, 22.

In Micah 4:4 the Bible says, "But they shall sit every man under his vine and under his fig tree; and none shall make them afraid: for the mouth of the Lord of hosts hath spoken it."

Friends, it will be a blessed time when Jesus returns to this earth, takes His rightful place on David's throne, and rules the nations with a rod of iron.

6. Satan will be chained and bound during the reign of Christ.

"I saw an angel come down from heaven, having the key of the bottomless pit and a great chain in his hand. And he laid hold on the dragon, that old serpent, which is the Devil, and Satan, and bound him a thousand years, And cast him into the bot-

tomless pit, and shut him up, and set a seal upon him, that he should deceive the nations no more, till the thousand years should be fulfilled."—Rev. 20:1-3.

Some say Satan is already bound. But a wise friend of mine said, "If he is bound, he is bound to me." When another fellow said, "He is already chained," someone suggested that if he is, he is on an awfully long chain.

No, Satan is not yet bound. He is called "the god of this world" (II Cor. 4:4). But when Jesus comes to reign, Satan will be chained and cast into the bottomless pit; a seal will be placed upon him; and he will deceive the nations no more until the thousand years are finished.

A number of other things will happen during the reign of Christ. I can only mention them.

7. Jerusalem will be the center of worship and knowledge for the whole earth (Micah 4:1, 2).

8. There will be no more wars. Men shall beat their swords into plowshares, according to Micah 4:3.

9. All Israel will know the Lord (Rom. 11:26).

10. Christ will reign on David's throne—the actual, literal throne from which David reigned.

11. Christians will reign with Him. Revelation 3:21 says, "To him that overcometh will I grant to sit with me in my throne, even as I also overcame, and am set down with my Father in his throne."

IV. THE PREPARATIONS FOR HIS COMING

In light of the fact that Jesus Christ is coming and could come for His own at any moment, I want to say two things.

First, if you have not accepted Jesus Christ as your personal Saviour, please trust Him today. There are two groups in the world today—the saved and the lost. If Jesus came in the next five minutes, everybody who has trusted Christ as Saviour would leave the earth.

Luke 17:34-36 says:

"I tell you, in that night there shall be two men in one bed; the one shall be taken, and the other shall be left. Two women shall be grinding together; the one shall be taken, and the other left. Two men shall be in the field; the one shall be taken, and the other left."

That is not spiritually speaking; that is actually, literally so. There will be two people at a mill grinding; one will leave and the other will be left behind. There will be two people in a field working; one will leave and the other will be left behind.

I have heard preachers spiritualize this passage and say that means the new man inside will leave and the old body will be left behind. But the Bible does not teach that the bodies of believers will be left behind. As a matter of fact, it teaches that the body will be changed, not left. Says Philippians 3:20, 21:

"For our conversation [citizenship] is in heaven; from whence also we look for the Saviour, the Lord Jesus Christ: Who shall change our vile body, that it may be fashioned like unto his glorious body."

It says nothing about getting a new body and leaving the old one; it says *this* vile body will be changed.

I'm afraid some of our doctrine is based on words we have heard in song. I remember singing,

> **This robe of flesh I'll drop, and rise**
> **To seize the everlasting prize.**

But we will not drop this robe of flesh and rise. This robe of flesh will be changed "in a moment, in the twinkling of an eye," and made exactly like Jesus' body.

First John 3:2, "Beloved, now are we the sons of God, and it doth not yet appear what we shall be: but we know that, when he shall appear, we shall be like him; for we shall see him as he is." So, when the Bible says "two men shall be in the field; the one shall be taken, and the other left," that does not mean the spiritual man inside the body will leave and the body will be left. It means exactly what it says: there will be two in a field; one will be taken and the other left.

When the trumpet sounds, the saved will be caught up to meet the Lord in the air and the unsaved will be left. The unsaved who are left could be divided into two groups: those who have heard the Gospel and had an opportunity to be saved, and those who have never heard the Gospel and have not had an opportunity to be saved. Those who have heard the Gospel and could have trusted Christ as Saviour but rejected Him will have their destiny sealed. A person who heard the Gospel and had an opportunity to be saved before the rapture of the church will not have an opportunity to be saved after the rapture. But those who had never heard the Gospel will have such an opportunity.

Notice II Thessalonians 2:7, 8:

"For the mystery of iniquity doth already work: only he who now letteth [hindereth] will let [hinder], until he be taken out of the way. And then shall that Wicked be revealed, whom the Lord shall consume with the spirit of his mouth, and shall destroy with the brightness of his coming."

Verse 10 continues,

"And with all deceivableness of unrighteousness in them that perish; [notice] BECAUSE they received not the love of the truth, that they might be saved."

Why do they perish? Because they "received not the love of the truth, that they might be saved."

Now, notice verses 11 and 12: "And for this cause God shall send them strong delusion, that they should believe a lie: That they all might be damned who believed not the truth, but had pleasure in unrighteousness."

Here the Bible says those who heard the Gospel but "received not the love of the truth, that they might be saved," would be sent a strong delusion "because they received not the love of the truth, that they might be saved." They are sent a strong delusion "that they should believe a lie: That they all might be damned who believed not the truth, but had pleasure in unrighteousness."

There are two groups in the world at this moment: the saved and the lost. If Jesus comes in the next five minutes, the saved will be caught out; the unsaved will be left behind. The unsaved who have heard the Gospel and had an opportunity to be saved will be given a "strong delusion, that they should believe a lie: That they all might be damned who believed not the truth, but had pleasure in unrighteousness." When they had an opportunity to trust Christ, they rejected Him; therefore the Bible says their destiny is sealed. On the other hand, those who never heard the Gospel and never had an opportunity to be saved would be given such an opportunity during the tribulation period.

This is not what some call a second chance for salvation, because these precious people never had the first chance. During the tribulation period, the Bible teaches that 144,000 born-again, blood-washed missionaries will preach the Gospel all over the world, and then many will be saved. In Revelation 7:14 the Bible speaks of those who "came out of great tribulation, and have washed their robes, and made them white in the blood of the Lamb." These are tribulation saints, those who trust Christ during the tribulation.

Let me remind you again that if you have heard the Gospel, and had an opportunity to trust Christ, you will not have an opportunity to be saved after the rapture of the church. If you have never trusted Christ as your personal Saviour, please trust Him today. In the words of Matthew 24:44, "Therefore be ye also ready: for in such an hour as ye think not the Son of man cometh." It could be today. If you are a Christian then, ". . .abide in him; that, when he shall appear, we may have confidence, and not be ashamed before him at his coming" (I John 2:28). Live for Christ that you may meet Him confidently and unashamedly.

The Believer's Threefold Judgment

CHAPTER SEVENTEEN

Past Judgment As a Sinner
Present Judgment As a Son
Future Judgment As a Servant

The believer's judgment is threefold—past, present and future. Our past judgment, as a believer, is our judgment for sin. Our present judgment is our judgment as a son. It is a self-judgment. And our future judgment is our judgment as a servant, when all Christians shall stand before the judgment seat of Christ to have our works tried by fire, according to I Corinthians 3:11-15.

I. THE BELIEVER'S PAST JUDGMENT: AS A SINNER

The Bible teaches that every sin we have ever committed—past, present and future—was laid on Christ two thousand years ago.

". . . the Lord hath laid on him the iniquity of us all."—Isa. 53:6.

"For he hath made him to be sin for us, who knew no sin; that

we might be made the righteousness of God in him."—II Cor. 5:21.

"Who his own self bare our sins in his own body on the tree."—I Pet. 2:24a.

Now, friends, two thousand years ago God took every sin you have ever committed or ever will commit and placed them on Christ, just like I lay my pencil on my Bible. "The Lord [that is, Jehovah, the Father in Heaven] hath laid on him [Jesus] the iniquity of us all" (Isa. 53:6).

It is difficult for the believer to understand how Jesus could die for his future sins. But, friends, when Jesus died, all your sins were future. God looked down through the telescope of time, saw every sin that you would ever commit, took those sins in one package and laid them on Christ. Christ actually became guilty for your sins; not that He was a sinner, but He bore your sins in His own body. While Jesus was bearing all your sins in His own body on the tree, He answered to God for them. And on the cross God actually treated Jesus just as He would have to treat the guilty sinner.

It is an interesting Bible study to read the story of the rich man in Hell, recorded in Luke 16, then the account of the crucifixion of Christ. As you go from one to the other, you discover that the experience of the rich man in Hell was a preview of Calvary and Calvary is a preview of Hell. In other words, on the cross Jesus suffered everything one would have to suffer if he died without Christ and spent eternity in Hell.

For instance, the rich man in Hell suffered the agony of separation. Abraham said to him, "Between us and you there is a great gulf fixed: so that they which would pass from hence to you cannot; neither can they pass to us, that would come from thence."

Then, on the cross, Jesus suffered the agony of separation from God. While hanging on the cross, He uttered seven things. Three utterances came before the darkness, three after the darkness, and one during the darkness. That utterance was, "My God, my God, why hast thou forsaken me?"

Jesus Christ was separated from God. Not only did the rich

man suffer the agony of separation; he suffered also the agony of thirst, crying, "Send Lazarus, that he may dip the tip of his finger in water, and cool my tongue; for I am tormented in this flame."

On the cross, Jesus Christ suffered the agony of thirst. The fifth cross utterance was, "I THIRST."

The man in Hell suffered the agony of darkness. We read concerning the wicked, "Bind him hand and foot, and take him away, and cast him into outer darkness; there shall be weeping and gnashing of teeth" (Matt. 22:13).

On the cross, Jesus suffered the very darkness of Hell. Between 12:00 noon and 3:00 in the afternoon, it became as black as an Egyptian midnight, so black you could feel it.

On the cross, Jesus Christ suffered everything that men will have to suffer if they die without Christ and go to Hell. Otherwise, He has not fully paid my sin debt. He did pay it.

He not only from the cross uttered, "I thirst," and "My God, my God, why hast thou forsaken me?" but He shouted, "It is finished!" That means nothing can be added nor taken from it; it is complete. When Jesus Christ died on the cross, He made full payment for the believer's sins. He suffered everything that we should have to suffer. He satisfied the just demands of a holy God and paid in full what we sinners owe.

I once heard a man say that nobody will ever know how much Jesus suffered on the cross except those who go to Hell. That sounded reasonable to me and I believed it. But after several years I changed my mind, because even those who go to Hell will not fully know what He suffered on the cross. Here is what I mean.

The suffering of Jesus was enough to pay in full what every sinner owes. He could justly cry out from the cross, "It is finished!" Men who go to Hell will be paying on the sin debt forever but will never suffer enough to pay in full. Men in Hell can never cry, "It is finished!" because it will never be finished.

John 3:36 says, "He that believeth not the Son shall not see life; but the wrath of God abideth on him." You cannot couple annihilation with abiding wrath. Men will be in Hell forever and ever and ever and ever paying on the sin debt, but will never get it paid completely.

On the cross, Jesus Christ paid in full what the sinner owes. The Bible says in Hebrews 9:26, "Once in the end of the world hath he appeared to put away sin by the sacrifice of himself." Since Jesus Christ died on the cross for our sins, we believers will never face God in judgment for sin. God will never again deal with me as a sinner. All His dealings will be as a son.

You say, "But there will be a judgment." Yes, there will be, "For we must all appear before the judgment seat of Christ" (II Cor. 5:10). Yes, believers will be judged, but they will not be judged for sin. The moment you trust Jesus Christ as Saviour, you are justified. "Therefore being justified by faith, we have peace with God through our Lord Jesus Christ" (Rom. 5:1).

That verse means God wipes your slate clean, and you stand before God as if you had never in your life committed a single sin. And if you were to die and go to Heaven and there remind God of some sin you had committed, He would remind you of this verse: "I, even I, am he that blotteth out thy transgressions for mine own sake, and will not remember thy sins" (Isa. 43:25). God forgets our sins.

When you trust Christ, the sin question is forever settled. Jesus Christ took care of your sins by bearing them in His own body on the tree; and God judged Jesus Christ in your place, as your Substitute. The result of that judgment was death to Jesus Christ and justification to the believer. Our judgment for sin is past.

I hear some argue, "Yes, but if we sin after we are saved, we must pay for it!"

Dear friends, if we had to pay for any sin we ever committed, whether small or great, we would have to spend eternity in Hell. God has only one payment for sin. In Genesis 2:17 He said to Adam, "In the day that thou eatest thereof thou shalt surely die." And in Ezekiel 18:4, "The soul that sinneth, it shall die." And in Romans 6:23, "The wages of sin is death." God's one and only payment for sin is death. And if we had to answer to God for any sin, no matter how small, we would have to go to Hell and stay there forever and ever. That is God's price for sin, and God never alters that price because He is immutable. He never changes; therefore, His price for sin never changes.

You ask, "What if the believer sins after he is saved? Doesn't God chastise the believer?"

Yes. "For whom the Lord loveth he chasteneth, and scourgeth every son whom he receiveth" (Heb. 12:6). But, friends, chastening is not payment for sin.

If I spanked my son for breaking a window, the spanking, or chastening, would not be payment for the window. After I had spanked him, I would take money out of my pocket and pay for the window to be replaced. And when God chastises the believer, it is not payment for sin, because Jesus Christ paid for all your sin two thousand years ago at Calvary; and, as a believer, you will never answer to God for any sin. You will be chastened; but the chastening is child training, not payment for sin.

II. THE BELIEVER'S PRESENT JUDGMENT: AS A SON

Since the believer's judgment for sin is past, does that mean he can live loosely, sinfully and immorally, and get by? Certainly not. And here is where the second phase of the believer's judgment comes in. I call it his judgment as a son, a present judgment, a self-judgment.

"For if we would judge ourselves, we should not be judged. But when we are judged, we are chastened of the Lord, that we should not be condemned with the world."—I Cor. 11:31, 32.

Now if we judge ourselves, we will not be judged. But if we do not judge ourselves, then we are judged of God and chastened that we should not be condemned with the world. Every believer should constantly look into his life to see what is wrong, then face his sins, confess them, and obtain forgiveness and cleansing.

David prayed in Psalm 139:23, 24, "Search me, O God, and know my heart: try me, and know my thoughts: And see if there be any wicked way in me, and lead me in the way everlasting." The Scandinavian word for "search" literally means ransack. David said, "Ransack my heart. Look under every corner of the rug. Pull out every drawer in the chiffonier. See if there is secret sin in my heart or any wicked way in me."

Friends, the believer is constantly to judge himself. "But let a man examine himself" (I Cor. 11:28). The purpose of this self-examination is to face up to sin and confess it that we may obtain forgiveness and cleansing.

"My little children, these things write I unto you, that ye sin not. And if any man sin, we have an advocate with the Father, Jesus Christ the righteous: And he is the propitiation [or atoning sacrifice] *for our sins: and not for our's only, but also for the sins of the whole world."*—I John 2:1, 2.

We are told not to sin; but if we do sin, we have an Advocate—Jesus Christ.

"If we say that we have no sin, we deceive ourselves, and the truth is not in us. If we confess our sins, he is faithful and just to forgive us our sins, and to cleanse us from all unrighteousness."—I John 1:8, 9.

I suppose one of the most difficult things for the believer is to honestly face his sins. In reading through the Bible, I find there are at least four things Christians do about their sins. First, they blame someone else. In the beginning, God gave Adam one prohibition:

"Of every tree of the garden thou mayest freely eat. . . . But of the tree of the knowledge of good and evil, thou shalt not eat of it: for in the day that thou eatest thereof thou shalt surely die."—Gen. 2:16, 17.

Now, when Adam sinned God came on the scene. "Adam, hast

thou eaten of the tree, whereof I commanded thee that thou shouldest not eat?" Immediately Adam responded, "The woman whom thou gavest to be with me, she gave me of the tree, and I did eat."

Someone rightly suggested that Adam was the world's first buckpasser. "It wasn't me; it was the woman You gave to me." He tried to excuse his sin by blaming his wife, Eve. Ultimately he blamed God because he said, "The woman whom thou gavest to be with me. . . . " When we sin, it is so easy to blame someone else.

Some time back I was preaching in a small church. My wife was with me. After the service, I realized I did not have the car keys. "Honey, do you have the car keys?" I asked.

"Oh, no. I gave them to you." She insisted that she had given me the keys. I insisted she did not. This went on back and forth, back and forth for several minutes. After a while I got out of the car, looked around and to my surprise saw the keys in the car door. I had just used them to unlock the car!

Was I embarrassed! Could I have gotten by with it, I believe I would have put the keys in her purse and accused her of misplacing them! I hated to face the fact that I was guilty.

It is difficult to say, "I have sinned." In the Bible, some blame others for their sins, while still others excuse their sins.

Take the case of Saul. Though he was instructed to slay utterly, when he came back he had some prize cattle and sheep and the king he had spared in war. When the man of God asked, "Did you obey God?" "Oh, yes!" Saul said. Then when the cattle began to low, and the sheep began to bleat, the prophet said, "What meaneth then this bleating of the sheep in mine ears, and the lowing of the oxen which I hear?" Saul tried to excuse his sin by saying, "The people spared the best of the sheep and of the oxen, to sacrifice unto the Lord thy God. . . . "

I heard about a woman who went to the preacher and said, "You must pray for me. I have a cross to bear."

"What is it?" asked the preacher.

"A bad temper," she replied.

"Nonsense," replied the preacher, "you don't have a cross to bear. You have a sin. Your husband has a cross to bear."

He was right.

There are those who blame someone else for their sin and those who excuse sin.

Then there are others who try to cover their sins. "He that covereth his sins shall not prosper" (Prov. 28:13).

How many attempts have been made to cover sin!

Not long ago I was with a church in South Carolina, and the pastor told me a funny little story that illustrates this point. A man was remodeling his home. He had a thin temporary wall in the bathroom. One day the children were wrestling and one of them fell through the wall and knocked a hole large enough for a child to walk through.

When the man came home and found the hole in the wall, he lined each of the children up and asked, "Did you knock that hole in the wall?"

"Oh, no," said the first child. He was dismissed.

To the second he asked, "Did you knock the hole in the wall?"

"Oh, no!" And he was dismissed.

And so with the other children until he came to the last little fellow, "Son, did you knock that hole in the wall?"

The little fellow who was not over two or three years old, asked, "What hole?" Man, the hole was big enough to slide the bathtub through, but that kid tried to cover it up!

When I was a child, I used to close my eyes and think no one could see me. I figured since I could not see myself, no one else could see me. We may close our eyes, but we cannot cover our sins.

Something else we can do about our sins is confess them. "If we confess our sins, he is faithful and just to forgive us our sins, and to cleanse us from all unrighteousness" (I John 1:9).

I must face my sin honestly and confess it. Maybe it is a sin of neglect. Then I say, "Dear Lord, I have failed to read my

Bible as I should. You promised if I would confess it, You would forgive and cleanse me; and You cannot lie." That's confessing and claiming the forgiveness and cleansing God promises in the Bible.

God not only forgives our sin when we confess it, but He cleanses it. In other words, He does away with it. It is one thing to forgive a child for falling into the mud. It is another thing to give that child a bath and fix him back like he was before he fell into the mud. That is forgiveness **and cleansing.**

Dear friend, when you come to Christ and confess your sin, wanting forgiveness, God not only forgives but cleanses. And the Bible says He is "just to forgive us our sins, and to cleanse us." He is just to forgive us because He bore that sin in His body two thousand years ago at Calvary. He doesn't sacrifice His justice in forgiving our sins, because justice was satisfied when He died at Calvary.

Somebody said the word "forgiveness" means literally to bear the burden. If you owe a man $1,000 and he forgives the debt, it means he bears the burden. When Jesus Christ forgives your sins, He bears the burden. The sin that you might commit tomorrow—He died for that one. If you sin after you are saved, it doesn't destroy your sonship, only your fellowship. "If we walk in the light, as he is in the light, we have fellowship one with another, and the blood of Jesus Christ his Son cleanseth us from all sin" (I John 1:7). As we keep our sins confessed, we keep fellowship with Christ.

Martin Luther once said, "Keep short accounts with God." By that he meant: Don't let sin pile up in your life. Don't let a day go by without confessing every known sin for the purpose of obtaining forgiveness and cleansing.

If you go to bed night after night without confessing sin, you allow it, like a brush pile, to accumulate in your life. And it is not easy to sweep it away with one prayer meeting. Remember, God's way to obtain forgiveness and cleansing is:

1. Be honest with God about your sins.

2. Confess your sins.

3. Claim the forgiveness and cleansing that God promised (I John 1:9).

4. Rest assured that any confessed sin is forgiven and cleansed because God promised and He cannot lie (Heb. 6:18).

Now, what happens if the believer does not judge himself? Let I Corinthians 11:31, 32 answer: "If we would judge ourselves, we should not be judged. But when we are judged, we are chastened of the Lord, that we should not be condemned with the world."

I don't have time in this message to share with you exactly what form the chastening of the Lord takes; but the Bible says if we refuse to judge ourselves, then we are judged of the Lord and chastened that we should not be condemned with the world.

I simply say this: the chastening sometimes takes the form of sickness. But that is not to say that all sickness is a result of sin. Sometimes it is, as in the case of I Corinthians 11:30; and sometimes it is not, as is the case of the blind boy in John 9:1-3. The chastening sometimes takes the form of financial reverses. Sometimes it is the loss of loved ones. In the case of King David who committed adultery with Bathsheba, it was the loss of a child and later problems with some of his other children.

Chastening takes various forms. It can mean premature death for the believer if he continues in willful, habitual sin (I Cor. 11:30; I Cor. 5:5). Someone has suggested that He speaks, spanks and calls Home.

IV. THE BELIEVER'S FUTURE JUDGMENT: AS A SERVANT

The believer's judgment as a sinner is past, and it resulted in the death of Jesus Christ and justification of the believer. His judgment as a son is present and is a self-judgment. The result of this judgment is when we confess our sins, God forgives and cleanses us; or when we fail to confess our sins, we are judged of the Lord and chastened.

The third phase of the believer's judgment is future. This is his judgment as a servant.

"For other foundation can no man lay than that is laid, which is Jesus Christ. Now if any man build upon this foundation gold, silver, precious stones, wood, hay, stubble; Every man's work shall be made manifest: for the day shall declare it, because it shall be revealed by fire; and the fire shall try every man's work of what sort it is. If any man's work abide which he hath built thereupon, he shall receive a reward. If any man's work shall be burned, he shall suffer loss: but he himself shall be saved; yet so as by fire." —I Cor. 3:11-15.

Now notice something very carefully in this passage. The Bible says nothing here about man being judged for his sins. Look at verse 13: "Every man's *work* shall be made manifest," not his sins. When a person trusts Jesus Christ as Saviour, the sin question is forever settled. This future judgment is for the believer's works. It is a judgment for our service. It is our judgment as a servant. "Every man's *work* shall be made manifest."

"If any man's *work* abide which he hath built thereupon..." (vs. 14). "If any man's *work* shall be burned, he shall suffer loss: but he himself shall be saved; yet so as by fire" (vs. 15).

You ask, "Do we work to be saved?" Oh, no.

D. L. Moody said,

> **I would not work my soul to save,**
> **For this my Lord hath done;**
> **But I would work like any slave,**
> **For love of His dear Son.**

"For we are his workmanship, created in Christ Jesus unto good works" (Eph. 2:10). God expects every believer to work. We are all to serve Christ. Now we don't all have the same opportunities, but God expects everyone to do something.

Somewhere I read this sign:

> I am only one, but I am one. I cannot do everything, but I can do something. What I can do, I ought to do; and what I ought to do, by the grace of God, I will do.

Now, friends, there are people you can reach with the Gospel whom I cannot reach. You have some service you can render that I cannot render. Every person should be doing what he can for the Lord. The measure of Christian service is found in that little expression in Mark 14:8, where it says of Mary of Bethany, "She hath done what she could." All God expects any of us to do is just what we can. One of the most frustrated persons in the world is the man whose ambitions exceed his abilities. Do what you can. Mary of Bethany did what she could.

Could you visit the jails? Could you distribute Bible tracts? Could you sing in the choir? Could you help keep the church building clean? Could you work as an usher? Could you drive a bus or visit on a bus route? There is some work you can do. Every believer is going to stand before God at the judgment seat of Christ and be judged as a servant. "For we must all appear before the judgment seat of Christ" (II Cor. 5:10). Your work will be tried.

Now notice something in verse 13: "The fire shall try every man's work of what *sort* it is." It says nothing about size, but it says something about sort. Quality is the important thing. The motive behind the service is important. Fire doesn't measure size; it tests quality. If He were trying for size, He would use a tape measure or scales; but it is tried by fire. The Bible says, "It shall be revealed by fire; and the fire shall try every man's *work*."

Did you know that service not motivated by love for Christ will not be rewarded at the judgment seat of Christ? The Bible says in I Corinthians 13:3, "Though I bestow all my goods to feed the poor, and though I give my body to be burned, and have not charity [or love], it profiteth me nothing." Paul said, "I could give all my goods to feed the poor, cash in my stocks and bonds, draw all my money out of the bank, sell all my real estate, give it all to feed the poor, be burned at the stake, and die a martyr's death; but if I have not love it profiteth me nothing."

The Lord is not only interested in what you do; He is also

interested in why you do it. Did you perform that service for the glory you received? Then you have your reward. Did you make that gift to be seen of men and to receive the praise of men? Then you have your reward. Or did you do it because you love Christ? If love motivated you, then you will be rewarded at the judgment seat of Christ.

Notice what the Bible says in I Corinthians 3:14, 15:

"If any man's work abide which he hath built thereupon, he shall receive a reward. If any man's work shall be burned, he shall suffer loss: but he himself shall be saved; yet so as by fire."

This is not a judgment to determine whether a man is saved or lost. This is a judgment of works, of service, to determine the believer's reward. Notice that neither man goes to Hell from this judgment. Both are saved. One man's works abide, and he receives a reward. The other man's works are burned, and he suffers loss; but the Bible says he is saved, "yet so as by fire." Both men are saved: one is rewarded, one suffers loss.

That word "reward" means payment for service rendered. That is not Heaven. I have heard preachers say at a funeral service, "Our dearly beloved has gone to his reward." Heaven is not a reward but a gift. Salvation is also a gift. Heaven was bought and paid for at Calvary two thousand years ago. And when a man dies, he does not go to his reward, because that does not come until after the judgment seat of Christ. And this judgment will not take place until the coming of Christ.

"Therefore judge nothing before the time, until the Lord come, who both will bring to light the hidden things of darkness, and will make manifest the counsels of the hearts: and then shall every man have praise of God." —I Cor. 4:5.

The Bible says God will judge the quick (living) and the dead at His appearing (II Tim. 4:1). The bodies of Christians who have gone on to be with Christ will be raised; the living saints will be changed and caught up with them to meet the Lord in the air, then all believers will appear before the judgment seat of Christ.

Second Corinthians 5:10 tells us, "For we must all appear before the judgment seat of Christ." The little pronoun "we" is found 26 times in that 5th chapter and each time refers to believers. We—every believer—must stand before the judgment seat of Christ, and our works will be tried. If our works abide, we will receive a reward; if our works are burned, we will suffer loss; but we will be saved "yet so as by fire" (I Cor. 3:14, 15).

The Bible mentions five different crowns that will be given at the judgment seat of Christ.

The incorruptible crown:

"And every man that striveth for the mastery is temperate in all things. Now they do it to obtain a corruptible crown; but we an incorruptible."—I Cor. 9:25.

This crown is for those believers who keep their bodies under subjection, who refuse to yield to the flesh, who do not live carnally, fleshly or worldly. Such a believer will receive the incorruptible crown at the judgment seat of Christ.

The crown of rejoicing:

"For what is our hope, or joy, or crown of rejoicing? Are not even ye in the presence of our Lord Jesus Christ at his coming? For ye are our glory and joy."—I Thess. 2:19, 20.

This crown is for the soul winner. Paul says of those he had won to Christ, "You are our crown of rejoicing." This crown will only be given to those who win souls.

The crown of righteousness:

"Henceforth there is laid up for me a crown of righteousness, which the Lord, the righteous judge shall give me at that day: and not to me only, but unto all them also that love his appearing."—II Tim. 4:8.

This crown is given to those who love the second coming of Christ, those who love His appearing.

By the way, we should distinguish between our disappearing and His appearing. Some folks are anxious for Christ to come simply to get away from their troubles, from under the pressure. They love their disappearing, but I am not sure they love His appearing. The crown of righteousness is for those who love His appearing.

The crown of glory, mentioned in I Peter 5:4: "And when the chief Shepherd shall appear, ye shall receive a crown of glory that fadeth not away."

This is the pastor or elder's crown, or for the person who surrenders himself for full-time Christian service and serves God faithfully.

"Feed the flock of God which is among you, taking the oversight thereof, not by constraint, but willingly; not for filthy lucre, but of a ready mind; Neither as being lords over God's heritage, but being ensamples to the flock. And when the chief Shepherd shall appear, ye shall receive a crown of glory that fadeth not away." —I Pet. 5:2-4.

The crown of life:

"Blessed is the man that endureth temptation: for when he is tried, he shall receive the crown of life, which the Lord hath promised to them that love him." —James 1:12.

"Fear none of those things which thou shalt suffer: behold, the devil shall cast some of you into prison, that ye may be tried; and ye shall have tribulation ten days: be thou faithful unto death, and I will give thee a crown of life." —Rev. 2:10.

The crown of life is the martyr's crown, given to those who sacrifice their lives for their testimony.

Now what will the believer do if he is rewarded with different crowns?

The Bible says,

"The four and twenty elders fall down before him that sat on the throne, and worship him that liveth for ever and ever, and cast their crowns before the throne, saying, Thou art worthy, O Lord, to receive glory and honour and power: for thou hast created

all things, and for thy pleasure they are and were created." — Rev. 4:10, 11.

These elders cast their crowns at the Saviour's feet. Perhaps believers, too, will stand before Christ and cast their crowns at His feet. But whatever the case may be, you will stand before the judgment seat of Christ and be judged for your work. You will be judged as a servant and either receive a reward, which will be in the form of five different crowns; or you will suffer loss. I don't believe believers will stand at the judgment seat of Christ, see their works burned, go up in smoke, and then shout and thank God for a life of unfruitful service.

Dear friends, what time you have ought to be spent wisely in serving Christ. As Mary of Bethany, do what you can. "Now, little children, abide in him; that, when he shall appear, we may have confidence, and not be ashamed before him at his coming" (I John 2:28).

Jesus is coming. If you have never trusted Him as your Saviour, then do it today. If you have trusted Him, then set out to be the best Christian you can possibly be.

Deciding Questionable Things for Believers

CHAPTER EIGHTEEN

"*For one believeth that he may eat all things: another, who is weak, eateth herbs. Let not him that eateth despise him that eateth not; and let not him which eateth not judge him that eateth: for God hath received him.*"—Rom. 14:2, 3.

"*One man esteemeth one day above another: another esteemeth every day alike. Let every man be fully persuaded in his own mind.*" —Rom. 14:5.

This week I received a letter from an honest, sincere Christian wanting to know if a certain thing was right or wrong. In the letter he stated that he had searched the Bible and could not find a clear Bible verse regarding the matter; then he said, "It is my purpose to do right and have my family do right. I am honestly in a quandary, or I would not write and ask for help."

This dear Christian was absolutely right—there is no verse in the Bible that gives a clear answer to his question. But one must remember two things regarding the Bible.

First, it was written for all people of all ages; therefore, everything could not be spelled out in detail. For instance, if there were a verse in the Bible that stated, "Thou shalt not smoke Camels [Camel cigarettes]," those old rabbis would have had a difficult time interpreting the passage; and it is doubtful they would have ever figured out exactly what it meant. Some would probably make sure they never built a fire near their camel lest the smoke blow in his direction.

And suppose there were a verse in the Old Testament that said, "Thou shalt not watch TV." Then those rabbis would have spent hours discussing what TV meant, and it is doubtful they would have ever reached an agreement. So since the Bible was written for all men of all ages, many things are not clearly spelled out.

Second, the Bible is a condensed Book. Let me explain what I mean.

The Scripture says in John 21:25, "And there are also many other things which Jesus did, the which, if they should be written every one, I suppose that even the world itself could not contain the books that should be written." So had everything Jesus did been written in books, no one would ever find time to read them all. God chose to reveal to Bible writers what He wanted men to know. The Bible is not a revelation of what God knows, but a revelation of what God wants men to know. If it were a revelation of what God knew, again the world could not contain the books, because there is nothing God doesn't know. He is omniscient.

Someone said, "Did it ever occur to you that nothing ever occurred to God?"

Since the Bible does not give detailed answers to every question the believer will ever face, then what does he do regarding things not spelled out in the Scriptures? It is often suggested that the Christian let his conscience be his guide. I have heard preachers say, "Follow your conscience," but this is not good advice. One's conscience is regulated by what he believes; and if he doesn't believe right, his conscience will mislead him.

For instance, a Catholic friend's conscience may bother him

if he doesn't attend Mass because he believes he should attend; but my conscience never bothers me for not attending Mass, and I have never attended. The difference is, I don't believe I should attend.

So you cannot follow your conscience nor let your conscience be your guide. The Bible never says, "Follow your conscience."

If one cannot follow his conscience and the Bible does not give detailed, clear instructions regarding every question the believer faces, then what is the Christian to do regarding questionable things?

Now while the Bible does not give all the specific details regarding what a Christian should and should not do, it does give guidelines by which every honest Christian can make the right decision regarding questionable things. In this message I wish to share eleven guidelines that will help the believer in deciding whether a thing is right or wrong.

I. ARE YOU WILLING TO DO WHAT IS RIGHT ONCE YOU KNOW GOD'S WILL?

We are the servants, and God is the Master. It is not the servant's duty to guess what the Master wants; it is only his duty to obey once the Master makes His will clear. When the believer doesn't know whether a certain matter is right or wrong, he should decide firmly and clearly that he will do God's will even if it goes against his wishes. John 7:17 promises, "If any man will do his will, he shall know of the doctrine." One cannot approach God with the attitude, *Lord, let me know whether this is right or wrong, and I will decide if I will do what is right.* He must have the attitude, *Lord, I don't know whether this is right or wrong; but if you will let me know for sure, I will do right regardless of what others say or what my preferences are.*

The person who wants God's very best for his life and will do what is right can know God's will regarding questionable things. But if you are not willing to do the right thing once you know it, then the rest of the guidelines are useless.

II. DOES IT AGREE WITH ALL THE SCRIPTURE HAS TO SAY ON THE SUBJECT?

The Bible says in II Peter 1:20, "Knowing this first, that no prophecy of the scripture is of any private interpretation." This verse does not mean that one cannot sit down in private and read and study his Bible. It simply means that one passage of Scripture is not to be isolated and interpreted without considering all that the Bible has to say on the same subject.

For instance, there may be a passage that seems to teach one thing; but a careful study of the Scriptures reveals many other clear passages that seem to contradict the obscure passage.

An example is found in Hebrews 6:4-6 which seems to teach that one could be lost after he is saved. If we had only this passage, we might not believe in eternal security; but when you study what other Scriptures say regarding eternal security, the matter becomes clear.

Verse after verse states that the believer has everlasting life—verses such as John 3:16, 3:36, and 3:14. Nothing can be clearer than John 5:24, "Verily, verily, I say unto you, He that heareth my word, and believeth on him that sent me, hath everlasting life, and shall not come into condemnation; but is passed from death unto life." Here the Bible not only states that the believer has everlasting life but promises that he shall not come into condemnation, that is, he will never again be under the sentence of sin.

A good rule to follow is: never use an obscure passage to contradict several clear passages. So whatever Hebrews 6:4-6 means, it certainly does not contradict the clear passages which teach the believer has everlasting or eternal life.

When the honest, sincere Christian is faced with the decision regarding whether a thing is right or wrong, he should ask, *Does it agree with all that the Scripture has to say on the subject?*

III. HAVE YOU PRAYED ABOUT IT?

Dr. A. J. Gordon once said, "There is more you can do after

you pray, but there is nothing more you can do until you pray."

The Bible indicates that we are to pray about all things. Philippians 4:6 says, "Be careful for nothing; but in every thing by prayer and supplication with thanksgiving let your requests be made known unto God." Again the Scripture promises, "What things soever ye desire, when ye pray, believe that ye receive them, and ye shall have them" (Mark 11:24). The expression, "What things soever ye desire," would certainly include the believer's desire to know God's will about a questionable matter.

One of the saddest verses in the Bible to me is James 4:2: "Ye have not, because ye ask not." It doesn't say what we don't have; it just simply says we have not because we ask not. That would certainly include the leading of the Lord regarding a questionable matter. If we don't have clear leading, the Scripture says we have not because we ask not.

When praying for the Lord's will about something questionable, don't give up if you don't receive clear leading after one prayer; just keep on praying until God makes it clear. The promise in Matthew 7:8, "For every one that asketh receiveth," means to continually ask. Then when God answers, He will not answer in an audible voice; He will lead you by the Holy Spirit. Which brings me to the next question:

IV. DO YOU HAVE THE LEADING OF THE HOLY SPIRIT?

When things are not spelled out clearly in the Bible, we can expect the Holy Spirit to lead us. The Bible says in Romans 8:14, "For as many as are led by the Spirit of God, they are the sons of God." In the New Testament, the Holy Spirit directed God's servants where to preach and work.

Acts 13:1,2 says,

"Now there were in the church that was at Antioch certain prophets and teachers; as Barnabas, and Simeon that was called Niger, and Lucius of Cyrene, and Manaen, which had been brought up with Herod the tetrarch, and Saul. As they ministered to the Lord, and fasted, the Holy Ghost said, Separate me Bar-

nabas and Saul for the work whereunto I have called them."

Here is a clear case where the Holy Spirit led men to a certain place to preach and work.

There is another case where the Holy Spirit led men not to go to Asia. The Scripture says in Acts 16:6-8,

"Now when they had gone throughout Phrygia and the region of Galatia, and were forbidden of the Holy Ghost to preach the word in Asia, After they were come to Mysia, they assayed to go into Bithynia: but the Spirit suffered them not. And they passing by Mysia came down to Troas."

Here is a clear instance where the Holy Spirit forbade men to preach in a certain place.

Someone suggested that the stops as well as the steps of a good man are ordered by the Lord. The two Scripture references I have called attention to certainly indicate that truth.

The Holy Spirit leads us in prayer. The Bible says in Romans 8:26, "Likewise the Spirit also helpeth our infirmities: for we know not what we should pray for as we ought: but the Spirit itself maketh intercession for us with groanings which cannot be uttered." Here the Bible says there are times when we do not know what to pray for nor how to pray.

Recently I spoke at a gathering where many unsaved people were present. Afterwards I asked those who would trust Christ as Saviour to come forward and make a public declaration of their faith in Christ. Forty people responded.

After the service, a dear man came to me and said, "I didn't know how to express myself to the Lord. I knew I wanted to go to Heaven, but I didn't know how to tell Him I was trusting Him." After thanking me for leading him in a simple prayer, he said, "That is what I wanted to say all along but didn't know how to say it."

Most believers who have been saved any length of time have experienced times when the Holy Spirit gave definite leading regarding a matter. I remember such an experience.

Late one night while driving through the state of South Carolina, I passed a hitchhiker and had a strange feeling that I should give him a ride and try to lead him to Christ. But after reasoning that I was alone in the car and it may be dangerous to pick up a stranger, I passed him by. However, I couldn't get him off my mind. Somehow the Holy Spirit was leading me to go back and get him. Now I heard no audible voice. I simply felt that I had made a mistake in not giving the man a ride. I even prayed, "Dear Lord, I have already passed him now, and it may be several miles before I can find an exit where I can turn around and go back." But that inner feeling would not leave. Finally I found an exit, turned around and went back. To my surprise the hitchhiker was still there. I stopped and asked if I could give him a ride. "Sure," he said, and he got into the automobile.

We had been riding only a few seconds before I explained what had happened. I told him how I felt strangely led of the Holy Spirit to pick him up. I even told him how I had passed him by and turned around and come back. In a few moments, I explained the simple plan of salvation; and the man trusted Christ as Saviour. We had a wonderful time of fellowship; and he promised to find a Bible-believing church, join it, and set out to live the Christian life.

Now when I talk about the leading of the Holy Spirit, I am not talking about hearing an audible voice or having strange visions. The Holy Spirit leads through our desires. Philippians 2:13 states, "It is God which worketh in you both to will and to do of his good pleasure." That is, God works in us the desire and then gives us the power to make the desire a reality. Rest assured that the Holy Spirit will never lead you to do something contrary to scriptural principles. The Bible says, "All scripture is given by inspiration of God, and is profitable for doctrine, for reproof, for correction, for instruction in righteousness." Since all Scripture is given by the inspiration of the Holy Spirit, the Holy Spirit would not contradict Himself in leading someone contrary to the Bible.

In any matter where we have questions, we have a right to
ask the Holy Spirit to lead us and to expect His gentle guiding.

V. DOES IT PLEASE GOD?

The Bible says in I John 3:22, "And whatsoever we ask, we
receive of him, because we keep his commandments, and do those
things that are pleasing in his sight." It is possible for one to
keep His commandments, but what if there is no clear commandment regarding the matter in question? Some things are clearly commanded.

For instance, the Bible commands, "Thou shalt not kill. Thou
shalt not commit adultery. Thou shalt not steal. Thou shalt not
bear false witness," etc. But since there is no commandment that
says, "Thou shalt not listen to rock music," or, "Thou shalt not
dance," then what does the believer do? When there is no commandment to obey, then the question is, "Does it please God?"
The Scripture says, "We keep his commandments, and do those
things that are pleasing in his sight." Though there may be no
clear command regarding the matter in question, does it please
God? Can you honestly and sincerely say, "This thing I want
to do pleases God"? "The way I want to dress pleases God"? If
the Christian cannot honestly say yes, then he shouldn't do it.
The Scripture says in II Corinthians 5:9, "Wherefore we labour,
that, whether present or absent, we may be accepted of him."
The marginal rendering is "well pleasing to him." The Christian should never do anything unless he is thoroughly convinced
that it will please the Lord.

VI. CAN YOU DO IT IN THE NAME OF THE LORD JESUS?

Colossians 3:17 states, "And whatsoever ye do in word or deed,
do all in the name of the Lord Jesus, giving thanks to God and
the Father by him." Notice carefully the words, "whatsoever
ye do in word or deed." That covers every word the believer will
ever utter and anything the believer will ever do. And accord-

ing to the verse, we are to do it "in the name of the Lord Jesus."

Let's take the matter of dancing. There are perhaps some Christians who feel there is nothing wrong with the dance. But can you honestly dance in the name of the Lord Jesus?

Can you smoke cigarettes in the name of the Lord Jesus?

Can you curse in the name of the Lord Jesus?

Can you listen to music with suggestive lyrics in the name of the Lord Jesus?

When the believer is faced with a matter and can't decide whether it is right or wrong, he should simply ask, "Can I do it in the name of the Lord Jesus?" If not, then it is wrong.

VII. CAN YOU GIVE GOD THANKS FOR IT?

Again, Colossians 3:17 says, "And whatsoever ye do in word or deed, do all in the name of the Lord Jesus, giving thanks to God and the Father by him."

Whatever the matter in question, can you honestly thank God for it?

Peter Cartwright, that old camp-meeting preacher of yesteryear, was passing over the Cumberland Mountains when he was compelled to stop overnight at a house where there was to be a dance. Many of the people had never heard a sermon. Cartwright sat in one corner of the room watching the dance. He made up his mind to stay over the next day (Sunday) and preach to the people.

"I had hardly settled this point in my mind," says he, "when a beautiful young lady walked very gracefully up to me, dropped a handsome curtsy and, pleasantly, with winning smiles, invited me out to take a dance with her.

"I can hardly describe my thoughts or feeling on that occasion. However, in a moment I resolved on a desperate experiment. I rose as gracefully as I could; I will not say with some emotion, but with many emotions. The young lady moved to my right side; I grasped her right hand with my right hand, while she leaned her left arm on mine. In this position we walked on the floor. The whole company seemed pleased at this act of politeness in the young lady, shown to a stranger.

"The black man, who was the fiddler, began to put his fiddle in the best order. I then spoke to the fiddler to hold a moment and added that for several years I had not undertaken any matter of importance without first asking the blessing of God upon it, and I desired now to ask the blessing of God upon this beautiful young lady and the whole company that had shown such an act of politeness to a total stranger.

"Here I grasped the young lady's hand tightly and said, 'Let us all kneel down and pray,' and then instantly dropped on my knees and commenced praying with all the power of soul and body that I could command. The young lady tried to get loose from me, but I held her tight. Presently she fell on her knees. Some of the company kneeled, some stood, some fled, some sat still, all looked curious. The fiddler ran off into the kitchen, saying, 'Lord have mercy, what's de matter? What does dat mean?'

"While I prayed, some wept and wept aloud. Some cried for mercy. I rose from my knees and commenced an exhortation after which I sang a hymn. The young lady who invited me on the floor lay prostrate, crying for mercy. I exhorted again. I sang and prayed nearly all night.

"About fifteen of that company professed religion, and our meeting lasted next day and next night and as many more were powerfully converted. I organized a society, took thirty-two into the church, and sent them a preacher. My landlord was appointed leader, which post he held for many years. This was the commencement of a great and glorious revival of religion in that region of the country, and several of the young men converted at this Methodist preacher's dance became useful ministers of Jesus Christ."

Here is a case where an old-fashioned preacher prayed about a matter in question and the result was a revival meeting and the establishment of a church.

Take the matter of attending movies. The Bible does not say,

"Thou shalt not attend movies," but can I thank God for the movies? If I can't, then I should not attend. "Whatsoever ye do in word or deed, do all in the name of the Lord Jesus, giving thanks to God and the Father by him." If you cannot sincerely give thanks to God for the matter in question, then it is best not to do it.

VIII. DOES IT BRING GLORY TO GOD?

The Scripture admonishes in I Corinthians 10:31, "Whether therefore ye eat, or drink, or whatsoever ye do, do all to the glory of God." Whatsoever we do, we are to do it to the glory of God. That would involve anything the Christian wants to do or is ever tempted to do, and the question is, "Can I do it to the glory of God?"

One translation reads, "If you eat or drink or do anything else, do everything to honor God."

Does the thing you have a question about bring honor to God? Does it glorify God? Does it give God a good name? If not, then it is wrong. For whether we eat or drink or whatsoever we do, we are to do all to the glory of God, to honor God, to give God a good name.

Psalm 23:3 states, "He leadeth me in the paths of righteousness for his name's sake." We are Christians. We bear His name. Our lifestyle, language, attitudes, and manner of dress reflect on His name. He leads us in paths of righteousness for His name's sake. Unless you are honestly convinced that the thing in question will bring glory to God, then don't do it.

IX. DOES IT OFFEND OTHER CHRISTIANS?

Paul said in I Corinthians 8:13, "Wherefore, if meat make my brother to offend, I will eat no flesh while the world standeth, lest I make my brother to offend." In I Corinthians, chapter 8, the Scripture deals with meats and the limitations of Christian liberty. According to I Timothy 4:3-5, there is nothing unscriptural about eating meat:

*"Forbidding to marry, and commanding to abstain from meats,
which God hath created to be received with thanksgiving of them
which believe and know the truth. For every creature of God is
good, and nothing to be refused, if it be received with thanksgiving: For it is sanctified by the word of God and prayer."*

The Apostle Paul knew there was nothing wrong with eating
meats; however, he would not exercise his Christian liberty at
the expense of offending another brother. He refers to a weak
brother in I Corinthians 8:11 and again in Romans 14:2 where
he says, "For one believeth that he may eat all things: another,
who is weak, eateth herbs."

It is clear from these passages that some weaker Christians
thought eating meats was wrong; and, though Paul taught that
"every creature of God is good, and nothing to be refused, if it
be received with thanksgiving," he said, "If meat make my
brother to offend, I will eat no flesh while the world standeth,
lest I make my brother to offend." The Greek word translated
"offend" means "to trip up." One translation reads, "Therefore,
if food causes my brother to stumble, I will never eat meat again,
that I might not cause my brother to stumble."

Now when I ask, Does it offend other Christians? I don't mean
that if you can find one single Christian anywhere in the world
who is offended by the thing in question, then you shouldn't do
it. You will probably find some Christian who would be offended
at almost anything you did. But if it offended several good and
respected Christians, then I wouldn't do it even though I thought
it was right.

There are things I have never done; not because I think they
are wrong (to be honest, I see nothing wrong with them) but I
refrain from doing them because I know Christians who would
be offended; and I would not use my religious liberty to cause
another believer to stumble.

A lady approached a great preacher of yesteryear and stated
that she was offended by his necktie. It was a small string tie
that the lady didn't approve of. He politely handed her a pair

of scissors and told her to clip it off, which she promptly did. When she handed the scissors back to him, he said, "I am offended by your tongue."

Offending a Christian brother is a serious thing. Jesus said, "It were better for him that a millstone were hanged about his neck, and he cast into the sea, than that he should offend one of these little ones" (Luke 17:2).

With position comes responsibility. There are certain things I cannot do because of my position, things which others may do and no one think anything about it. Relationship also brings responsibility. Because of their relationship to me, my children have a certain responsibility that other children do not have. They also have a responsibility to each other that they do not have to other children.

As children of God, we have a responsibility to every other born-again believer. We must do everything possible to help him on in his Christian life and be careful never to do anything that offends him.

If the thing in question offends other Christians, then it is wrong.

X. AM I FULLY PERSUADED THAT IT IS RIGHT?

In Romans 14:5 the Bible says, "One man esteemeth one day above another: another esteemeth every day alike. Let every man be fully persuaded in his own mind." The word "persuaded" in this verse simply means "convinced." In other words, if you are not thoroughly convinced that the thing is right, then it is best not to do it.

Dr. Bob Jones, Sr., told a story of a man who was getting ready for Sunday school. He picked up a shirt that had been worn before; and raising his voice so his wife could hear him in the other room, asked, "Honey, is this shirt dirty?" She calmly replied, "If it is doubtful, it's dirty."

Romans 14:23 warns, "Whatsoever is not of faith is sin."

As pastor of the same church for twenty-one years, I counseled with thousands of people. Through the years people have asked, "Pastor, is it wrong for me to do so and so? The Bible doesn't say clearly whether it is right or wrong, and I really don't know."

In many cases I have asked, "Do you have doubts about it?" If their reply was, "Yes," I showed them Romans 14:5 and Romans 14:23, then explained that it is best to give God the benefit of the doubt. I always counsel people never to do anything unless they are thoroughly convinced that it is right.

In connection with this, Colossians 3:15 is a very helpful verse: "Let the peace of God rule in your hearts." The word translated *rule* means to "govern," to "prevail." In other words, let the peace of God govern, let it decide. If you don't have peace about the matter, don't do it.

The worst decisions I ever made were made when I didn't have peace about them. I well remember buying an automobile. It was beautiful, and I really wanted it. However, when it came time to sign the sales contract, I felt very uneasy. I had no peace. I ignored these uneasy feelings and purchased the car anyway.

Boy, was that a terrible mistake! In three months we had spent more on the automobile than we originally paid for it. Time and time again I said to my wife, "I wish I had never seen that car!" If I had followed the scriptural principle in Colossians 3:15, I would have avoided much unhappiness.

When the believer is faced with a decision regarding a questionable matter, he should never proceed unless he has complete peace about it. If there is nothing wrong with it, then God is able to give complete peace. You can rest assured that every time you violate the scriptural principle of Colossians 3:15 you will regret it. When deciding questionable things, a Christian should have complete peace about it and be thoroughly persuaded or . convinced that it is right.

Finally,

XI. DO THE BEST CHRISTIANS I KNOW AGREE THAT IT IS RIGHT?

Those are blessed words of advice in Proverbs 24:6, "In

multitude of counsellors there is safety." There have been instances in my life where I have had a difficult time deciding about a matter. After using all the guidelines above, I still wasn't satisfied. My last resort was to seek the counsel of good, godly Christians.

I usually get a good Christian alone and ask, "What would you think if I were to do so and so?" Then I assure him that I want his honest opinion. I have learned a lot through my counselors.

Just two weeks ago I approached at least eight different Christians regarding a matter I had a question about and asked their advice. Not one knew that I had talked to the other, and in this way I got the honest feelings of eight individuals.

It has been my practice for years never to make an important decision without getting the opinion of several good, godly Christians. And I can testify that "in multitude of counsellors there is safety." I feel God has protected me through the years because I sought the counsel of wise and good Christians.

When you are faced with a questionable matter, approach several Christians individually and get their opinions. Their counsel is valuable in helping make the right decision.

Heaven, the Believer's Home

CHAPTER NINETEEN

Bible Answers to Questions Most Often Asked About Heaven

"Let not your heart be troubled: ye believe in God, believe also in me. In my Father's house are many mansions: if it were not so, I would have told you. I go to prepare a place for you. And if I go and prepare a place for you, I will come again, and receive you unto myself; that where I am, there ye may be also."—John 14:1-3.

When I was a small boy, I heard the preacher talk about Heaven. He said when the Christian dies he goes up to Heaven. I used to lie on my bed at night and wonder: *Is Heaven a real place? If Heaven is a real place, where is it? If I were to die as a Christian, would I go to Heaven immediately? If I did, how long would it take me to make the trip? And when I got to Heaven, would I know my friends? would they know me? What would I look like in Heaven? Would I have a body? could I eat in Heaven? would my loved ones know me? Would I know my loved ones? would I know my grandmother and grandfather who had already* gone to Heaven? These and many other questions went through my mind—death and Heaven were mysteries to me.

One of the greatest causes of sorrow, when our loved ones pass away, is a lack of knowledge concerning the dead. The Bible says in I Thessalonians 4:13, "I would not have you to be ignorant, brethren, concerning them which are asleep, that ye sorrow not, even as others which have no hope."

On today's broadcast, I will try to answer several questions about Heaven.

I. IS HEAVEN A REAL PLACE?

Yes, the Bible teaches that Heaven is a real, literal, physical place. Jesus said in John 14:2, 3, "I go to prepare a place for you. And if I go and prepare a place for you, I will come again, and receive you unto myself; that where I am, there ye may be also."

I mention that Heaven is a place because some think that Heaven is a state of the mind. Jesus said:

"Lay not up for yourselves treasures upon earth, where moth and rust doth corrupt, and where thieves break through and steal: But lay up for yourselves treasures in heaven, where neither moth nor rust doth corrupt, and where thieves do not break through nor steal."—Matt. 6:19, 20.

Now, friends, that could only be said of an actual, real, literal, physical place.

If I had time to read Revelation 21 and 22, you would see a beautiful description of the Holy City, the New Jerusalem, which is the eternal home of the saved. In those chapters the Bible says that Heaven has foundations, and the foundations are garnished with all manner of precious stones. The Bible says the walls of the city are made of jasper. It goes on to say that there are three gates on the east, three on the west, three on the north, three on the south; and it says the gates are made of pearl; and every several gate is of one pearl.

Say, that could not be said of a state of mind but only of a real, literal place.

In Revelation 21 and 22, the Bible gives the measurements of the Holy City in cubits. If you were to take the cubits and multiply them into feet, then divide them into miles, you would find that the Holy City, the New Jerusalem, is fifteen hundred miles square—fifteen hundred miles in four different directions!

Now, friends, there is no way to measure the state of a man's mind. You could not measure Heaven unless it was a real, literal, physical place.

II. WHAT KIND OF PLACE IS HEAVEN?

First, Heaven is a place of indescribable beauty and glory. The Bible says in I Corinthians 2:9, "Eye hath not seen, nor ear heard, neither have entered into the heart of man [or crossed man's mind], the things which God hath prepared for them that love him."

Wait a minute. The Bible says it has never crossed man's mind; there is no way to imagine the indescribable beauty of Heaven! I suggest you read Revelation 21 and 22, and you will have then only a little glimpse of the beautiful place called Heaven.

One night a young boy was walking with his grandfather. It was a beautiful night. The sky was deep blue, and it seemed like a million stars were on parade. The little boy, pulling at his grandfather's coattail, said, "Grandpa, Grandpa, if Heaven is so beautiful on the outside, what must the inside look like!"

The songwriter was correct when he wrote:

How beautiful Heaven must be, must be,
Sweet home of the happy and free.

Heaven is a place of indescribable beauty and glory.

But Heaven, too, is a place of perfect rest. The Bible says in Revelation 14:13, "Blessed are the dead which die in the Lord from henceforth: Yea, saith the Spirit, that they may rest from their labours; and their works do follow them."

Most people here never know what it is to experience complete and perfect rest, with no worries, no schedules to meet, no time clocks to punch, no alarm clocks to awaken early in the morning.

When my mother died, I was out soul winning. Some friends found me and told me Mother had passed away. Hurrying home, I entered the bedroom where she had been for several weeks due to illness. And there on the bed lay my mother's body. When I looked at her, my first impression was, "Mother, this is the first time in my life I've ever seen you relaxed." She always had a burden of some kind to carry; now she was resting from her labors. The burdens were gone.

Heaven is a place of indescribable beauty, a place of perfect rest. But Heaven, too, is a place of open vision.

Often people say, "When I get to Heaven, there are things I want to ask the Lord." And I always reply, "When you get to Heaven, you will know everything the Lord knows and there will be no need to ask Him anything."

There are so many things I cannot explain here.

I remember a young couple with three small children. I was called to conduct the funeral of one of those little ones. A few months later the second child died. And in less than a year the third child was dead. They all had unrelated diseases. It was an unusual thing, and I had never had an experience like it. As we walked away from the grave of their last child, the mother said as she wept, "Explain to me why this happened; why did God take every child we had while other families never lose a one?"

Friends, I could not explain it, because I cannot see the end from the beginning. But God knows. Romans 8:28 is true. It is the Word of God. It is a fact. "All things [DO] work together for good to them that love God."

I said to that young couple, "You may not always be able to *trace* God, but you can always *trust* Him."

> **My Father's way may twist and turn,**
> **My heart may throb and ache;**
> **But in my soul, I'm glad I know**
> **He maketh no mistake.**

God knows what He is doing. I cannot explain everything now, for I cannot see as God sees. But in Heaven I'll know. Heaven is a place of open vision with no glass between, and there I will understand it all. First Corinthians 13:12 says, "Now we see through a glass, darkly; but then face to face: now I know in part; but then shall I know even as also I am known."

I read the story of a young boy in England who, due to his father's death, had to drop out of school and go to work to make a living for his family. This ten- or eleven-year-old boy sold papers to help his mother provide for other family members.

Each day after selling his papers, he stopped at a toy store on his way home to look at some beautifully painted toy soldiers in the window. The storekeeper had noticed this.

Then one day after missing the boy, he inquired of those in the street, "Has anyone seen the little paper boy who used to stop and look at the toy soldiers?"

Someone said, "Oh, haven't you heard? He was hit by an automobile the other day, and he lies in the hospital unconscious."

The storekeeper was moved: he gathered up the little toy soldiers and took them to the hospital. He told the boy's mother how the boy had looked wishfully at the soldiers every day, and then he asked permission to give them to him.

The boy was unconscious; so the man placed the beautiful, little soldiers across the foot of the bed. They stayed there several days.

One morning when the boy regained consciousness, the first thing he saw was the toy soldiers. He could hardly believe his eyes. He began moving forward. Reaching with his little hands to touch the soldiers, getting closer and closer, until finally the soldiers were in his hands. With a smile he exclaimed, "Oh, look, Mother! Look! Here are the soldiers, and there is no glass between!"

III. DO THE SAVED GO TO HEAVEN IMMEDIATELY?

The answer is yes. The Bible says in II Corinthians 5:8, "to be absent from the body" is "to be present with the Lord."

There are only two places a Christian can ever be: in the body or with the Lord.

In Philippians 1:23, Paul said, "I am in a strait betwixt two, having a desire to depart, and to be with Christ; which is far better." Depart and be with Christ. Man is not a body; he is a soul. He has a body. The Bible says that God created man in His own image, and that God breathed into his nostrils, and he became a living soul (Gen. 2:7). My body is not me. It is mine. My body is my possession. If I bump my head, I say, "I bumped *my* head." It is my head, my hands, my feet, my ears, etc. But it is also my watch and my coat. My coat as well as my body is my possession. The body is simply the house in which I live. I am the soul and spirit on the inside. In I Thessalonians 5:23, Paul said, "I pray God your whole spirit and soul and body be preserved blameless unto the coming of our Lord Jesus Christ." When a man dies, his soul and spirit leave his body and go immediately to be with Christ.

In London, England, there is a tombstone with an unusual epitaph. A man named Solomon Peas gave instruction before he died to put these words on his tombstone:

> **Beneath these clouds and beneath these trees,**
> **Lies the body of Solomon Peas;**
> **This is not Peas; it is only his pod;**
> **Peas has shelled out and gone Home to God.**

When I read that, I wished my name were Solomon Peas; I would like to have that on my tombstone.

When the Christian dies, he goes immediately to be with Christ: absent from the body; present with the Lord.

IV. WILL WE KNOW EACH OTHER IN HEAVEN?

The Bible indicates we will. Jesus said, ". . . when ye shall see Abraham, and Isaac, and Jacob, and all the prophets, in the kingdom of God." Here the Bible teaches that we will know Abraham, Isaac and Jacob.

On the Mount of Transfiguration, Moses and Elijah appeared with Christ. Now, keep in mind that Moses lived and died long before Elijah was born. But on the Mount of Transfiguration, Moses knew Elijah; and Elijah knew Moses. They not only knew each other, but they still had the same names.

Someone asks, "Will we have our same name in Heaven?" I don't know. I know Moses was still Moses, and Elijah was still Elijah, Abraham was still Abraham, Isaac was still Isaac, and Jacob was still Jacob. Perhaps we will. I may still be Curtis Hutson.

Will we know each other in Heaven? Yes. Moses knew Elijah, and Elijah knew Moses, though they had never met on earth. They not only knew each other, but they knew what would happen in the future. And the Bible says in Luke 9 that they discussed the death that Jesus should accomplish in Jerusalem. First Corinthians 13:12: "Now we see through a glass, darkly; but then face to face: now I know in part; but then shall I know even as also I am known."

Yes, dear friends, I will know my mother in Heaven. I will know my dear grandfather who died when I was a little boy. I will know my grandmother who lived to be 99 years of age.

V. WILL WE HAVE A BODY IN HEAVEN?

The Bible seems to indicate that we will. In Luke 16, when Lazarus died and was carried by angels to Abraham's bosom, the rich man looked across a great gulf and saw Lazarus in Abraham's bosom. And in the conversation with Abraham he asked that Lazarus dip his finger in water. That implies that Lazarus had a body.

In II Corinthians 5:1, Paul says, "For we know that if our earthly house of this tabernacle were dissolved, we have a building of God, an house not made with hands, eternal in the heavens." He goes on to say that in this tabernacle we groan, desiring to be clothed upon with our body or tabernacle which is from Heaven.

The Bible does indicate that there will be a body between death and resurrection. It is a body that will be occupied until Jesus comes and this body is raised.

Friends, the Bible teaches that Jesus is coming. When He comes, the bodies of Christians will be raised from the dead. First Thessalonians 4:16 says, "The Lord himself shall descend from heaven with a shout, with the voice of the archangel, and with the trump of God: and the dead in Christ shall rise first." Christians are going to come out of the graves.

The Bible says in Acts 24:15, ". . . there shall be a resurrection of the dead, both of the just and unjust."

In John 5:28, 29, Jesus said,

"Marvel not at this: for the hour is coming, in the which all that are in the graves shall hear his voice, And shall come forth; they that have done good, unto the resurrection of life; and they that have done evil, unto the resurrection of damnation."

In Job 19:25-27, Job said,

"I know that my redeemer liveth, and that he shall stand at the latter day upon the earth: And though after my skin worms destroy this body, yet in my flesh shall I see God: Whom I shall see for myself, and mine eyes shall behold, and not another."

The Bible teaches that when a man dies, his soul and spirit leave the body and go immediately to be with Christ. And based on II Corinthians 5, that soul and spirit occupy a temporary body between death and resurrection while awaiting the resurrection of this body. So I suppose the body of II Corinthians 5 is a temporary body that the believer occupies between death and resurrection; but when Jesus comes, the Bible says that the dead in Christ shall be raised first. And when this body is raised, the Bible teaches that it will be a body exactly like Jesus'.

First John 3:2:

"Beloved, now are we the sons of God, and it doth not yet appear what we shall be: but we know that, when he shall appear, we shall be like him; for we shall see him as he is."

Philippians 3:20, 21:

"For our conversation [or citizenship] *is in heaven; from whence also we look for the Saviour, the Lord Jesus Christ: Who shall change our vile body, that it may be fashioned like unto his glorious body."*

Now here is the picture: the Christian dies; his soul and spirit leave his body and go immediately to be with Christ; his body is buried; it goes back to dust. It may be a hundred years before Jesus comes, or a thousand years. On the other hand, it may be only a year or maybe a day. Nobody knows when.

But when Jesus comes, the Bible says He will come with a shout, with the voice of the archangel and with the trump of God and the dead in Christ shall be raised first. The body of that Christian will be raised from the dead. The soul and spirit that have been with Christ since death will be brought back.

"But I would not have you to be ignorant, brethren, concerning them which are asleep, that ye sorrow not, even as others which have no hope. For if we believe that Jesus died and rose again, even so them also which sleep in Jesus will God bring with him."—I Thess. 4:13, 14.

When Jesus comes the saints who have died will come back with Him. The body will be raised, and the soul and spirit will be reunited with the resurrection body, and in eternity the person will be with Christ.

First Thessalonians 4:17 says, ". . . and so shall we ever be with the Lord."

Now I raise the question,

VI. DO THE SAVED IN HEAVEN KNOW WHAT IS HAPPENING ON EARTH?

The answer is yes, as I will show you from a number of Bible verses. The saved in Heaven are conscious and awake. Some think that when a man dies he goes to sleep and knows nothing until the resurrection. The Bible does say that man sleeps, but "sleep" has reference only to the body.

First Thessalonians 4:13: "I would not have you to be ignorant, brethren, concerning them which are *asleep*." In John 11, Jesus spoke of Lazarus as being asleep. But that has no reference to the soul and spirit. There are other Bible verses that teach that those in Heaven are conscious and know what is happening on earth.

Here is a good rule to follow when interpreting the Bible: Never use an obscure passage to contradict a clear one.

Let me show you several verses that teach that those in Heaven are conscious and awake.

Luke 15:7 and 10 say there is more rejoicing in Heaven over one sinner who repents than over ninety-nine just persons who need no repentance. The rejoicing is not by the angels, because angels do not know what salvation is. The only ones who can rejoice are those who know about salvation.

Up in Heaven, the saved look down on earth. They see friends and loved ones who accept Christ as Saviour, and they rejoice over their salvation.

We read in Revelation 6:9, 10, when the fifth seal was opened,

"I saw under the altar the souls of them that were slain for the word of God, and for the testimony which they held: And they cried with a loud voice, saying, How long, O Lord, holy and true, dost thou not judge and avenge our blood on them that dwell on the earth?"

Now, these people in Heaven are those who had been martyred or slain. The Bible says they cried out with a loud voice. They were not asleep. Rather, they were talking to the Lord and asking Him how long before He would do something about those who had martyred them.

Notice several things here. These people in Heaven could look back on earth, and they saw the people who had martyred them were getting by without punishment. So they asked the Lord, "How long . . . dost thou not judge and avenge our blood on them that dwell on the earth?"

Notice something else. The Lord spoke back to them, and verse 11 says, "And white robes were given unto every one of them; and it was said unto them, that they should rest yet for a little season, until their fellowservants also and their brethren, that should be killed as they were, should be fulfilled."

Now do the saved in Heaven know what is happening on earth?

Hebrews 12:1: "Wherefore seeing we also are compassed about with so great a cloud of witnesses...." These witnesses are those mentioned in Hebrews 11, which lists at least seventeen names: then Hebrews 12 begins, "Wherefore seeing we also are compassed about with so great a cloud of witnesses...."

In the original manuscripts, there were no chapter-and-verse divisions. These were added by men. Spurgeon complained about those who chopped up the Bible into chapters and verses. I think his complaint is justified. Now if we stop at the end of Hebrews 11, we miss a very important truth because Hebrews 12:1 teaches that those in Heaven know what is happening on earth. We are "compassed about" with such a great cloud of witnesses.

Do the saved in Heaven know what is happening on earth? Yes. How much do they know? I am not sure they see all the sin and sorrow. I am not sure they see all the murder and wickedness. But I do know they know when unsaved people trust Christ as Saviour, because Luke 15:10 says they rejoice in the presence of the angels of God over one sinner who repents.

Man's existence is divided into three stages—the present, the intermediate and the eternal. The present is from the time a man is born until he dies. The intermediate is from the time a man dies until he is resurrected. And the eternal is from the time a man is resurrected on through eternity. I say through because it is a common expression. Of course, there is no such thing as going through eternity. When a man is resurrected, from that point on is the eternal state.

I am living in the present. If I were to die right now, my soul and spirit would leave my body and go to be with Christ. My body would be buried. And the intermediate stage would be the time between death and resurrection, while awaiting the coming of Christ.

There are several theories concerning this intermediate time. Some say there is soul-sleep, that people don't know what is happening. Our dear Catholic friends say there is a purgatory where unconfessed sins are purged before going on to Heaven. But the Bible says that between death and resurrection a man is with Christ, that he is conscious, that he has a body, and that he does know what is happening on earth.

Now there is another question I want to ask regarding Heaven:

VII. WHERE IS HEAVEN?

When I was a little boy, I used to say "up to Heaven." When I got older, someone reminded me that if I died in China and went up, I would be going an opposite direction from a man who died in America and went up. Since the world is round and China is on the other side of the world, that seems reasonable. But I have discovered from the Bible that Heaven is in a fixed location in the sides of the North beyond the highest star.

Here is an interesting passage: "Promotion cometh neither from the *east*, nor from the *west*, nor from the *south*. But God is the judge: he putteth down one, and setteth up another" (Ps. 75:6, 7).

Isn't it strange that the word "north" is left out? Why? Because promotion does come from the North. It comes from God. "He putteth down one, and setteth up another."

In Isaiah 14:12-17, we have the story of Lucifer, who became Satan. He said, "I will exalt my throne above God's throne." He said, "I will ascend above the heights of the clouds." He said, "I will go into the sides of the north."

Heaven, then, is in a fixed location in the sides of the North. According to Isaiah 14, it is beyond the highest star.

Here in Isaiah 14, Satan said, "I will ascend into heaven, I will exalt my throne above the stars of God." If he is talking about literal stars, he is talking about going out beyond what we call the second heaven.

There are three heavens, Paul said in II Corinthians 12:2, 4,

"I knew a man in Christ above fourteen years ago, (whether in the body, I cannot tell; or whether out of the body, I cannot tell: God knoweth;) such an one caught up to the third heaven. . . . How that he was caught up into paradise, and heard unspeakable words, which it is not lawful for a man to utter."

If there is a third Heaven, there is a second and first heaven. The first heaven is the atmospheric heavens where the birds fly. Says II Peter 3:10, ". . . the heavens shall pass away with a great noise." He is speaking of the atmospheric heavens. Psalm 19:1 says, "The heavens declare the glory of God." This is talking about the second heaven—the starry or planetary heavens. And the third Heaven, the Paradise of God where Christians go and where Jesus is, is somewhere out beyond the last star, beyond the second or starry heaven.

I am told that the farthest star man has been able to locate through his most powerful telescopes is 500 million light years away. Light travels a little more than 186,000 miles per second. That means if you could go 186,000 miles per second, it would take 500 million years to reach the last star that man has been able to locate; and Heaven is somewhere out beyond the highest star, in the sides of the North, according to Isaiah 14.

So when I said "up to Heaven" as a little boy, I was right; though I did not understand it. Any time you go North you are going up. Everybody says "up North" and "down South." And the North Pole is the top of the earth. So Heaven is up.

Heaven is real. It is in a fixed location in the sides of the North, beyond the highest star.

VIII. WHO IS GOING TO HEAVEN?

Suppose I ask you, Who is going to Heaven? Some would say the man who reads his Bible and prays. Others would say the man who lives good and keeps the Ten Commandments. Still others would say the man who attends church faithfully or the man who has been baptized. I have even heard people say if a man suffers enough here, he goes to Heaven when he dies.

When I was a small boy, there was a great fire in Atlanta, Georgia. The Winecoff Hotel burned, and many people lost their lives. Someone wrote a song (it was supposed to have been a gospel song) about the Winecoff fire. One verse of the song went like this:

> **Surely there's a Heaven**
> **For folks who die this way;**
> **And we'll go Home to see them**
> **In Heaven some sweet day.**

The implication is, since they suffered in a fire, they would go to Heaven. Yes, people have different ideas about how to go to Heaven.

When I worked at the Post Office, a lady came in and said, "Preacher, the way I see this business about Heaven is: we are all at the Post Office this morning. You came up Covington Highway and out Candler Road, and you are here. So-and-So came through Panthersville, and he is here. I came through East Lake Park, and I am here." She went on to describe how a number of people had all arrived at the Post Office, none having come the same way. When she finished, she said, "Now that is the way it is about Heaven. We are all working for the same thing; and as along as we are sincere, we will all go to Heaven when we die." Then she asked, "What do you think about that?" I replied, "There is only one thing wrong with it: when we die, we are not going to the Post Office."

There are many ways to the Post Office, but only one way to Heaven. John 14:6: "I am *the* way, *the* truth, and *the* life: no man cometh unto the Father, but by me." Acts 4:12: "Neither is there salvation in any other: for there is none other name under heaven given among men, whereby we must be saved."

Now, who is going to Heaven? Let's see what the Bible says. In Revelation 7 we have a heavenly scene. There is an innumerable host, clothed in white robes. Revelation 7:13 says, "And one of the elders answered, saying unto me, What are these which are arrayed in white robes? and whence came they?"

Now, notice the question of one of the elders: "How did these people get here? From whence came they?" John answered in verse 14, "Sir, thou knowest. And he said to me, These are they which came out of great tribulation, and have washed their robes, and made them white in the blood of the Lamb." These people in Heaven were there because they had washed their robes and made them white in the blood of the Lamb.

Friends, only those who have been washed in the blood are going to Heaven.

But what does it mean to be washed in the blood? There is no way we can take the blood of Jesus and put it into a basin and wash our hands. We have never seen that blood. Let me briefly explain.

The Bible teaches that all men are sinners. Romans 3:23: "For all have sinned, and come short of the glory of God." The Bible says in Romans 3:10, "As it is written, There is none righteous, no, not one." Not all men have committed the same sins or the same number of sins, but all have sinned. Since all men are sinners, all men owe a penalty. Sin demands a price. Ezekiel 18:4: "The soul that sinneth, it shall die." Romans 6:23: "The wages of sin is death. . . ." James 1:15: "Sin, when it is finished, bringeth forth death."

Now, here is the picture: I am a sinner. I have sinned. And being a sinner, I owe a penalty. The penalty for sin is death. But that death is more than dying with a gunshot wound or cancer. That death is described in the Bible as the second death, the lake of fire. Revelation 20:14: "Death and hell were cast into the lake of fire. This is the second death." If I pay what I owe as a sinner, I must go into Hell and stay there forever and ever and ever.

Now, here is the bright side of the story. The Bible teaches that two thousand years ago God took every sin I have ever committed and all I ever will commit and placed those sins on Jesus. That is not just preacher talk but exactly what the Bible says in Isaiah 53:6, "...the Lord hath laid on him the iniquity of us all." Two thousand years ago God looked down through the telescope of time and saw every sin that I ever would commit, and He took those sins—one by one—and placed them over on Jesus. And I Peter 2:24 says, "Who his own self bare our sins in his own body on the tree." The Bible also says in II Corinthians 5:21, "He hath made him to be sin for us, who knew no sin; that we might be made the righteousness of God in him."

Now, you can never change the fact that two thousand years ago God took every sin you have ever committed, all you ever will commit if you live to be a thousand years old, and placed those sins on Jesus; and while Jesus was bearing our sins in His own body, God actually punished Him in our place to pay the debt we owe.

Someone said the Jews killed Him. But that is not so. Others say the Roman soldiers killed Him. They are wrong. The Bible says, "For God so loved the world, that *he* gave his only begotten Son." And Romans 8:32 says, "He that spared not his own Son, but delivered him up for us all...." God actually punished Jesus in our place to pay the debt we owe; so that, when we die, we won't have to pay it.

That sounds like everyone is saved, doesn't it? It sounds like everyone will go to Heaven because He died for everyone. But everyone is not saved. The death of Jesus Christ on the cross is sufficient for all, but it is efficient only to those who believe.

Here is what happened. God transferred your sins to Christ, and on the cross Jesus Christ died for you. He shed His blood. Leviticus 17:11 tells us, "The life of the flesh is in the blood." Blood in the body means the man is alive. Shed blood speaks of death. When Jesus shed His blood, He gave His life for you. He paid what you and I owe. He suffered what we should have suffered.

That is what we mean when we sing:

What can wash away my sin?
Nothing but the blood of Jesus.

Hebrews 9:22 says, "Without shedding of blood is no remission." When Jesus died in our place, He shed His blood. That is what it means when it says they "have washed their robes, and made them white in the blood of the Lamb." It means they believe that Jesus Christ died for them, that He suffered their death and paid their debt; and they are trusting Him as Saviour.

Now let me briefly sum up what I have said. We are sinners. We owe the sin debt. God transferred our guilt to Jesus. Jesus shed His blood. He died on a cross. He paid what we owe. That is what He meant when He cried out from the cross, "It is finished." Now for us to be washed in the blood or to accept the payment, we must do it by faith. John 3:16 says, "For God so loved the world, that he gave his only begotten Son, that whosoever believeth in him should not perish, but have everlasting life."

The main hang-up is over that little word "believe." Everybody says, "I have always believed in Christ. I'm not an atheist." But the Bible word "believe" does not mean to accept the historical fact that He was a person who lived and died. To "believe" means to trust, to depend, to rely on.

I have often illustrated faith by an airplane.

We go to the airport. You say to me, "Is that a plane?"
"Yes."
"Do you believe the plane will fly?"
"Yes."
"Do you believe the plane will take you to California?"
"Yes."

But I never make the trip. I must not only believe it is a plane, that it will fly, that it is going to California, but there must come a time and point when I make a decision that I will definitely trust that plane and that pilot with my physical life. When I get on the plane, I am depending on the pilot to take me to California. My physical life is in his hands.

That is what it means to believe on Christ. It means I admit that I am a sinner, I believe that I do owe the sin debt like the Bible says, I accept the fact that Jesus Christ has already died, and that with His death He paid what I owe as a sinner; and finally, it means that I will fully trust Him to get me to Heaven. Just like I put my physical life in the hands of a pilot to take me across America, so I must put my eternal life in the hands of Jesus to take me to Heaven.

If you can pray this prayer honestly and sincerely, I promise you that when you die you will go to Heaven: "Dear Lord Jesus, I know that I'm a sinner. I do believe You died for me, and here and now I do trust You as my Saviour. From this moment on, I am fully depending on You to get me to Heaven."

If you will trust Him, I promise that you have everlasting life. And you can know that when you die you are going to Heaven.

How can you know it? In John 3:36, Jesus said, "He that believeth on the Son hath everlasting life." God said it. He cannot lie. Hebrews 6:18 says it is impossible for God to lie. If you are trusting Him completely for salvation, you have everlasting life; and you have God's Word for it. If you will write and tell me you have trusted Him, I have some free literature I would like to send you that will help you as you set out to live the Christian life. All you need do to receive your free literature is simply fill out the decision form below and send it to me.

(Please see next page for decision form.)

Decision Form

Dr. Shelton Smith
SWORD OF THE LORD
P. O. Box 1099
Murfreesboro, Tennessee 37133

Dear Dr. Smith:
I have read the sermon on Heaven in *Bread for Believers*. I do want to go to Heaven when I die. I know that I am a sinner and do believe that Jesus Christ died for me. The best I know how I trust Him as my Saviour. From this moment on, I am depending on Him to get me to Heaven.

Please send me the free literature that will help me as a I set out to live the Christian life.

Date _____

Signed _____

Address _____

City_____ State _____

Zip _____

For a complete list of books available from the Sword of the Lord, write to Sword of the Lord Publishers, P. O. Box 1099, Murfreesboro, Tennessee 37133.